ANXIOUS PARENTS

PETER N. STEARNS

ANXIOUS PARENTS

A History of Modern Childrearing in America

New York University Press • *New York and London*

NEW YORK UNIVERSITY PRESS
New York and London

Library of Congress Cataloging-in-Publication Data
Stearns, Peter N.
Anxious parents : a history of modern childbearing in America / Peter N. Stearns
p. cm.
Includes bibliographical references and index.
ISBN 0-8147-9829-2 (cloth : alk. paper)
1. Child rearing—United States—History—20th century.   2. Parenting—United
States—History—20th century.   3. Parent and child—United States—History—20th
century.   4. Child development—United States—History—20th century.   I. Title.
HQ769 .S76 2002
649'.1'0973—dc21   2002152802

New York University Press books are printed on acid-free paper,
and their binding materials are chosen for strength and durability.

Manufactured in the United States of America

10 9 8 7 6 5 4 3 2 1

For my children and stepchildren.
Are you o.k.?

Contents

Preface

THIS BOOK IS DESIGNED to inform the challenge of contemporary parenting by discussing some significant changes in child-adult relations in the past several decades. It is not a how-to book, of the sort that dominates parenting shelves in the bookstores. Rather, it is an orientation to the history of modern parenting and to the connections of past to present; as such, it offers considerable understanding of how-not-to, which is important in its own right.

Why is it that American parents so often get caught up in worries that they lose perspective on some of the basic goals and pleasures of parenting? Understanding the sources and locations of some key anxieties can help us decide what's worth worrying about. And the process that brought us to our current anxieties is interesting and revealing in its own right, which adds to the pleasure of contemplation. We need to know, and we can know, how we got to where we are today, distresses and all.

The basic argument is not complicated. Several decades back, many American parents, and those who advised them, began to change their ideas about children's nature, attributing to it a greater sense of vulnerability and frailty. This new view then influenced the handling of matters within the family, such as discipline and chores. It also affected the ways parents tried to mediate between children and other experiences that affected them, such as schooling or recreation. Some of our most striking practices, from grade inflation to worries about children's boredom, result from the intersection of beliefs in vulnerability and the influence of wider social institutions.

American parents have been dealing, and continue to deal, with some tough issues, which are complicated by the fact that they're of fairly recent origin. The equation between childhood and schooling is the focus of one set of concerns, and the increasing separation of children from work is another. The effort to manage the place of children in a consumer society, surrounded by commercial media, presents another set of challenges. The contemporary environment for children has taken on additional complexity deriving from the worries about emotional and physical vulnerability that gained center stage from the 1920s onward. These worries reflected not only new ideas but also significant changes in the ways children were behaving and in the lives of parents themselves.

The book aims at better understanding of what contemporary parenting is all about. It does not prescribe—parents get enough prescriptions from the many books on the parental advice shelf. It does provide a basis for thinking about appropriate reactions to pervasive worries and for acquiring some perspective on the season's dominant fads and the experts who push them. It aims at providing a better understanding of the evolution of parenting, in the process helping parents themselves to chart their own course a bit more on a sea of advice.

Acknowledgments

MANY FAMILY MEMBERS and scholars have contributed to this study, intentionally or not. Sincere thanks to my children and stepchildren for a host of insights and much support. A number of suggestions by Deborah Stearns, Eryq Dorfman, Paula Fass, and my wife, Meg Brindle, were unusually helpful. Derek Coryell and Luke Brindle provided invaluable research assistance, and I am grateful as well to Megan Barke, Joseph Devine, Matt Weiss, and Lawrence Beaber for the information they provided. Rachel Blanco and Kaparah Simmons supplemented my computer in preparing the manuscript.

I

Anxious Parents

A 20th-Century History

SYMPTOMS OF PROBLEMS may shift, but the anxiety remains the same. A rash of new child-rearing manuals began to appear in the United States in the 1920s, followed shortly by *Parents Magazine*; the publications were designed to provide answers to parental concerns but also to offer standards that might lead parents to feel concerns where none had existed before. *Parents Magazine*, in fact, became both a stimulus and an outlet for a range of parental worries, from children's physical health to their performance in school to their personality development. Polls in the late 1930s, exploiting a new capacity to probe public opinion, encouraged parents to rank-order a long list of worries. Post–World War II parents wondered, in cyclical fashion, whether bad marriages or divorces were worse for children. Surveys in the 1970s and 1980s suggested declining parental satisfaction with children, in part because of the troubles involved in raising them. By the 1990s, anxious parents increasingly sought new targets, arguing that schools and teachers should rate their kids highly regardless of performance, lest the child's or the parents' self-esteem be damaged as a result of an adverse opinion.

The 20th century, once rated the "century of the child,"[1] became rather a century of anxiety about the child and about parents' own adequacy. And children did not necessarily benefit from this process of adult debate and self-doubt.

To be sure, a few worries soared for a time, only to recede. Strictures about children's posture, high on the anxiety scale during the first third of the century, ultimately fizzled, as adults gave up on slouch. The need to identify and correct left- handedness disappeared by the 1950s. But new problems were discovered. Hyperactivity, for example, though discussed by experts in the 1920s, became a widespread concern only in the 1970s. The list of targets did not shrink.

In one sense, the level of anxiety was surprising, for the 20th century ushered in some unprecedented gains. American children were far less likely to die in the 20th century than were their counterparts in centuries past. Key childhood diseases were conquered. Thanks to improvements in adult life expectancy, children were also far less likely to be orphaned. Standards of living and educational access improved for most children, though there were continuing pockets of poverty and periods of concern. Child labor abuses receded under the twin glare of regulation and economic change. Opportunities for entertainment expanded.

Against these gains, obviously, two countercurrents surfaced. First, the very successes achieved in improving children's lives led to an escalation in what came to be seen as the minimal standard for children's well-being, which brought its own set of anxieties. Second, successes were not clear-cut: the ubiquity of mass entertainment brought new worries, and even the decline in child labor raised unexpected issues about children's functions and identities. Levels of anxiety experienced by parents did not correlate with what might have been registered as historic progress in children's quality of life.

This is a book about the emergence and evolution of key parental worries during the past century. It does not ignore the joys, but it deliberately concentrates on the anxious undercurrents. It focuses on concerns not only about children but also about parental adequacy. It seeks to explain what caused these anxieties and why objective gains did not enhance parents' self-confidence.

The basic argument is simple: it was during the past century that some of the key uncertainties about modern childhood were clearly deployed. The key question was what children's role should be, as traditional functions were progressively stripped away. While elements of the question had been posed in the 19th century, particularly for sectors of the American middle class, its prominence is a 20th-century phenomenon. For it was only during the past hundred years that it became fully clear that children could not be expected to contribute significantly to the family economy, that in truth they were primarily economic burdens, and that, as a result, other measurements of function had to be developed. Given the fact that children had literally always worked in the past, usually for the family directly, this fundamental redefinition posed a tremendous challenge, one that has not fully been resolved to this day. The fact that many parents sensed the definition dilemma only vaguely, believing instead that their concerns stemmed from more specific problems such as adolescent growing pains, compounded the difficulty.

A host of other new issues have drawn parental attention. Worries about cars, and the need to drive children to essential destinations, constitute a case in point. An array of new consumer products, ranging from comic books to violence-laden video games, was aimed at children, and it proved difficult to restrict access to these devices despite parental disapproval. New disease entities, like Sudden Infant Death Syndrome, and fears of adolescent suicide framed a new set of physical concerns that extended literally from birth to adulthood. Changes in family structure reduced parental confidence, as well, particularly when the rising divorce rate made clear the lower priority society placed on children and created new waves of adult remorse.

For it was in the 20th century that parents grasped, more fully than in the previous decades, when it seemed easier to shelter middle-class children, that the modern world was a dangerous place for children. There was no easy transition from childhood innocence to successful adulthood, even for women—perhaps particularly for women. As a mother of an overfriendly toddler wrote to an advice columnist at the century's end, "How can I teach my daughter that the world is dirty and evil?"

There were less tangible changes, as well. The fundamental image of children shifted for a number of reasons, including parents' guilt over their failure to provide traditional levels of care (whether these levels were real or imagined) and the new, intrusive sources of childrearing expertise. Like Victorian observers, 20th-century commentators saw childhood as a separate experience, not just a prelude to adulthood. But the similarity ended there. Unlike the 19th-century view of children as sturdy innocents who would grow up well unless corrupted by adult example and who were capable of considerable self-correction, 20th-century rhetoric viewed children as more vulnerable. Contemporary children were seen as more fragile, readily overburdened, requiring careful handling or even outright favoritism lest their shaky self-esteem be crushed. Notions of children's fragility obviously caused new levels of parental anxiety, but they were also a reflection of these anxieties.

Both mothers and fathers were involved in new kinds of self-doubt. For many men, the notion that one satisfied parental obligations by being an adequate breadwinner declined in salience, at least from the Depression onward. Supporting the family remained essential (of course, some men defaulted on this), but, amid growing prosperity and particularly with the increase in the number of women at work, it was no longer a big deal. As early as the 1920s, many men tried to develop new kinds of contacts with their kids. But, while this was an encouraging and potentially rewarding trend, the question was how to do so. Many fathers continued to feel a bit awkward around their children, deferential to mothers' expertise, in a situation ripe with new opportunities for self-doubt.

Burdens on the mothers' side were at least as acute. The huge change came in the 1950s and 1960s, when the majority of white mothers went out to work amid crushing anxieties about whether they were abandoning their children. (African Americans had faced this dilemma for decades.) But, even before this, as early as the 1920s, 19th-century assumptions about mothers' instinctive suitability for their task had been challenged, amid cutting attacks on maternal overprotectiveness and "smother love." It was harder than before to know whether one was performing correctly as a mother.

Parents' doubts about their own adequacy were sharpened by a number of new dilemmas. In the chapters that follow, we discuss worries about school, about work, and about leisure. New kinds of concerns emerged in these areas, derived from dramatically novel situations; in all three cases, the concerns were enhanced by a characteristic tension, a set of question marks. Was school too much for kids, or was the main anxiety making sure that kids were ready? If formal work for children was now mostly inappropriate, what about chores at home—was there a family variable in the definition of work? And what was the main problem in the entertainment field—shielding children from the inappropriate or providing fun at all costs? All these dilemmas produced really interesting compromises, but the compromises did not eliminate the extra anxiety involved.

In this book I hope to improve our understanding of the kinds of parental concerns and doubts that have become commonplace in our time, despite some changes in how they are manifested. The key tool is historical perspective; I treat the 20th century as a new period in the generation of worries about children and argue that a better comprehension of the origins of these worries and of prior patterns will illuminate not only the recent past but the present, as well. History will help us understand ourselves.

The result does not provide explicit formulas for behavior. It may encourage some parents to worry a bit less, but others may decide quite reasonably that even though some of their concerns are products of a particular history, they will cling to them all the more. The goal is greater freedom from the assumption that our standard worries are absolutely inevitable or natural so that we can step back from them, think about them through a historical lens—regardless of what we then decide to do, or not do, about changing them. Besides, the highlights of 20th-century parenting are simply interesting and provide a means of exploring why certain paths were chosen during the past three or four parental generations and others rejected.

WHERE THE BOOK FITS

A brief history note: this book is based on research by many different scholars, historians but also sociologists and others. Readings suggestions at the end of each chapter encourage further exploration of the major topics. A number of chapters are also based on original research; I have previously worked on some of the topics in chapter 1, which I now apply to the parenting field, and for this book I undertook additional research, particularly on children's work and consumerism.

There are few comprehensive reviews of 20th-century parenting practices. There is a terrific book by Viviana Zelizer on the early 20th century; I want to add to its main thesis, but I value it greatly. There are some splendid histories of fathering, but, interestingly, they apply more to the 19th than to the 20th century. Histories of children and, particularly, three really good studies on the history of adolescents provide useful material. Social historians have offered other crucial insights, as they expand our understanding of what the past is; I depend greatly on what they have discovered on various aspects of schooling, on anxieties about new media, on the impact of birth control, and on many other areas. Still, on many specific topics and on the larger perspective, this book breaks new ground. The purpose, to be sure, is not to provide an exhaustive history of all aspects of parenting but rather to explore some intriguing features of the recent past and to use them to shed light on the present.

PRELIMINARIES AND ASSUMPTIONS

Before turning to the main task, I must take up a few other issues. First, the personal. Any historian writing about a topic of this sort inevitably brings some individual baggage. I am trained as a social and cultural historian and have written on a number of topics in American, European, and world history. A study of parenting fits my intellectual interests in aspects of the recent past, in dealing with ordinary people and their beliefs and practices, and in trying to link historical patterns with current concerns. Previous work I've done on topics ranging from the history of aging to changes in emotional standards of behavior or self-control obviously sets up aspects of this study. And I've also done some previous work specifically on childhood.

But I also was a child, of course, and have been and am both parent and stepparent. I had a deep relationship with my father (and with my mother, also, but she died when I was fairly young—an atypical 20th-century pattern) and with my sister and half sisters. I always wanted to be a parent and have had four children, in two different batches; I also have four stepsons. All of this has undoubtedly shaped my historical perceptions. I have long been interested, for example, in part because of my experience (yes, also exasperation) not only with my own offspring but with myself, in the problem of deciding how much family work children should do and in how our views on this subject have changed and become more complicated. I believe in objective history, but of course we choose historical topics in part because of personal experiences, and undoubtedly our objectivity is colored by these same experiences, particularly around a topic such as parenting. So: this book is not a personal story, and I'll be describing some parental concerns I've never experienced personally. But there is a personal element that I cannot always tease out myself.

(I should add, for the record: despite trials and tribulations on both sides, I've largely enjoyed my experience as parent and am immensely proud of what my children and stepchildren have become or are becoming. This is not a sour- grapes history. Nor, I hope, is it the kind of history that aging observers sometimes write, lamenting the deterioration of our youth. This genre has a hoary history of its own, bemoaning the deteriorating virtue and the follies of the young. We have had this approach aplenty in the 20th century; it is one way to express adult concern about children and about Americans' own performance as parents. Indeed, we live in a period in which blasts at wayward or misled youth are particularly common, as part of the resurgence of social conservatism. This book must comment on approaches of this sort, and about some very real changes in young people's behavior. But I do not, for the record, think that our recent history is a story of clear decline, and I've rather pitied some eminent historian-colleagues who, at relatively late ages—later than mine—have indulged in this kind of lament.)

Issue number 2: race, class, and ethnicity. Generally, middle-class ideas about children and parenting received wide dissemination in the 20th century. Middle-class guides shifted from a 19th-century emphasis on the distinctions between families that were respectable and those that were not to a claim that proper child-rearing standards should be urged or imposed on everyone. The distinction, of course, was not complete: key groups might still be singled out for their apparent neglect of the appropriate standards. But the missionary impulse ran strong. During the 20th century, ever-larger segments of American society, nearly 85 percent of all citizens by the 1950s, claimed to be middle class. Consumerism, which played a considerable role in shaping both childhood and adult concerns, pervaded society, affecting the middle class and also centers of urban poverty. Some of the most interesting anxieties about children and parenting, finally, emerged from broadly middle-class settings. Despite prosperity and generally good health conditions, parents worried loudly and extensively about their own children and/or children in general. This book focuses heavily on this middle-class experience, relying extensively on the literature that the middle class generated and accepted and on the growing breadth of middle-class identity.

Of course, the middle class was not the whole story. Even many people who claimed middle-class membership in fact had varied experiences. And distinctive anxieties were likely to arise in African American communities where the fear of police violence against the young loomed large, or in immigrant settings where the characteristic gaps between second-generation children and their parents added so much to some of the standard generational tensions in American society.

Rural-urban divisions, though declining, also entered into the picture regarding, for example, children's work obligations. This book does not cover every major variant and does not follow trends in all the major subgroups consistently. But the issue of diversity is vital, and it imposes qualifications on some of my main points. I propose generalizations at the expense of some subtle distinctions, and some readers may dispute the resulting balance.

Issue number 3: the 20th century as a period. I try to show that the early decades of the 20th century ushered in several new kinds of concerns about kids, helping to produce parental anxieties that have proved quite durable. But some cautions apply. Some of the anxieties began to take shape in the 19th century. The concept of adolescence, for example, which has focused so much attention on a troubled period of late childhood, was a 19th-century product, emerging around midcentury and then taking on a more formal definition beginning in the 1870s. The concept reflected the fact that late childhood was becoming in some ways more difficult for several reasons, including extended schooling and consequent later work entry for middle-class children and earlier sexual maturity, which conflicted with increasing pressure to restrict sexual activity in order to avoid unwanted children. In our worries about teenagers, we build on a clear 19th-century legacy. On another front: while concerns about schooling increased in the early part of the 20th century, the modern schooling experience had begun to take shape beginning in the 1820s and 1830s; no break with the past occurred as if by magic after 1900. On yet another point: John Demos has plausibly argued that the 19th-century middle class family's intense emotional relations and expectations set up the context for the 20th-century interest in therapy. Here, shifts in the 20th century merely built on a pre-existing impulse relevant to parenting and marital relationships alike. And, certainly, while 20th-century divorce rates soared—an important aspect of parenting—it was already clear by the 1890s that American family instability was commonplace.

Fundamentally, it was in the late 19th century that urban parents began to realize that the world their children would face as adults would be quite different from their own, that it would be unusual (and perhaps undesirable) to expect them to follow literally in their parents' footsteps. This situation, unusual in human history, inevitably complicated parental clarity and confidence—and, of course, the realization would deepen and spread in the 20th century. I do not always dwell on the various antecedent trends, but I have no wish to oversimplify the relationship between contemporary parenting and earlier experiences in what was already an increasingly urban and industrial society.

Further, the 20th century itself was not monolithic. While, again, not focusing on some of the oscillations and internal periodizations for their own sake—I do not, for example, have an explicit section on the Depression or on World War II, though both events shaped some particular versions of 20th-century parenting—I provide some indication of political and social changes that took place over time. Certainly, in arguing for some dominant themes throughout the century, I am not trying to ignore the complexity of generalizing about an entire century.

There have been many kinds of changes within the 20th century. Shifts in the political climate have not been negligible. Parents who worried about the undue repression of children in the 1960s were replaced (amusingly, in some ways) in the 1990s by these same children transmogrified into more conservative parents who worried about character and indulgence. The 20th century has seen two periods of high immigration, with its huge impact on the interaction between parents and children, with decades of measurably increasing homogeneity sandwiched in between. The difference between the baby boom period and the preceding and succeeding decades of low birth rate is obvious and important in any examination of parental outlook.

Changes in parent-child contact have been significant, and not always in expected directions. A study in 2001 revealed a 25 percent increase in the amount of time children spent with both mothers and fathers between 1981 and 1997, with parents claiming to be aware of devoting new levels of attention to their offspring and limiting their use of such devices as playpens, which reduced the need for direct interaction. Similarly, children's TV watching declined markedly during this time in favor of a major increase in sports participation (up by 27 percent), with the emergence of frenzied soccer moms and dads. Overorganized kids seemed to supplant the underorganized, particularly in the middle class, during this two-decade span. Some observers began to talk of "postmodern" parenthood. While the term was more trendy than useful, it's clear that change and fluctuation are part of the contemporary experience of parenting. In later chapters I explicitly take up modifications in adaptations to school and in attitudes toward work.

Indeed, internal change within the 20th century is built into this account. It took time for the basic themes outlined, as established in chapter 1, to become part of parents' reactions to the key aspects of their children's lives. The key problems, in areas such as schooling and consumerism, were present early in the century. But there were important adjustments in parental formulations by the 1940s and 1950s; new ideas about disciplining and even schooling coalesced at that point. The development of "child-intensive" suburban patterns, related to the baby boom, the cold war, and even some shifts in personality norms toward more other-directed approaches, did have meaning.[2] It was at this point that child-rearing advice, and consequently many middle-class parents, focused on socialization goals aimed at developing the skills needed in corporate management and social economy. A closer look at parenting makes clear the considerable changes that evolved around mid-century, and the minor fluctuations that occurred later on.

The book argues that, despite some internal shifts, there were overarching themes to the twentieth century's approach to child rearing as a whole, based on the general recognition of children's vulnerability and the need to accommodate children as economic liabilities whose main functions involved schooling and who deserved explicit entry into the world of consumerism and escapist entertainment. We play these consistent themes against clear points of transition, for example, the advent of greater permissiveness and heightened school commitments in the 1950s or the turn in the 1980s to greater conservatism. I do not always belabor the subtle tensions between basic continuities and internal markers and oscillations. I draw evidence from different decades and argue that late 20th-century concerns, though more conservative than those of the late 1960s, were more closely linked to the anxieties of that earlier era than we often realize. Other historians—for we love to debate this sort of thing—might quarrel both with the claim of some fundamental unity and with my decision not to prove the continuity every step of the way. They might contest the internal change points that I emphasize, in favor of more familiar markers such as economic depression and war. At least the assumptions should be clear.

I should note also that I see the main themes of the 20th century, in terms of parental anxieties, emerging full force only in the 1920s, after several transitional decades in which the signs of incipient change intensified. My 20th century, in other words, has lasted not quite one hundred years, though it began to take shape 120 or so years ago. Further, though this is a minor point, I don't see decisive changes developing in the first years of the 21st century, which suggests that the main themes persist in defiance of the tidiest chronological convenience.

Issue number 4: the 20th century as distinctive. Comments here shade off from the previous discussion of chronology, but the focus is more sweeping. I argue that many key parental anxieties of the 20th century differed from those in earlier times, whether the 19th century or before. On the other hand, some older problems receded in importance. In some ways, furthermore, I contend that parents in the 20th century were more anxious, not just differently anxious. But I cannot prove this claim definitively—I don't think levels of anxiety can ever be subjected to precise historical measurement. And, while I suggest that parental anxiety reached a greater magnitude in the twentieth century, I wish to be somewhat cautious, leaving aside questions about specific evidence and measurement.

Historians who deal with new topics—and, while parenting isn't brand new, it certainly does not have a massive historical literature— often tend to exaggerate the nature of change. When scholars first began dealing with family emotions, for example, there was an initial argument that premodern Western families were unemotional, whereas from the 18th century onward parents began to display warm feelings toward their children. This description turned out to be far too stark— which does not, however, mean that no change in parenting style occurred. I do not wish to fall into that tempting but oversimplifying trap. Parents in the 19th century, and always, worried about their kids. A well-established 19th-century fictional theme, for example, dealt with growing boys who abandoned their loving mothers for a period of dissipation (though happy endings insisted that they later saw the light and returned to reward maternal devotion). Concerns about fallen girls, though directed particularly against the unrespectable lower classes, could also apply to girls in one's own class. And there were massive worries about children's illness and death, and more than enough parental guilt, when death occurred, to go around. As noted earlier, it was in the 19th century that concepts such as adolescence began to reflect adult anxieties about the impact of schooling, declining work opportunities, and changing sexuality—anxieties that would inform the 20th century, as well.

All this said, two aspects of 20th-century concerns are distinctive simply on their face. First, the concerns flourish, despite the changes in context that have made childhood in many ways so much more secure. By key 19th-century standards, we should be worrying less, and yet there is no sign that this is so. Second, while levels of anxiety can't be measured exactly, the 20th century has certainly produced a far more abundant literature chronicling parental anxieties, promoting new levels of concern as a means of selling expert solutions, and providing reassurance that the anxieties can be survived. This may result simply from the expansion of literacy and the undoubted rise of new types of expertise and more abundant popularizations that actively seek a market. But parents have bought into the game, which may suggest that they are not merely dupes but are seeking advice because of the extent of their worry. Certainly some established guidelines have become less available, which has opened the door to popularizing experts and may have directly augmented anxieties. Notably, a new gap has opened between older parents and their young-parent offspring. While older parents are more likely to be alive for all or part of their grandchildren's childhood, they are less likely than in the 19th century to live in the same household and more likely to encounter objections from their young-parent offspring that their advice is irrelevant or intrusive. The trend for grandparents to move out of households started in the 1920s, while the belief in the irrelevance of the past generation's advice began to be systematically noted in the 1940s.

The 20th century, then, has seen changes in the precise nature of many parents' concerns. These concerns have flourished despite the diminution of some of the classic causes of parental worry, notably in the area of children's health and life expectancy. The level of concern is highlighted by the decline of certain traditional guideposts and the emergence of a massive market for outside advice, which is sought both for reassurance and for precise guidance on what should be worried about. Parental confidence has often dipped below the levels apparent in the 19th century, and some of the reasons for this can be demonstrated. The idea of the vulnerable child, which replaced earlier convictions about children's sturdiness, reflects an anxious century. More anxious than before? Quite probably. Oddly anxious, all things considered? Without a doubt.

Issue number 5: comparative perspective. While arguing for the 20th century as distinctive, without absolute proof, we also argue that American parenting in this century was somewhat distinctive, though without the careful comparative treatment that can make this claim conclusive.

Signs of a somewhat distinctive American approach to childhood go way back. By the late 18th and early 19th centuries, European visitors noted that American children were less rigorously disciplined and given more voice in family affairs than was common in the old world, and these comparative impressions have persisted. Some commentators commended the American approach, as freer and as allowing children more creativity, while others deplored it, but the difference seemed pronounced to both sets of observers. And there were reasons for this. A less entrenched sense of hierarchy, a more deeply engrained sense of democracy among the society at large, may well have been in place by the revolutionary era and beyond. Certainly American parents vitally needed their children for work in an economy that was short of labor, which may have increased their desire to please their offspring. And there was an unquestionable related anxiety that children, if disaffected, could simply scoot off to the frontier. The abundance of land also reduced some of the sources of generational tension common in Europe, again making it easier for parents to please their children. In sum, by the 19th century a strong American tradition seems to have developed that encouraged parents to be very sensitive to their children's health and happiness. This could, in turn, have undergirded an unusual anxiety to please—an obvious facet of 20th-century parenting.

European parenting was not, of course, static. By the late 20th century, some of the same child-rearing manuals that had won huge sales in the United States, such as Dr. Spock's, also had a European audience. Particularly among teenagers, the increasingly transatlantic culture of consumerism, including movies, fashions, and music, has also generated some common responses among parents. Some degree of convergence has undoubtedly occurred. But convergence is not identity. Middle-class Europeans have been much less worried about entrusting their children to institutional childcare than have their American counterparts. While most accounts note a real shift away from traditionally authoritarian parenting in Germany and Holland, for example, since the late 1950s, the emergence of a 20th-century parenting style in the United States dates back at least thirty years before that, built on the existing tradition of greater family democracy. Scandinavia, to be sure, seemed to move beyond American flexibility, particularly in its more widespread opposition to traditional disciplinary methods such as spanking. American traditions also included a considerable commitment to chastisement, particularly in the strictest Christian households. Even here, however, the American mixture was distinctive: Scandinavian fathers remained more reserved, less playful than their more experimental American counterparts, who have since the 1920s often sought to be "pals" with their children, even as they remained likely to spank them once in a while. Revealingly, the characteristic American resorts of the second half of the 20th century, the Disney complexes, were designed to please and entertain children above all, whereas the most successful entry of distinctively European origin, Club Med, was much more heavily adult focused, with children entertained separately. Americans' anxiety to ensure their children's happiness showed even at the institutional level.

Judith Warner, a feminist journalist writing in the Washington *Post*, puts the comparison this way regarding mothering. On the surface, French women seem notably less liberated than their American counterparts, greater slaves, for example, to fashion and to sexuality. But take a look at what happens when one has children. On this side of the Atlantic, one faces pressing advice about the dangers of working and about the need to be available, almost around the clock, to drive kids to their games, lessons, and entertainments. "This über-momming represented a level of selflessness that would have been considered downright neurotic in France." And it is more than greater fatigue on the American side: it is constant guilt about whether the right choices are being made, whether the children are being adequately tended. The French simply do not feel this kind of guilt. "The word wasn't in the air. Had I expressed it [in France], it would have sounded, once again, like sheer neurosis." The contrast is clear, but only a more extended inquiry can discuss how the pressures here have developed (for some fathers as well as mothers) and what we might do about it. (Interestingly, Warner suggests the need for laws to limit work time as the readier alternative to really rethinking American parental culture.)[3]

Explicitly comparative studies are a desirable goal in such fields as the history of parenting. This book does not quite rise to that ambition. But there is reason to believe that there are a number of distinctive features in the anxieties it traces that have to do with specific American traditions, compounded by the changes that produced the

20th-century pattern of anxiety. Recurring comparative references renew this claim.

Anxious Parents approaches its subject on several levels. It discusses a number of specific worries, from concerns about accidents and automobiles to worries about sibling rivalry and what they portend for children's safety and adult development. It deals also with the consistent tendency to exaggerate concerns beyond demonstrable need—to expand, for example, the number of kids suspected of having Attention Deficit Disorder or to make minor posture deviations the subject of anguished correction. It discusses some larger, often unexpected, characteristic worries, such as the recurring sense that schooling is really too much for kids, whether because of the homework assigned or because of the meting out of less-than-superlative grades. It interprets adult behaviors in terms of what they suggest about attitudes toward children. The characteristic declining birth rate, for example, allowed parents to lavish more attention on individual children (which meant more time as well to indulge anxieties), but it also caused guilt (why are we not having more children, and is recreational sex really all right?), and it ultimately reflected some real ambiguities about how enjoyable and rewarding children are.

For, beyond specific behaviors, many 20th-century American adults set very high standards for what they expected from their children and from parenthood itself. Behind many worries has lurked the guilty suspicion that having children was not as satisfactory as had been expected, a thought whose subversiveness could heighten anxiety in its own right. Adulthood itself was involved. In some ways, at least, it became more complex. Certainly, in an increasingly white-collar economy, it demanded more training. Amid greater sexual temptations and complex behavioral rules, it might also require new subtlety. Here, too, were tensions that could easily be cast back on children, in the name of preparing them for maturity in a society that claimed to adore childhood but did not, in the main, appreciate childishness.

FURTHER READING

Viviana Zelizer, *Pricing the Priceless Child: The Changing Social Value of Children* (New York, 1985), provides a crucial introduction. See also the essays in Joseph Hawes and N. Ray Hiner, eds., *Childhood: A Research Guide and Historical Handbook* (Westport, CT, 1985), that deal with periodization, especially, on the post–World War II changes, Charles Strickland and A. M. Ambrose, "The Changing Worlds of Children, 1945–1963;" and David Macleod, *The Age of the Child: Children in America 1891–1990* (New York, 1998). See also Elliott West and Paula Petrick, eds., *Small Worlds: Children in America 1850–1950* (Lawrence, KS, 1992); Harvey Graff, *Growing up in America* (Detroit, 1987); Lloyd de Mause, *The History of Childhood: The Evolution of Parent-Child Relationships as a Factor in History* (London, 1980); and the additional references following chapter 2. On generational conflict over child rearing, B. Q. Mills, *Not Like Our Parents* (New York, 1987), provides some data. For discussion of maternal anxieties and blame, see Paula Caplan, *Don't Blame Mother* (New York, 1990). An important general overview is Steven Mintz and Susan Kellogg, *A Social History of American Family Life* (New York, 1988).

2

The Vulnerable Child

WORRIES ABOUT CHILDREN and anxieties about their potential deficiencies surface in most societies, and certainly were present in earlier periods of American history. The concept of original sin once organized a host of concerns, and for some groups in the United States these concerns remain. In a real sense, many 20th-century anxieties constitute a secularization of problems that used to be described within the context of sin. Nineteenth-century culture, already moving away from convictions about original sin, produced another rhetoric of anxiety, especially around the theme of maternal responsibilities and mothers' deep concerns for their children's wellbeing. Without attentive mothers, children might be misled by strangers or fall into ill health. Efforts to monitor possible masturbation were one outcome of the concern that children, and particularly boys, might go astray. Twentieth-century anxiety literature unquestionably built on these older traditions.

There was change as well, however, and not only because some customary concerns, for instance in the health arena, became objectively less necessary. The image of the vulnerable child, the subject of this chapter, is one way to bring the change into focus. The concept of the vulnerable child, potentially overwhelmed unless parents provide protection, has some similarities to the view of the sinful child in provoking parental attention, but there are crucial differences, as well, including the extent to which threats came to be seen as forces outside the child's obvious control, and without any fault on the child's part. The differences help explain a more anxious, and far less harsh, parental response. And, while motherhood and worry went hand-in-hand in much 19th-century imagery, society also had a good bit of confidence in the sturdy child, capable, unless felled by disease, of learning from experience, surmounting obstacles, and heeding good advice. Even prodigal sons returned, in one standard Victorian story line.

New levels of concern in the 20th century resulted in part from the increasing value placed on each child, at least in principle. Viviana Zelizer has legitimately called our attention to how "priceless" children had become by the 1890s. As the birth rate declined, each child seemed more precious. Parents who found themselves incapable of having children became more loudly desperate than ever before, and considerable industries developed throughout the 20th century around trying to enhance fertility or find children for the involuntarily childless. But the same value inevitably provoked new levels of concern about children: what if these priceless entities were swept away or went astray? How could parents not only control the environment to make sure that they had children but also make sure that children prospered? The theme of control on the part of parents who knew that having children was now a choice runs through the emergence of the concept of the vulnerable child. New expertise, and especially psychological discoveries about children, helped differentiate 20th-century responses from those of the 19th century, but the desire to reduce the role of change and accident played a central role. This desire warred against new forces from the outside, from schools to the purveyors of children's goods, that threatened to reduce the parental function.

A SEA CHANGE IN PARENTING ADVICE

In 1901, Felix Alder issued a revised edition of what was in effect the last widely popular 19th-century manual on childrearing, entitled *The Moral Instruction of Children*. It went through a number of printings, as many of its predecessors had. Then there was a publishing pause, as if both authors and audience needed a moment to shift gears to a different type of operation. Only one major source, the government-sponsored pamphlet *Infant Care*, suggested a new approach before 1918, and, while widely popular, the manual initially focused only on health issues. Then, in the 1920s, springing in part from authors associated with the same Children's Bureau that continued to issue *Infant Care*, a new generation of literature began to emerge. This was capped, as noted earlicr, by the establishment of *Parents Magazine*, which enshrined the new approach to child- rearing advice on a regular, reach-into-your-home basis.

Child-rearing literature is tricky evidence. It is not aimed at everyone but normally reflects the values of a dominant group—in this case, a white, urban middle class. Not everyone reads it (though an audience can develop beyond the group of origin), and not everyone who reads it agrees with it or pays serious attention. Child-rearing literature does not, in other words, clearly predict child-rearing practice or even parental attitudes. At the same time, people who buy such publications—who provide the subscriber base for an outlet like *Parents Magazine*—clearly feel they have some need, and they are likely to assimilate some of the material presented to them.

This means, in turn, that this new generation of literature, as it emerged in the 1920s, was a meaningful development. It reflected a new type of author, calling on medical and psychological rather than moral expertise (more on this a bit later). It also reflected some new concerns on the part of a reading audience, which was open to advice that explicitly differentiated itself from what was available in older-type manuals. Change in signals, change in needs—a decade-plus after the century's chronological inception, a distinctive 20th-century parenting style was off and running.

There were two huge contrasts between the dominant 19th-century manual, published between the 1820s and 1910, and its 20th- century analog. First was authorship: the 19th-century manual was issued by proponents of moral common sense, usually clergymen writing in a nondenominational (but Protestant) vein or their wives or daughters. The 20th-century manual drew on professional expertise, usually from psychology or medicine, or on popularizers trained in and reliant on these disciplines. The second difference involved size and content: the 19th-century manual was brief, rarely more than 150 pages. It had a small number of chapter headings, on the importance of piety, obedience, the need for good parental example, the different natures and obligations of boys and girls, and the basic dictates of good health. The 20th-century manual could easily be double the size of its predecessor (already in the 1930s, the average was more than three hundred pages), and it encompassed a huge range of topics, now usually phrased as problems. Emotional and psychological risks competed for attention with a variety of health and hygiene concerns; parental obligations could be met but imposed major demands. A 1930s book caught the new tone in its title, *Big Problems on Little Shoulders*. More than authorship was changing here: so was the characterization of the child's nature. Parental example remained important, but it was no longer enough. Because of children's fragility, a larger array of protective devices and manipulations now became essential. More detailed guidance was a key concomitant.

Even government publications caught the new tone, and indeed helped launch it. D. H. Thom, writing for the Children's Bureau in the mid–1920s, referred to the "problems of childhood," with the child a "delicate organism." *Infant Care*, by 1929, wrote of the "helpless infant" and how "problems come up about his care," in physical terms but even more as part of character development. The list of issues requiring attention included constipation, disease, selection of the right home, clothing, bathing, teeth, sleep, shoes, play, and emotional manifestations—all this in the most widely sought, frequently reissued brochure the federal government ever commissioned.[1]

The transition in actual attitudes about children was surely less stark than the shifts in the child-rearing manuals. Parents reacted variously to mainstream advice in both the 19th and the 20th centuries, depending on class, race, religion, and personality. There is no need to pretend that some facile equation exists between a cultural artifact and people's real beliefs and behavior. But the need for a new kind of guidance was obvious in some quarters; otherwise, the new approach would not have succeeded. And the persuasiveness of the new arguments, the bombardment of warnings about children's fragility, was hard to resist entirely, as it was conveyed not only in reading matter but also in schools, in pediatricians' offices, and in other settings.

New manuals and the inauguration of magazines explicitly directed at parents formed only part of this new bombardment. During the 1920s and 1930s, experts also established a host of classes for parents, not only through schools but also in women's clubs, settlement houses, and other agencies, reaching rural and immigrant populations, as well as the urban middle class. The movement reflected deep concern on the part of experts that many parents did not know their job and that parenting was hardly a natural act, save in the most rudimentary biological sense. But the movement also reflected, as well as stimulated, beliefs among parents themselves that old habits and assumptions had to be revisited, in a context in which not only parenting but also children themselves became more problematic.

THE TRANSFORMATION OF CHILDREN

As beliefs in original sin declined, a dominant image of children's innocence emerged in the 19th century. Children were seen as fundamentally good, and, though they could be led astray, if not corrupted by bad example they would grow naturally into their great potential.

There was dispute about this, of course. Ideas of original sin persisted in some groups, and even parents who had converted to what one historian has dubbed the "moderate" camp in the late 18th century continued to harbor some doubts.[2] Some boys and girls turned out to be "bad." Examples of lower-class children who did not measure up to character standards provided ready reminders of the possibility of deviation. Sexuality attracted new levels of concern, in a middle class increasingly concerned about respectability and a lower birth rate. Anxiety about masturbation, particularly among boys, might easily undermine the confidence in children's fundamental good nature.

But the confidence was there in most respects, on the assumption of a properly supportive middle-class family environment. Children would go up strong, with good characters, as long as they were allowed to do so. Good examples would help, of course, but the main point was to prevent the bad, to let nature take its benign course.

Gender beliefs reinforced this approach. While children of either gender could turn sour if misled, girls were by nature pure, even-tempered, prepared for the roles that awaited them as women. Boys had a natural spunk and competitiveness that at most needed a bit of fine-tuning to turn into the qualities needed for sound business or political life. Youth was another sturdy category. While the idea of adolescence as a time of some trouble originated in the 19th century, adults continued to assume that the process of educating and guiding children could continue into youth; not everything had to be instilled while the child was still very young. The prodigal-son-returned theme reminded adults that fundamental goodness could overcome even transitional setbacks.

Natural sturdiness shone through in a variety of settings. The American Institute of Child Life, shortly after 1900, issued a pamphlet on anger that sketched how parents needed merely to present their sons with illustrations of constructive reactions. Thus, one mother took her son to a town meeting at which shoddy treatment of the poor was being denounced. The boy immediately took the point, his face eager, his capacity for outrage permanently trained on bad public behavior. "His eyes flash with righteous indignation," as he builds on a natural emotion to channel feeling toward acceptable energy and action. There were no huge cautions here, no great anxieties about ungovernable impulse, just the opportunity to provide gentle guidance to a natural process of emotional maturation and social responsibility.[3]

The 20th-century approach, as it began to emerge after 1910, was different. Children were still seen as innocent in a sense, certainly worthy of love. But their natures were no longer viewed as reliable. Inner psychological demons and even physical failings could bring them down, through no fault of their own. Gender became less reliable as a predictor of behavior. Boys might turn out to be too girlish, at their worst falling into the pit of homosexuality (a new anxiety of considerable proportions). Girls were not naturally sweet; jealousy, for example, could make them dangerous to siblings at a shockingly young age. Individual propensities varied, of course, but there was no core sturdiness to call upon across the board. Flaws could emerge in the best of homes, without the provocation of bad example, and could poison the adult personality. Indeed, in the emotional sphere, an image of festering vice became widespread; children were seen to carry corruptive agents that must be drained lest they gain ascendancy. Without active adult intervention and manipulation to inhibit the flaws of character, emotional imbalances might intensify and lead to a totally dysfunctional adult personality. The problem could be anger, or jealousy, or even obsessive love. The root would lie in some distortions of children's nature, exacerbated by bad adult example and inadequate remediation. In summary, children were fragile; childhood, if not itself a problem, was problem- filled.

One of the great selling points of Dr. Spock's hugely popular book *Child Care*, which first appeared in 1946, was of course its reassurance—one historian, indeed, has dubbed Spock the "confidence man" because of his encouragement to parents.[4] After three decades of dire warnings, it was comforting to read a manual that suggested that parents might be able to handle the problems they encountered. But Spock was no reversion to 19th- century generalities. His book detailed a daunting list of potential issues in its several hundred pages, and it hardly assumed that parents' natural instincts would always carry them through the litany of health, emotional and environmental issues their children would generate. Some parents, in fact, complained that Dr. Spock heightened their anxiety. Spockian recommendations about such simple acts as bathing a child, with a huge list of do's and don'ts about what to wear, how to regulate temperature, and so on, could fluster far more than reassure: parenting seemed very difficult. Parents' panic might decline, but not their sense of childhood fragility.

THE CASE OF FEAR

Victorian attitudes toward fear and childhood were fairly straightforward and coincided largely with the confidence in the emotionally sturdy child. Girls, as part of their femininity, might be somewhat fearful, but this was not a major issue. A bit of feminine timidity could be charming. Boys, for their part, would face the idea of fear (if not necessarily the fact) as part of their manly development of courage, a key value. Boys' stories, correspondingly, were filled with tales of bravery; books like the Rollo series, where young Rollo routinely faced fear and conquered it in the interests of rescuing a sister or staring down a bully, echoed the same theme. Not only books but also boy culture itself stressed courage as a key male characteristic.[5] "Train up your children to be virtuous and fearless," one prolific child-rearing author wrote.

Here, obviously, was a key standard. Like all standards, it might fail of achievement. Parents could worry that an individual boy lacked pluck (that great 19th-century word), and there was a new term, sissy, to label the result. So there is no reason to claim that courage was a worry-free attribute. But the point here is that no sense emerged that children faced systematic problems with fear. There was no natural impediment to courage. The only issue that deserved systematic attention involved parents who used fear in discipline, but this was the kind of bad example (derived from misguided beliefs in children as evil) that could send even sturdy children astray. Otherwise, fear existed, and its conquest was something boys at least should learn about; for the most part, simply presenting the standards and providing examples of appropriate reactions would do the trick.

As early as 1904, before wholesale revisions to the 19th- century child-rearing approach, authors began sounding new notes of caution about fear and children. Mrs. Theodore Birney reported psychological research that showed that infants might be terrified by darkness or animals even if their parents had done nothing wrong. Children might, in other words, have some innate flaws where fear was concerned. And this meant that parents now faced a double burden. First, they had a problem where none had existed before. Second, the characteristic Victorian response, in which they themselves had been raised, was now seen as radically wrong. Children should not be blithely urged toward courage, after all, for they might become even more terrified, their fears "hardening" into a durable emotional weakness. While courage was not yet dropped as a goal, parents were best advised to help children avoid fear-provoking situations, rather than urging even reading matter on children that might upset them. Evasion was replacing natural maturation as a response. Words like pluck began to seem quaint.

Behavioral psychologists picked up this theme in the 1920s, with their stark claim that, in John Watson's words, "at three years of age the child's whole emotional life plan has been laid down, his emotional disposition set. At that age the parents have already determined for him whether he is to grow into a happy person or . . . one whose every move in life is definitely controlled by fear." Building on late 19th-century psychological research on children, which revealed the pervasiveness of fear- induced dreams, the behavioral psychologists argued that children did possess a few innate fears, which were often deepened and supplemented by careless parental behavior. Helping children avoid their objects of terror, using bribes rather than injunctions of natural courage to cover further deficiencies—these were the paths toward a healthy adulthood. The problems, in other words, could be fixed, but only with anxious parental attention and a realization that, by themselves, children might well be unable to work themselves out of the emotional swamp.[6]

By the 1930s, according to leading manual writers, the goal of courage itself became fairly remote, given the level of childish fears. More to the point was the capacity to bring fears out in the open for ventilation and discussion, and here parental assistance was vital. The vulnerable child, male or female, needed coddling. As Sidonie Gruenberg, an indefatigable manual writer, put it, "There is always the danger that the fear resulting from [simple insistence on courage] will reach the 'overwhelming' stage and leave its mark for a long time." Coping, not courage, was the more realistic goal. As *Parents Magazine* put it, going well beyond earlier behaviorist research, "The fact is that a child can get to be afraid of almost anything."

This was no abstract change. Parents were now urged to devise elaborate stratagems, involving great care and considerable periods of time, to help children overcome fears of animals or darkness. Sometimes, simple avoidance should be maintained: the child did not have to have a dog, darkness could be dissipated by a night light. Bad dreams were less avoidable and required lavish attention, with parents sitting up with the sleepless child for long stretches of time. It was Dr. Spock who cautioned, "Don't be in a hurry to sneak away before he is asleep . . . this campaign may take weeks, but it should work in the end." Delay travel plans when children seem anxious, Spock advised. Don't push toilet training to the point of causing fear. Love even older children who evince fear, because "the child is scared enough of his own mental creations."[7]

The point is clear and important: childhood self-sufficiency had been redefined away. Parental obligations increased immeasurably in the process, as confident emotional remedies gave way to demanding strategies: "The main job of the parent should be to prevent fears, since some fears are difficult to cure."[8] Success was possible, but it was neither easy nor automatic. And parents, as they wrote anxious letters to *Parents Magazine*, largely agreed: the list of sources of fear grew steadily as they recounted their own children's woes.

THE CHILD AS EMOTIONALLY NEEDY

Children's emotional problems could go well beyond their encounter with fear, of course. Once the research orientation developed, all sorts of possibilities were uncovered (some of which, it should be noted, have since been disproved). A spate of 1920s research, for example, revealed the extent of bitter sibling rivalries, on the part of girls and boys alike. Here was another inherent situation from which children could not necessarily extricate themselves. Jealousies could endanger other children and again could fester into adult dysfunction. Parental vigilance was required, and parents dutifully reported, in late-1930s surveys, that the sibling rivalry problem was one of the most difficult they had to contend with. Grief became another emotion that children were too fragile to handle, and a major campaign to keep children away from the sight of death and from funerals developed, again reversing a standard Victorian pattern. Manipulation was easier here, given the increasing isolation of severely ill people in hospitals, from which children were normally excluded. But there were some additions to parental anxieties, even so. Above all, parents must conceal their own emotions, such as grief, lest the vulnerable child be contaminated.

It was in this context that the uses of therapy for middle- class children began to be explored. It was no longer strange to believe that individual children might develop levels of psychological difficulty such that experts must intervene. More widely still, parents were encouraged to evaluate a host of developments for their potential to impinge on children's tender psyches. World War II, for example, generated not only formal studies but also extensive popularizations warning of potential damage to children's emotional development. The idea of childhood as vulnerability was easily extended to new situations.

Another change in emotional signals is interesting, though less dire. By 1920, experts were no longer urging that children be guided to suppress envy and find contentment. This was too stressful and also, now, unnecessary. Instead, children should be helped to conquer envy through a greater abundance of consumer goods and recreations. Here was a link between the vulnerable child, no longer safely constrained, and the culture of leisure, which we take up in chapter 6.

THE PHYSICAL CHILD

While emotional and psychological life most clearly revealed a new paradigm for children, worries about children's physical wellbeing took on a new slant, as well. Here, too, new knowledge and new standards combined. The contrast with the 19th century was slightly less stark, in that Victorian parents had also worried about children's health. But the sense of overall fragility increased here as well, for nature was no longer automatically benign.

Posture provides an interesting, if ultimately transient, example. From the late 18th century on, middle-class people had been urged to pay attention to careful posture as a badge of the capacity to control bodily whims. Standards in this area were thus not new. But child guidance literature had paid little attention to the issue, aside from some injunctions about table manners, for it was not assumed that children, properly dressed in stiff clothing and sitting in rigid furniture, would have much problem measuring up in formal settings. Aside from a bit of medical comment, there was no pervasive sense that children's bodies and proper posture were at odds.

This happy situation began to change by the 1890s, in part because clothing began to become less formal and furniture more lavishly upholstered, giving children more opportunity to slouch. A host of medical and school experts emerged to contend that children's posture was naturally bad unless corrected through elaborate adult efforts at home and in the classroom. The argument paralleled to a remarkable degree the burgeoning beliefs about children's emotional fragility. Children were not naturally aligned—a manual of 1894 trumpeted, "it is seldom that a completely normal figure is met with." Children's spontaneous activities, in addition to those forced on them in unnatural school settings, would make the matter worse in modern society. "We are forever engaging in activities which tend toward asymmetry and derangement of our architecture."[9]

This was not a matter of aesthetics alone. For several decades, posture experts contended that organs could grate against each other in the posture-poor body. Even character might suffer. As a *Parents Magazine* article put it, "Mental slackness is not necessarily caused by a bad walk, but almost invariably when this condition exists, the bodily movements are uncertain."[10] Once again, from babyhood on, nature was playing games with children, which only careful testing and remediation could counter.

Here was another problem for the responsible parent to add to the list of psychological risks. Parents were urged to watch children closely for signs of bad posture. Ubiquitous testing in schools and colleges drove the point home, making it clear that the inadequate parent would be readily found out. The array of devices used in schools to make children worry about their posture, such as tests against some ideal standard and probings by physical education personnel, multiplied through the 1940s. Thousands of middle-class college freshmen were photographed in the nude to check for deficiencies. Elite colleges not only tested but imposed grades and posture training courses to make good what nature and parents had neglected.

To be sure, this particular anxiety began to fade as doctors began to note, by the 1950s, that most children did in fact have adequate posture when judged by realistic standards. In this case, lessened rigor reduced parental anxiety, but only after several decades of active concern precisely when the idea of childhood as problem was taking root.

Furthermore, other issues rushed into the void. Most obviously, it was increasingly urged that children did not by nature know how to eat right and that modern social conditions exacerbated the problem. The science of nutrition gained ground, and its adepts emphasized the gap between proper standards and natural appetites. A growing drumbeat, throughout the early 20th century, stressed children's tendency to ignore foods vital for their physical and dental health, while overindulging foods that would do them harm. Again, watchful parents and nagging discipline must correct for willfulness. By the 1970s, concern about endemic overeating began to swell the chorus. American children were underexercising and growing too fat—except for those tragic cases, also ensnared by modern lures, where they radically underate, in the throes of anorexia nervosa. Whatever the excess, it was clear that natural distortions were being exacerbated by the temptations of modern life.

It was germs, of course, that added most acutely to parental concerns about children's health in the 20th century. Here was another set of natural villains, conspiring to undermine the child. And, while germs, unlike nasty emotions, were not of the child, they were within it, endemic, requiring careful vigilance and, in early childhood, placing the parent in direct conflict with the child's natural impulses. Admittedly, the measures taken to combat germs built on prior concerns about cleanliness. This aspect of children's vulnerability was more fully prepared by 19th-century standards than was the idea of children's psychological frailty. But, while 19th-century adults in the middle class sought cleanliness for respectability, they did not see it as part of a battle against unseen enemies, and their anxiety did not approach the intensity that became standard by the 1920s.

Timing here was crucial, particularly given the overlap with the new discoveries about children's emotional burdens. Germ theory began to be applied to focused concerns about the organization of home and family in the last years of the 19th century. Scare tactics proliferated, with "death calendars" that charted infection rates and admonitions about not letting strangers touch a baby adding to parental anxiety.

Children's lack of natural protection against this new threat was obvious, creating a potentially overwhelming responsibility for parents.

"In 92 percent of the deaths caused by communicable diseases the organism enters or leaves the body through the mouth or nose; and it is the human hand, in many instances, that carried it." So began a pitch, sponsored in the mid–1920s by a soap company, for a school campaign for child-focused hygiene standards, aimed at health and "decency" alike. Schools must teach that "all the children wash their hands regularly after toilet and before lunch"; "the object should be not merely to make children clean, but to make them love to be clean."[11]

Hygiene messages, school programs, and advertisements all urged that parents begin the fight against germs early by insisting that initially recalcitrant infants be given regular baths. Again, it had to be admitted that natural impulses, particularly among little boys, warred against this essential discipline, but there should be no concessions. And baths were to be accompanied by regular toothbrushing, another unnatural act but essential for dental health and people-pleasing smiles. The first widely used American dental cream, Dr. Sheffield's Crème Dentifrice, came on the market in 1892, and new kinds of brushes soon followed. The regimen became standard, imposing another year or two of careful guidance on the part of parents. Obviously, the campaigns worked: most children did become attached to this kind of hygiene, making parental guidance a temporary requirement. For the early years of life, at least, the need to monitor children's bodies unquestionably increased, adding to the understanding of children as vulnerable in the absence of anxious adult guidance.

Furthermore, enforcement standards in this area were quite clear, well beyond the presentations to neighbors that might punctuate a child's life in the 19th century. As with posture, school supervision was intense, spreading well beyond the middle class. As the New York Times explained, in 1927, "All the soiled and sotted children, backyards, restaurants and streets of the country are to be sought out, imbued with the desire for soap and scrubbing brushes, and turned loose with appearance and self- respect improved by several degrees." Children themselves were encouraged to tattle on home conditions as part of the schools' commitment to drive the new standards home. "Have children report on days they take baths at home. The type of home will determine whether to expect more than two baths a week." Here was a modest concession to different class standards, but the fact was that even the benighted immigrant was now expected to impose more frequent bathing than the respectable middle class had required forty years earlier.[12]

Further, led again by middle-class parents, the practice of regular checkups with pediatricians (an expanding medical specialty) also began to spread in the 1920s. Here was another mechanism by which parents' efforts to compensate for children's physical vulnerability would be checked, confirmed, and often, in the process, intensified.

We noted earlier that 20th-century developments created new worries even amid the rapid improvements in children's health. Campaigns to promote new levels of hygiene, building on the fears understandably associated with the germ theory and its unseen legions, were central to the intensification of this anxiety. The idea of steadily raising standards that increased work and worry, despite the potential for some relaxation, was hardly new to American or middle-class life. But the focus on children gave the process a somber human meaning, checked as it was by outside authorities and health specialists.

Finally, of course, and again as with concerns about emotional frailty, the general anxiety was readily supported by specific discoveries, in particular the intensified concern associated with key childhood diseases. During the middle decades of the 20th century, recurrent reports of polio epidemics, carried by germs in turn associated with public contact and dirt, helped keep parental anxieties at fever pitch. Tragic stories of children killed or crippled by a disease that seemed to single out young people provided ample motive for parents who fearfully kept their children inside during summers of crests in polio's incidence. Here was a stark vulnerability that began to win attention only in the 1880s. The epidemic of 1916, with its six thousand deaths, set the standard pattern in motion, the first of many summers that parents, particularly but not exclusively in the cities, would face a widely noted threat. Well-publicized illnesses of prominent Americans, such as the socialite Catherine Page, in 1916, and soon thereafter Franklin Delano Roosevelt, drove the danger home still further. March of Dimes campaigns continued the focus on innocent children: "Each year [polio] makes its awful visitations. Each year it seeks to maim and cripple our helpless babes, our happy youths. . . ."[13] The seriousness, chronology, and publicity associated with polio did much to solidify the image of children's physical vulnerability to germs.

The spur of specific epidemics and the more general informational campaign about germs—what one historian has called the "domestication of germs" between the 1890s and the 1920s, with vivid images of the millions of unseen demons that could cling to clothing and kitchen crevices[14]—provided one of the key links binding immigrant and working-class Americans to the theme of childhood vulnerability. The details of what was prescribed for psychological health might seem remote to immigrants, but health threats were another matter. The 1916 polio epidemic drove Italian-American mothers to shut their children in, sealing windows in stifling tenements in an effort to block the entry of germs. Cleanliness standards received sometimes obsessive attention, as mothers sought to protect children from infection.

Underlying the whole process of hygiene and disease threat—beyond the blandishments of self-interested soap advertisers, school-based Americanizers, and pediatricians—was the unprecedented unacceptability of death or serious illness among children. Here, too, changes transcended barriers of class and ethnicity. A child's death almost always causes anguish. The stakes had already gone up by the 19th century, when middle-class parents had been urged to wonder what fault they might bear for a child's tragic death. Always before, however, the understanding that some children would die, despite the best efforts of parents and doctors, had provided some cold comfort. Now this prop was withdrawn. Children rarely died (by 1920 the infant death rate was well below 5 percent and still falling), and they should not die. Here was the clearest way in which the new pricelessness of children shone through.

This valuation of children meant, for those few parents actually confronted with death, an almost unbearable sense of sorrow and guilt. Revealingly, few marriages in the 20th century survived the death of a child, so great was the sense that someone had done something wrong. After 1945, clubs formed for bereaved parents, because ordinary adults could simply not understand the emotions involved. But there was spillover even to the vast majority of parents who would not face the issue directly: there was always the question "what if?" It was hard to avoid an anxious monitoring of children's health given the intolerable burdens of error. And these stakes created an obvious context for well-intended but market-minded publishers to trot out one health threat after another, despite their usually low statistical incidence. Parents must be kept on guard, and, indeed, parents seemed to relish the reminders of their offspring's fragility.

SIDS: A CASE IN POINT

The history of Sudden Infant Death Syndrome reveals the power and extent of parental anxiety and guilt about children's death, and also the complexity of contemporary medical innovation in dealing with this same anxiety.

Infants have died mysteriously for many centuries. In the 19th century, a number of deaths were attributed to suffocation, with parents held morally but not legally responsible. It is possible that the rate of these mysterious deaths increased in the 20th century, thanks to separate infant sleeping arrangements, different bedding, and the survival of many infants who historically would have died at birth in an earlier era who had a particular vulnerability. With all this, the main cause of the invention or discovery of SIDS was middle-class parents' unwillingness to accept the customary designations of cause of death because of the intense guilt attached and their ability to influence responsive but also ambitious medical researchers in their cause.

In 1948, *Women's Home Companion* published an article by an anonymous parent who had lost a child and was convinced that the infant had died because physicians had advised him to place the boy on his stomach for sleep. Parental concern about this type of infant death was mounting, if only because so many other, more virulent problems had receded. Interestingly, fathers took at least as active a role in the campaign as mothers did, reflecting a level of parental anguish that may be less gender-specific than we sometimes imagine. Age-old questions— "why did my baby die?"; "what did I do wrong?"—were gaining new urgency and becoming less acceptable. When the questions were exacerbated by clumsy police interrogations in respectable middle-class homes, the results became less acceptable still.[15]

In 1958, Mark Roe, the six-month old son of a New York stockbroker, died. The Roes were devastated by grief but also convinced that there must be some explanation beyond mysterious suffocation. They were also convinced they had done nothing wrong, but they wanted reassurance. The organization and funding campaigns they inspired led to additional medical attention to the problem. Washington State politicians were soon brought in, in this case as a result of agitation by a be-reaved but savvy mother, again eager to demonstrate that there was some disease entity involved that would exonerate parents but that should also be investigated in the interest of better infant safety. It was in the 1960s that SIDS began to be defined as a distinct cause of death, still insufficiently explained but definitely not the result of parental fault. National legislation followed in the 1970s, directing that SIDS be taken seriously in infant death inquiries. Research funding increased. By this point, alert parents everywhere were quite aware of SIDS (its popular name was crib death). What began as an effort to reduce guilt had revolutionized a corner of medicine and medical law.

The results were not, however, clear-cut, in relation to the parental anxieties that had spawned them. In the first place, SIDS has still not been entirely explained, much less prevented. In the second place, what began as a desirable, certainly understandable effort to reduce guilt at a time when parental anxieties concerning infant fatalities were mount-ing may have turned into a new way to accuse. Claims here are contro-versial, sometimes tinged with racism. Initially, SIDS diagnoses were disproportionately applied to infant deaths in the white middle class, which reflected the social origins and anxieties of the whole movement. By the 1980s, however, minority and lower-class families were generat-ing the bulk of the diagnoses, which led some observers to wonder whether parental neglect was not sometimes more involved than the now convenient disease label implied. Here, certainly, was another rea-son to worry lest the tragedy, however infrequent, strike home, lest the finger of guilt find another parental target.

Another irony emerged: research, by the 1980s, suggested that SIDS children might have congenital defects. This put affected parents right back at square one; they might have caused the problem, however in-advertently, after all.

Most important, however, was the anxiety that the popularization of SIDS generated. Growing understanding that accidental deaths could occur, bolstered by reams of popular articles, left many parents nervously checking on their offspring frequently during the night—even through there was almost nothing they could do. Hyperbole en-tered in, as is so common in contemporary American problem identifi-cation. By the 1970s, public claims that SIDS was responsible for up to thirty-thousand deaths per year were common, although this number represented five times the actual number annually diagnosed. (At six to seven thousand deaths per years, SIDS claims at most 3 percent of all children born.) Pediatricians eagerly distributed warnings, which further raised anxiety to potentially disproportionate levels. Or, as the *Saturday Evening Post* put it, in 1966, again inaccurately, though with the best intentions: "this silent invisible killer is the leading cause of death among infants."

Parental anxiety, growing to new and less tolerable levels, helped create SIDS. The disease, in turn, fueled parental anxiety. It was easy to claim progress in knowledge where children and disease were concerned, but it was harder to alleviate guilt or worry.

OTHER THREATS

Psychological and physical vulnerability hardly exhausted the 20th-century list of parental anxieties. There was a recurrent new fear of the impacts of crime on children. Widely heralded kidnapping cases, such as the abduction of Charles Lindbergh's son in the 1930s, helped generate new panic about strangers and children, and a host of accompanying admonitions. Ransom kidnapping emerged as an American phenomenon late in the 19th century, and, while it focused on the wealthy, it encouraged wider fears. The same held true for widely publicized crimes by and against children, such as the random murder of a Chicago boy by Leopold and Loeb in the 1920s. By the 1970s, runaways and disappearances brought another reminder of how the social environment might overwhelm parental control. The milk carton campaign, featuring pictures of lost children, began in 1979, after an appealing New York boy was abducted (he was never found). Soon, campaigns were claiming that fifty-thousand abductions by strangers took place each year (the actual figure was between two and three hundred). Hyperbole and deep fear combined, and the faces of lost children on milk cartons and postcards drove the point home: the world was not secure for children. In urban and suburban settings, fears could push parents to restrict their children's freedom of movement, as it became unclear how to get children safely from one place to another unless parents themselves provided the transportation. Here was another area, as well, in which children's natural impulses, for example in responding to strangers, were unreliable, another area where vulnerability had to be matched by new levels of parental vigilance. Similar panics developed at several points in the 20th century (the decades from the 1950s to the 1970s were the main exception) about sexual predators who targeted children, with greatly exaggerated accounts of pedophile rings and other threats from outsiders. A University of Pennsylvania study in 2001 contended that one child in 220 was sexually exploited, the authors claiming that there was an epidemic in a well-intentioned attempt to jolt parents and policymakers into action. But the report proved hastily done, the figures apparently involving significant double counting. The shock was administered, another vulnerability to worry about, but the actuality and the longer-term results were cloudier, in what became a characteristic zigzag pattern.

The dramatic conversion of Halloween from a chance for children to revel in their spontaneity to a new and anxiety- provoking parental responsibility showed the new fear of the outside world—in this case, including neighbors. Reports spread widely in 1982 about poisoned candy and razorblade-filled apples given to children when they were trick-or-treating. It was not clear that any of the poisoning reports were true, though there were three cases of pins stuck in candy bars in the Long Island area. But accuracy was not the point where children's vulnerability was concerned. Parents began dutifully going with their kids on trick-or-treat outings, while cities increasing regulated them. The new pattern was going strong a quarter- century later, the anxieties as fresh as when the rumors were first launched.

What was happening here, obviously, was an interaction between assumptions of vulnerability and the new range and immediacy of media accounts. Rumors about dangers to children are common in many societies, but their frequency is limited by the fact that they spread within particular regions. Now, with the press, radio, and, soon, television at the ready, any predation, anywhere in the United States, became grist for the anxiety mill. Events like the Leopold and Loeb murder became coast-to-coast reality, vividly detailed, demonstrating how children might fall victim to random crime. Parental grief could be disseminated as never before, and it could prove contagious.

It was the growing threat of accidents, however, that most clearly showed the gap between children's vulnerability and their surroundings in modern society. Here, too, media accounts had a key role, but there were new realities, as well. While teenage driving did not become widespread until after World War II, except in rural areas, the potential both for cars and for the growing array of home appliances, electrical outlets, chemicals, and medicines to cause damage to children emerged clearly by the second decade of the 20th century. Here, obviously, the new emphasis on children's frailty focused on changes in the home and neighborhood, not on some new weakness on the part of children themselves. But, in combination with other new concerns about vulnerability and the coincidence in timing, it all added up to a powerful package.

In 1922, fifteen thousand New York children were paraded up Fifth Avenue to honor a new Child Memorial constructed to memorialize victims of street accidents. A special division of 1,054 boys represented an equal number of children accidentally killed during 1921, while fifty mothers who had lost their offspring marched behind. The city's Health Commissioner intoned: "We are here to dedicate a monument to the martyrs of civilization—to the helpless little ones who have met death through the agencies of modern life." Safety campaigns urged mothers to be more attentive, while teaching children basic pedestrian rules. By 1932, 86 percent of all schools had safety training, in what became a truly emotional community focus (in contrast to more diffuse efforts directed toward road safety more generally). Many families responded, where resources permitted, by reducing the time children spent on the street and building indoor play facilities, including formal playrooms, to diminish children's vulnerability. Park playgrounds served much the same function in disciplining and constricting fragile children. Urban children, particularly, were kept close to home.[16]

But home had its own problems. The National Safety Council, formed in 1914, soon began to issue regular reports on domestic injuries and fatalities to children. By the late 1920s, it was hard to avoid a sense that new levels of care were essential to protect young children. Insurance companies chimed in. In 1929, the National Bureau of Casualty and Surety Underwriters offered a fellowship for a "study of home safety as an index of good home management." By the 1930s, the Federation of Women's Clubs got into the act, urging "the responsibility that resets on the shoulders of women for the elimination of home accidents." By this point, more than thirty-thousand deaths per year were being reported from home accidents, disproportionately involving children. The Red Cross began calling for programs of home inspection, and, in 1935, the federal government summoned a conference on the subject. The focus was on parental, primarily maternal, awareness and discipline. "Prevention of accidences in the home," a Red Cross official wrote in 1947, "is largely the responsibility of the homemaker," and both good domestic arrangements and careful supervision of children flowed from this responsibility.[17]

Children themselves were blameless victims in this scenario, the concept of childish innocence clearly applied. But the ideas of risk and accident were also being redefined in favor of a nearly explicit position that accidents were not really accidental—they flowed from parental fault. And this was new. While 19th-century manuals, though focused primarily on character issues, worried about health, they expressed little concern for accidents, which continued to be regarded as largely unavoidable. But, by the 1920s, this attitude was changing, even as the potential sources of household danger increased. Ida Tarbell put it this way, in 1922: "By analyzing some of the accidents to children, the mother's responsibility is clear enough. None but she could have prevented them. Who else can keep a child from falling from a window, from pulling over a vessel of boiling water?" The attribution of parental obligation even moved into law; as a White House conference put it in 1960, when the child first begins to be exposed to dangers such as "moving vehicles, fire, sharp instruments, and other hazards . . . his parents are totally responsible for his protection against accidental injury of whatever nature."[18]

To be sure, other options besides parental watchfulness were exploited, particularly from the 1960s on, to reduce children's vulnerability. "Childproof" devices for electrical outlets and medicine bottles and the advent of car seats helped tone down the rhetoric somewhat. But the fact remained that most of the engineering gimmicks depended on parental implementation, and accident rates stayed high, unlike the rates for many of the most troubling diseases. By World War II, accidents formed the leading cause of death among children. When this fact was combined with the reasonable assumption that adults could be doing more by way of protection, the challenge to ongoing parental anxiety was obvious. Ironically, even some commonsense qualifications, urging that parents not become too overprotective, simply increased the burden: it was almost impossible to strike a successful balance for children who were physically vulnerable to safety hazards but also psychologically vulnerable to excessive parental zeal.

The susceptibility to concern also took a distinctive national twist that deserves more systematic attention. An American society normally hostile to government regulation became obsessively safety conscious, with warning signs, railings, every conceivable intervention between children and danger. The contrast with a freer-wheeling European approach was fascinating: whatever the commitment to freedom in the abstract, American children must be surrounded with safeguards. By 2001, even traditional games like dodge ball came under scrutiny for their threats to physical and moral wellbeing; perhaps, experts and parents argued, they should be banned (and this despite the fact that softer balls had already been introduced). Neither children nor, perhaps, their parents had either the common sense or the natural instincts to take proper care of themselves.

STAGES OF CHILDHOOD

The emergence of the vulnerable child, in its several aspects, helped generate new approaches to the phases of children's development and their relationships to parents. The extensive focus on very young children was a striking facet of the shift toward vulnerability. Protection of infant health and safety required new attention, because of novel hazards and also because of the unprecedented unacceptability of infant death. The Children's Bureau publication *Infant Care* offered official sanction. From 1929: "His future mental health, as well as physical health, will depend largely on the habits he builds during the first year of life, especially the early months." But the notion that babies required anxious monitoring in terms of emotional behavior was an important innovation. The two-year-old who lashed out at a sibling was not just a nuisance, in this mode, but a target of careful redress in the interest of future development. The baby who was late in walking or talking might need active remediation, lest low intelligence be involved. A vivid feature of the new-style child-rearing manuals, in contrast to their much more generalized 19th-century counterparts, was the provision of precise measurements by which babies might be assessed—and found wanting unless parents stepped in.

The focus on infants both reflected and caused the larger turn toward vulnerability. Babies were helpless, and, as they loomed larger, their helplessness could easily seem to characterize childhood more generally.

The vulnerability theme had implications for other phases of childhood, as well. Parental anxiety, and the desire to keep children close to home, could readily complicate children's efforts to gain identity and independence. Teenage defiance was hardly a 20th-century invention, but its range unquestionably expanded. By the 1920s, dating began to replace courtship, moving heterosexual contact away from home and parents to more commercial and school settings—strike one against parental influence. After World War II, aided by the ubiquitous automobile, adolescents' contacts with their parents decreased still further; even a common mealtime became negotiable. While all sorts of factors affect this pattern, the desire to escape well-intentioned but patronizing parental influence deserves attention. The impact on parents, accustomed to focusing on their children's vulnerability but now incapable of the kind of monitoring that might minimize the danger, was considerable. Teenagers, particularly on the road but also with the opposite sex, seemed vulnerable still; but parents' capacity to act on their concern diminished steadily. Public service announcements began to play on this tension by the 1970s most famously with the slogan "Do you know where your child is?"

WHAT CAUSED THE NEW PERCEPTIONS?

Whether the issue is the recasting of the parent-adolescent debate over dependence or the attempt to confine younger children to playrooms and playgrounds, the replacement of the concept of the sturdy child with that of the vulnerable child was a cultural shift of major proportions. We will return to the question of its significance at the conclusion of this the chapter. But there's a step in the analysis that must come first, though part of the answer is obvious from the accounting of the change itself: what caused the new image of children?

A number of factors enter in. They first took on significance around the turn of the century, though many persisted over the decades, helping to explain not only the initial transformation but also its staying power. The role of outside experts is obvious but needs a bit of additional commentary. Changes in environment and, to a degree, in children themselves provide a second set of ingredients. Part of the new perception of childhood resulted from the fact that childhood and its context, particularly with regard to sexual maturity, refused to hold still, and new realities in day-to-day life also had their impact. Finally, other adult anxieties fed the mix, as adults transposed to children some new anxieties about their own lives.

Expertise and Changes in the Environment and in Views of Children

The new expertise that redefined child-rearing manuals contributed greatly to the new appreciation of problems in childhood. There are several angles here. The community of relevant experts and popularizers expanded, with the growth of academic research, family-related publishing, and so on. Finding and keeping an audience depended on identifying needs and refuting the previous generation's advice. This operated, of course, in a larger capitalist-consumerist framework in which people were encouraged to recognize lacks that could be ameliorated by buying some product or service. A certain faddish quality entered into the process: thus, permissiveness early in the century was replaced by behaviorist strictness, only to yield to Spockian permissiveness. The idea of vulnerability was not itself faddish, in that it underlay most of the cyclical fashions. But it was amplified by the sense of fluctuation and the urgent need to find new issues to pontificate about. A key cause of the intensification of posture concerns was the emergence of physical education instructors as an aspirant professional group, requiring a cause to justify their existence. More generally, pediatricians and psychologists needed clients, and their claim that only they had the knowledge needed to resolve otherwise crippling deficiencies in children went a long way toward redefining the larger images of childhood. Without question, the number of stakeholders in the belief in children's vulnerability, and the need for professionals who could guide parents as a result, increased steadily.

In fact, knowledge expanded; it was not just a matter of aggressive professionalism. A simple answer to why the change—too simple, in the final analysis—was that children's hitherto unknown traumas were laid bare, after a century of facile optimism, by new research on dreams, repressions, rivalries, and germs. Simply collecting and publishing accident statistics could have a great impact. American children became one of the most widely studied groups in the world, from a host of disciplinary vantage points.

Collectively, the research that began to be directed toward children, by people like William James, G. Stanley Hall, and Earl Barnes, late in the 19th and early in the 20th centuries, has been called the "child study movement." Its premises involved a belief that scientific principles had never been applied to the study of children and that people were therefore amazingly ignorant about what children were like. The goal was to promote child development and happiness, but the findings emphasized troubles and deficiencies, including both ignorance and strain. Thus, educators must realize how little children know, even after schooling. Employers and teachers alike should realize that children should not work too hard. The results added to knowledge, but they altered common assumptions in the process; the link between the two is difficult to disentangle. They also tended to elevate even semi-experts, like teachers, over parents, who seemed to fall to the bottom of the adult heap in terms of scientific understanding—another entry for the self-proclaimed authorities and their popularizers. At the same time, parents gained new responsibilities. Increasingly precise identification of handicapped and mentally deficient children, for example, prompted growing numbers of parents anxiously to screen their babies for the first signs of trouble—another prod toward anxiety.

Research findings were supplemented, and sometimes dominated, by new intellectual models. While the popularity of Freudianism in the United States has been debated, and not all Viennese theory found favor, Freudian ideas extended the belief in unconscious forces that could overwhelm children. They also confirmed the central importance of early childhood. Behaviorists explicitly disputed Freudian premises in many respects, but they echoed many of the points that could help convince parents that children were fragile creatures.

Darwinian premises entered in, providing a vivid connection between natural humans—and children were the most natural humans around—and animals. G. Stanley Hall explicitly argued that children must pass through the stages of evolution, from savagery on up, as part of their reach toward childhood. Small wonder that children, faced with this awesome climb, were easily overwhelmed, in experts' estimation.[19]

Professionalism replaced sentimentality. Parents continued to be very sentimental about children—this was part of the priceless-child formula—but experts prided themselves on hardheaded realism, removing the rose-covered glasses. This was a current that applied well beyond the child-rearing sphere, to social work, for example, where presumably scientific research was meant to replace female-directed charity. The shift involved some explicit attacks on older feminine rhetoric and its argument that mother's love and childhood innocence could solve all problems. Women experts themselves, in order to establish their professional status, turned against maternalist panaceas. The idea that parenting or mothering was a natural instinct suffered in the process.

Professional needs and new kinds of research produced the redefinition of child-rearing manuals, and this in turn helped generate new parental attitudes more generally. What's debatable is how much this expertise factor counted. Some historians have argued that parents' bombardment by expert opinion, not only in popular books but also in school programs and newspaper columns, undermined parental confidence. This contention was a significant part of Christopher Lasch's critique of American culture in the 1960s.[20] This argument suggests that parents came to see children as vulnerable not only because experts listed one problem after another but also because their own sense of competence diminished. The whole parent-child relationship became more questionable and fragile.

We have already argued that too much emphasis on the outside expert factor would be misplaced. Parents were influenced, though in diverse ways. But they also sought and accepted expertise because their own sense of who children were was changing, which is precisely why they needed new quantities of advice and why they bought into the childhood-as-problem formula.

New kinds of expertise contributed to the change. The continued outpouring of manuals, the endless procession of news article identifying one new childish weakness after another, helped maintain the new paradigm. But all of this built on other factors, which created the opportunities for reliance on expertise in the first place.

Changing Views of Childhood and Sexuality

On the borderline between expertise and parental realities was the gradual transformation in attitudes about sex. Middle-class standards in the 19th century were clear: children and sex should not mix. Childish innocence was explicitly asexual, and there were strong hopes that this innocence would shield children from contacts with this aspect of life. This assumption could founder, creating significant anxieties, for example, about masturbation. Boys occasioned particular concern, though adult ire was even stronger where deviant girls were involved. But the hope for innocence nevertheless burned bright.

From the 1920s on, attitudes about children's sexuality began to shift, in part because of the various scientific discoveries about children's sexual impulses. It was in this decade, for example, that sex education programs began to emerge in some schools. It was no longer assumed that childhood could or should be free from all connection to sexual issues.

In one sense, this gradual change could reduce parents' anxieties, in the area of masturbation, for example. And individual parents, hailing the possibility of a new openness about sexual pleasure, could rejoice in new latitude and new frankness where children were concerned. Sex was not an arena where 20th-century anxieties clearly outstripped those of the 19th century.

But, among American parents more generally, a profound ambivalence developed. On the one hand, children could not be shielded entirely. On the other, parents remained intensely uncomfortable about sexual discussions or about tolerating sexual behavior. The heightened tensions about homosexuality constituted one symptom of this, but the unease applied to heterosexual areas, as well. It was extremely difficult, as one result, to win agreements on anything but the most rudimentary, and usually negative and cautionary, approach to sex education in the schools. Children's sexual interests constantly seemed to be outpacing parents' tolerance levels. Sexual maturity occurred at ever younger ages, forcing adults to confront sexuality, even in sex education classes, in preadolescents. There was an obvious set of issues with regard to commercial entertainments available to children, as we discuss in chapter 6. But this ever younger sexuality affected the more general image of vulnerability, as well. For, while full innocence was gone, there was no entirely acceptable, generally agreed-upon model to put in its stead. So parents worried that their children faced new dangers, even as a certain degree of change seemed unavoidable. Fears of venereal disease or, later, AIDS obviously fed anxiety as well.

New Realities in Day-to-Day Life

Several components of the new emphasis on the need to protect children reflected objective changes in children's lives. By 1920, the United States was a predominantly urban society. Automobiles and other manifestations of contemporary technology were not child-friendly. Indeed, there was a deep tension between the high rhetorical value now placed on children—the priceless child—and the fact that contemporary life created new hazards in the home and new impediments to the free movement of children outside the home. The issue went beyond safety specifics, though these were important. The larger parental realization that modern society endangered children could motivate wider protective impulses. More than technology was involved. We will see, in later chapters, how a concern about children's vulnerability applied to large, impersonal bureaucracies—for example, the contemporary school systems—and to consumer agents preying on children—for example, the comic book industry.

Enthusiasts liked to argue that the 20th century was unprecedentedly focused on the child, that it was indeed the "century of the child." In fact, key realities pointed in the opposite direction, leading to new levels of parental anxiety and an objective grasp of children's frailty, at least in this new context. Even aside from the danger of new technology, Americans were not fully comfortable with the society developing around them. The 1920s, for example, saw the peak of the Chicago school of sociology, which emphasized the pathologies of urban life. The deep American commitment to suburbanization was a key reaction to discomforts of this sort, though it did not resolve major aspects of the gap between children and modernity.

For the many immigrants adjusting to American life in the first quarter of the century, urban unfamiliarity was compounded by strangeness in language and culture. How could parents care for children exposed to so many alien influences? It was easy for critics of immigrants, but also for immigrant parents themselves, to find new problems in childhood in this setting, for, in terms of cultures of origin, children were in fact more vulnerable in the new environment.

There were other new realities, as well, even closer to the middle-class home. The early 20th century saw the reduction of three traditional buffers between parents and children in middle- class households. The use of live-in domestic servants declined. This development was welcome in some ways; complaints about how crudely servants treated children was a staple of 19th-century women's conversation. But the fact was that, with servants less available, mothers and, to some extent, fathers had to put more time into the child-rearing process.

Simultaneously, in the 1920s, the common 19th-century pattern of older parents, particularly mothers, living with one of their adult children and helping out with the grandkids began to unravel as older people increasingly lived separately. Grandparents might still be within hailing distance, by phone or via a weekend drive, but they were not available for daily assistance. Again, the results were mixed, and there were no loud complaints about what was a major household change. One obvious outcome was the need for more outside advice and the greater readiness to believe that the past generation's standards were this generation's hit list. By the 1940s, a majority of American parents, when polled, claimed that it was vital to raise their kids differently from the way their own parents had raised them. Here was an attitude that was repeated often in subsequent decades and that in fact exaggerated generational change (as in the recurrent inventing of the "new fathering"). But here was an attitude, regardless of accuracy, that both reflected and encouraged the growing distancing of grandparents.

Finally, the steady reduction in the birthrate, again led by the middle class, reduced the number of older siblings available to help take care of the younger ones. Increased school and activity requirements contributed to the same result. Siblings were few in number, often quite close in age (a particular and odd feature of the baby-boom generation from the mid-1940s to the mid-1960s); and there was a decreasing sense that it was legitimate to ask for babysitting help too often anyway (part of the new confusions about work that we deal with in chapter 5).

A comment that appeared in the *Literary Digest* in 1925 suggests the effect of changes in the household in increasing parental anxiety: "In these days when parents have more time to observe their children, and have fewer children to observe, unusual attention is being given . . . to the natural activities of children. This leads to alarm on the part of those who may not be sufficiently informed as to what is normal child conduct." The author went on to note how stylish children's behavior problems were becoming in this context. "The mother who dares admit that her children have no behavior problems casts doubt upon her ability to recognize one."[21]

In sum: a key new reality of the early 20th century is that parents confronted children, particularly babies, more directly, with less assistance and fewer intermediaries, than had been the case in the 19th century. This could easily contribute to a sense that children had problems—partly reflecting the fact that parents had more problems with them. When combined with a rhetoric that insisted on children's preciousness, the tensions could readily translate into a sense of vulnerability. And children themselves became more emotionally attached to parents, precisely because of the lack of other figures in their young lives. Studies of small families, with few children, suggest a common pattern of sibling rivalry for parents' affection and attention, in contrast to more cooperative sibling relationships in larger broods. Yet the small family was now the norm. Reports of emotional vulnerability, particularly where sibling jealousy was concerned, thus reflected not just new expertise but also newly emphasized qualities within the children themselves.

Adding to domestic innovation, finally, was the question of sleep practices. Child-rearing advice in the 19th century reveals little concern about children's sleep. Recommendations about amounts of sleep were offhand, surprisingly permissive, in part no doubt because it was fairly easy for children to take naps on their own. Not so in the 20th century. Sleep became another issue where nature could not be relied upon. It was vital for parents to help children sleep soundly; the number of hours of sleep advised for young children went up steadily. Here, as in so many other aspects of children's lives, a new problem was being discovered, a new area in which children might be vulnerable.

Obviously, new expertise played a role here, particularly from pediatricians. But there were new realities, as well. Noise and artificial light created disturbances in contemporary urban environments (though the night light was a potential palliative for fears). Here was another area in which modern life and children really did not mix well. Behaviorists, who helped push sleep issues to the fore, insisted on the importance but also the difficulty of providing "quiet and serenity of environment." More broadly, the idea that sleep was a problem in a context of potential nervousness and anxiety on children's part reflected some of the wider concerns about modernity.

More important still was the increasing insistence, from about the 1880s on, that young children should quickly learn to sleep alone. Traditionally, babies had been placed in cradles, sleeping near either parents or domestics, until they were old enough to graduate to a common sleeping room with their siblings. These patterns now changed. Cradles gave way to cribs, which allowed infants quite soon to be placed in their own room, alone. And then, after cribs were outgrown, most authorities, and increasing numbers of parents, argued that a separate bedroom was vital for children's development and autonomy. As a children's magazine article put it, in 1923: "Do you sleep in a bed all by yourself? It is much better to sleep by yourself. You can rest better and breathe fresher air if you have a bed all your own." This fascinating formula reflected growing affluence, first on the part of middle-class families. It reflected a dramatic increase in the valuation of individuality on children's part, as well as concerns about sexual development and the ubiquitous fear of germs. It markedly increased the sleep difficulties of young children, particularly when accompanied by the new insistence that the child should learn to sleep uninterruptedly for ten hours or more. Loneliness, insecurity, and crying increased—which was why the self-appointed experts jumped in with new strictures and guidance.[22]

Needing to care for children with little or no additional help, parents, and particularly mothers, could easily translate their own concern about sleep-troubled children into a sense of childish weakness more generally. Here was another area in which the experience of childhood really was changing.

The environmental shifts around children provided the most obvious contribution to the new sense of children's vulnerability. They were balanced, to some degree, by the decline in health threats, but parents were not encouraged to perceive this tradeoff, given the heightened anxiety about germs. Less tangible, but at least as compelling, were the changes in child care and the needs that young children now conveyed to parents, thanks to changes in the parents' emotional focus and in the handling of issues such as sleep. The changes in children's behavior are not easy to assess, and of course they varied from one individual to the next. But they do help explain the extent of the paradigm shift, and why the new breed of expert had so much room to maneuver.

Some of the changes, finally, contributed as well to a parental sense of guilt. One of the reasons for the new sleep arrangements for children reflected the wishes of husbands and wives to have more time alone, free from rocking a baby, in a brightly lit room, possibly with the radio on. Child-centeredness at home, at night, decreased, and adult-child separation in this sense grew. The results were dressed up with new furniture such as cribs and new beliefs in the moral and health gains of sleeping alone, but the fact was that, at some point around 1900, parents began taking care of children at bedtime in ways that differed from their own upbringing. It was hard not to feel a tug of guilt about this shift in priorities, and this is turn could feed a more general anxiety about what parents themselves were contributing to children's well-being.

Adult Standards and Self-Reproach

The final set of causes for the change in how children were perceived involved new adults concerns that could be displaced onto children, both individually and as a category, making it easier to discern new weaknesses in children. The drop in the birth rate is a factor here. One historian has argued that turn- of-the-century parents felt obscurely guilty about their reluctance to have the traditional number of children (and, often, about their wish to indulge in purely recreational sex as birth control devices began to gain acceptance). This is hard to prove, but it falls into a category of adult distractions that might promote feelings of guilt about their devotion to their children, which in turn would generate a sense of children's neediness. Were parents being selfish in limiting the number of children they wanted to take care of? In seeking some separate adult time at night and defining marriage partly in terms of shared adult entertainments? The need to hire babysitters—a 1930s neologism—and worries about their inadequacy reflected the new desire for separate marital leisure, but also new problems it created. Selfishness might enter again, by the 1950s and 1960s, as mothers entered the labor force, particularly when self- fulfillment was the goal. How much of the loud devotion to the "century of the child" reflected a sneaking belief that children were not in fact receiving their due? Parental guilt made it easy to perceive new frailties in children.

Concern about the divorce rate could add impetus to this emotional change. The first public discussion of an American divorce crisis occurred in the 1890s, and the subject continued to loom large. Adults participating in divorce (a small minority until after World War II), those for whom divorce seemed an attractive option at some point, and those who simply observed what seemed to be the weakening of the American family could all wonder about the impact on children. And worry could easily translate into a fear that children were not being properly served, were less important in adults' views; from this to a belief in more systematic vulnerabilities was not a huge step. The same connections might apply to mothers' increasing interest in public activities and in recreations outside the home—and, soon, in formal employment itself. Were children being slighted? The link between uncertainties about the validity of new adult interests and a sense that children had weaknesses that must be indulged could be direct, and it intensified after World War II as family life was more systematically redefined.

Finally, in this category of transposed anxieties, adulthood itself became more complex in many ways, which meant that children must adjust accordingly. Educational standards increased; we will see the echoes of this when we deal with anxieties about the pressures of modern schooling on children. Emotional subtleties increased. One of the reasons adults came to believe in endemic jealousy among children was that their own experiences of jealousy were tested as co-education and other informal contacts between the sexes became more common. New needs to control adult jealousy easily confirmed the new belief that children were likely to be dangerously jealous unless controlled by their parents. Emotional health itself was redefined, becoming harder to achieve. Whereas Freud had posited the capacity to work and to love as the core definition of mental health, by mid- century many Americans sought more elaborate feel-good goals. With adult well-being more challenging, childhood inevitably came to be seen as more problematic as well; it would take more input for a good result.

Guilt about new adult interests, concerns about modernity, self-doubts displaced onto children (e.g., jealousy), and a sense that the socialization of children must meet new standards all could add up to a sense that childhood must be tacitly redefined, with growing emphasis on the problems involved. Here again was a source of the openness to cautions by experts, which readily played on a fear that traditional standards of child rearing were not being met. Here, finally, was another reason that some real changes in the experience of childhood could seem troubling, even ominous.

THE CONSEQUENCES OF THE VULNERABLE CHILD

Dominant imagery of children is a cultural construct and subject to change. Earlier in American history there had been a significant shift, from an emphasis on original sin and even on the animal-like qualities of children (though this was never played up as much in colonial America as in early modern Europe) to a belief in the innocent, benign, and lovable child. The growing focus on frailty built on the ideas of innocence and emotional value but added a vital new ingredient that could, indeed, predominate. The change was important.

It was also largely implicit. Experts were quite aware that they were offering new warnings about children's frailties and attacking older, presumably misguided views. During the Progressive era, there was also an understanding among experts and middle-class parents more generally that "other people's" children needed new protections against various dangers: what Anthony Platt has called the "child-saver" approach in settlement house and playground movements, directed at urban immigrants and the working classes. But the extent to which new anxieties were developing about one's own children, about children in the middle classes, was rarely articulated. A full statement of the concept of vulnerability and its contrast to 19th-century perceptions of children did not emerge. It was clear, nevertheless, not only that beliefs about original sin were wrong but also that undue reliance on a belief in the sturdy innocence of children was wrong, as well: children could be ensnared by psychological demons or physical threats, without being at fault but also without being able to right themselves without substantial assistance.

The factors that fed this new view accumulated, as we have seen, in the first quarter of the new century, building on some earlier preparation. New psychological research, the new fear of accidents, the impact of new kinds of birth control or sleep patterns all clustered together. Some of these factors lost a bit of force, or simply became routinized, by the middle of the 20th century. Accidents remained a deep concern, but they were no longer novel, and increasing attention shifted to engineering solutions, in contrast to the earlier emphasis on parental responsibility and fault. The number of spectacular ransom kidnapping declined, though fears about children's disappearance and abduction continued, and anxiety about child suicide mounted. Use of birth control no longer caused so much guilt (particularly after the baby boom showed the drawbacks of having too many kids). Psychological discoveries no longer surprised the public, and Freudianism began to lose favor.

But the idea of fragility persisted: there was no new paradigm to replace it. Specific evaluations did oscillate. Self- serving hopes in the 1960s that children could easily survive parental divorce yielded to more conservative views, and new data, that returned to the vulnerability model, arguing that children could be badly hurt by parental splits. New findings muted the potential for relief of ongoing concerns. Thus, while household equipment became safer, parents were warned of the dangers of keeping young children in confining playpens, so the task of monitoring toddlers around the house did not necessarily ease.

Some childhood diseases were eradicated, or nearly so, by inoculations, but there were new scares, such as Sudden Infant Death Syndrome. And growing realization of the ways fetuses could be damaged before birth by maternal overindulgence added to the image of children's vulnerability.

A humble example suggests the fundamental persistence of childhood as a time of vulnerability. From the 1970s on, well- meaning school programs often asked teenagers to carry a raw egg around with them for several days, in order to learn what an awesome responsibility a baby would be. The symbolism was particularly interesting because no one questioned it: but why such an easily breakable object? Was this really a useful representation of young children? The association made sense because Americans were so ready to accept the primacy of fragility (and of course were delighted by the possibility teenagers would be sufficiently deterred to keep their own eggs in check).

Again, new discoveries both used and confirmed the image of vulnerability. In 2001, newspapers trumpeted a growing concern about bullying in school. Findings that school shootings were often caused by kids who had been pushed around anchored this campaign. The San Diego *Union Tribune* picked up the new standards: "Think back to the third grade. . . . Maybe you were too short, too thin, too fat . . . too smart. Too . . . whatever 'they' decided. They who tripped you, mocked you, grabbed your lunch. Stole your dignity, your confidence, your spirit." Small wonder that the Los Angeles *Times* called bullying a "national pestilence," noting that 39 percent of all fifteen-year-olds said they had been bullied or were bullies themselves. A number of California authorities urged school to crack down on even minor acts of intimidation, like nasty gestures, "which can be precursors to bigger conflicts."[23]

The formula is familiar in American anxiousness: a legitimate concern—the school shootings—prompts a larger search for symptoms, which in turn easily is absorbed into the debate over the extent to which children are flawed and/or frail in face of threats. Then come the efforts to regulate behaviors, in this case despite evidence that almost all children survive some bullying phase (many of them both recipients and agents at various phases of childhood) and that actual child violence is diminishing. The image of the vulnerable child remained readily available. As another 2001 artifact—a popular bumper sticker—put it: "children need encouragement every day."

More generally, Americans maintain their readiness to accept specific new findings that both use and confirm the vulnerability theme. We will see in chapter 4 how easy it was to convince American adults of deficiencies such as Attention Deficit Disorder that would provide a specific vocabulary for a weakness that in turn would explain why many children were overwhelmed by school. The particularly American fascination with genetic explanations had much the same flavor, in the final decades of the 20th century. Genetics confirmed the belief that many children were flawed, either physically or mentally or both. Genetic causality might also, of course, provide some hope for redress, which was always welcome.

Genetic explanations of why children were depressed, or unruly, or fat also maintained the ambiguous relationship to parental responsibility that the fascination with frailty had always implied. Flaws were not the fault of children. They were also not the result of parental misbehavior. But they suggested a need for parental compensation, and they implied some responsibility, as well. Parents did not deliberately cause genetic misfiring, but they did provide the genes. They did not cause fearful nightmares, but they were culpable if adequate reassurance were not provided. It was difficult, faced with vulnerable children, not to feel some guilt.

The new image did not preclude exceptions. Different parents evinced different degrees of acceptance of the frailty model. In addition, larger cultural values could enter in. Authorities reported a continued impulse among fathers to urge sons to face up to their fears, to "be a man," in contrast to the more protective attitudes of mothers. Protestant fundamentalists still punished children on the assumption of original sin; the frailty rhetoric largely passed them by.

Even mainstream approaches could waver. We will see that American parents, otherwise open to vulnerability concerns, accepted several disciplinary settings where assumptions of sturdiness still prevailed; the fulminations of sports coaches were the most obvious case in point.

Parents did not act on their beliefs in children's frailty as decisively as might be expected in two key areas. Americans were slow to pick up the concern about overeating. In part, this resulted from an older image of childhood frailty: the underfed, skinny child, which continued to dominate concerns into the 1940s, exacerbated by the imagery of the Depression. Even later, hesitancies continued because of the potency of the anorexia fear, even though, statistically, the problems posed by anorexia were minor compared those posed by child obesity. It remained hard, in sum, for parents to act on an understanding that children did not spontaneously eat well, that in modern conditions at least they were prone to overindulgence.

There was also some interesting hesitancy over teenage drivers, despite the pervasive and understandable concern about accidents. The issue of teenage driving was defined by the 1930s, with abundant commentary on the need for traffic rules, license tests, and school training. These approaches were quite consistent with the realization that young drivers were extremely vulnerable. And Americans readily accepted regulations over other, related signs of weakness: for example, a brief experiment with treating eighteen-year-olds like adults by allowing them to purchase alcohol was ended quickly, and the United States ended the 20th century as one of very few societies around the world trying to defend a drinking age of twenty-one.

But, despite the larger imagery of vulnerability, despite the abundant evidence that teenage drivers were often the cause and the victims of accidents, direct regulation of teen drivers remained fairly lax. It was far easier to obtain a driver's license in the United States, at a younger age, than in other industrial societies. The assumption that adolescents should drive overwhelmed the reality of vulnerability. Here, even more than with overeating (where the issue revolved in part around what kind of frailty should be emphasized), we need to explain the exceptions to the rule—a promise for later chapters.

Overall, however, the image of the vulnerable child did win wide acceptance. It helped redefine parental and adult approaches in a variety of areas. It reshaped discipline, in warning against undue harshness. It dramatically colored attitudes toward school, which now could easily be seen as too taxing. It affected attitudes toward children's work and even toward the application of consumerism to childhood. The following chapters take up these effects, building on the theme of the vulnerable child but also further illustrating its power and sweep.

New beliefs in children's vulnerability also entered into discussions of adoption procedures, contributing greatly to the increasingly strict professional standards developed for adoption from the 1920s on. Fragile children needed careful protection so that suitable parents could be identified. The only problem was that knowledge of adoption—of rejection by one's birth parents—might in itself cause "serious narcissistic injury" even in the best of cases, making the task of navigating childhood successfully all the harder.

There were larger orientations, as well. The assumption of the vulnerable child interacted extensively with the increasing and unusual openness of American society to psychological explanations and remedies. If childhood was simultaneously flawed and causal, parents bore a huge responsibility for outcomes. Americans were distinctive, by mid-century, in their willingness to attribute personal problems to parental mishandling. Am I too fat? My parents must have dropped the ball somewhere, not only in failing to guide my eating but in generating other insecurities that I eat to compensate for. As the *Ladies' Home Journal* put it, in 1951, "the obese woman's very dimensions reflect her need for strength and massiveness in order to deny an image of self that she brings from childhood, an image felt to be basically weak, inadequate and helpless." Do you have problems with anger at work? Somehow, your parents did not help you learn to identify and control a dangerous emotion.

The American temptation to blame parents for providing inadequate help in growing up safe and sound obviously affected parenting itself. If I as an adult understand some of the damage my parents did to me, how can I do things differently for my own fragile brood? How can I avoid having my children think of me as I think of my own parents? It was not an easy task.

Not surprisingly, the charm of being child*like*, an image often evoked in the 19th century, particularly for women, now faded, yielding to the more unfortunate consequences of being child*ish*. Adulthood warred with immaturity: adult success meant that the debilitating features of childhood were overcome; yet these same weaknesses made the process arduous.

The implications of the image of vulnerable childhood for the prospect of parenting were complex and intimidating. Several reactions could coexist. The task of parenting became more daunting: it was a huge responsibility to deal with creatures still seen as lovable, but requiring so much remedial attention. Awe might slide over to dislike: though hard to articulate in a culture still eager to glorify children, the sheer responsibility of parenting might seem to outweigh any rewards. This was a theme that could justify not having children, against the common norms; or seeking adult spaces where children could not enter; or simply telling pollsters that parenthood had been a mistake—

all themes that emerged recurrently by the 1970s. Most obvious was the guilt reaction, the fear that, whatever one did, it would be inadequate to help the child through its sea of troubles. The goal of happiness and success for children was not new, but now it was clouded by the understanding that its achievement was not automatic, that more than childish self-help was essential. And who was at fault when the goal proved elusive?

Vulnerable childhood, as perceived and managed by parents and other adults, had its impact on children, as well. This deserves attention in its own right, after we follow some of the practical consequences in key areas of children's lives, such as school and work.

FURTHER READING

On the rise of vulnerable child, Joseph Kett, *Rites of Passage: Adolescence in America, 1790 to the Present* (New York, 1979); Theresa Richardson, *The Century of the Child: The Mental Hygiene Movement and Social Policy in the United States and Canada* (Albany, 1989). On emotions, Joel Pfister and Nancy Schnog, eds., *Inventing the Psychological: Toward a Cultural History of Emotional Life in America* (New Haven, 1957); Peter N. Stearns, *American Cool: Constructing a Twentieth-Century Emotional Style* (New York, 1994) and *Jealousy: The Evolution of an Emotion in American History* (New York, 1989). On disease and hygiene, Tom Gould, *A Summer Plague: Polio and Its Survivors* (New Haven, 1995); Naomi Rogers, *Dirt and Disease: Polio before FDR* (New Brunswick, NJ, 1992); Nancy Tomes, *The Gospel of Germs: Men, Women and the Microbe in American Life* (Cambridge, MA, 1998); and Vincent Vinikas, *Soft Soap, Hard Sell: American Hygiene in the Age of Advertisement* (Ames, IA, 1992). On nutrition and fat, Peter N. Stearns, *Fat History: Bodies and Beauty in the Modern West* (New York, 1997). On accidents, Joel Tarr and Mark Tebeau, "Managing Danger in the Home Environment, 1900–1940," *Journal of Social History* 29 (1996): 787–816; John Burnham, "Why Did the Infants and Toddlers Die?" *Journal of Social History* 29 (1996): 817–36. On crime, Ernest Alix, *Ransom Kidnapping in America, 1874–1974* (Carbondale, IL, 1978); Philip Jenkins, *Moral Panic: Changing Concepts of the Child Molester in Modern America* (New Haven, 1998); and Paula Fass, *Kidnapped: Child Abduction in America* (Cambridge, MA, 1999). On child-rearing literature, Daniel Miller and Guy Swanson, *The Changing American Parent* (New York 1958); Joseph Hawes and N. R. Hiner, eds., *American Childhood: A*

Research Guide and Historical Handbook (Westport, CT, 1988); Alexander Siegel and Sheldon White, "The Child Study Movement," *Advances in Child Development and Behavior* 17 (1982); and Stephanie Shields and Beth Koster, "Emotional Stereotyping of Parents in Childrearing Manuals, 1915–1980," *Social Psychology Quarterly* 52 (1989): 44–55. On parent education Steven Schlossman, "Philanthropy and the Gospel of Child Development," *The History of Education Quarterly* (1981): 275–99. On sleep, Peter N. Stearns, Perrin Rowland, and Lori Giarnella, "Children's Sleep: Sketching Historical Change," *Journal of Social History* 30 (1996): 345–66. On parents and adolescents, Beth Bailey, *From Front Porch to Back Seat: Courtship in Twentieth-Century America* (Baltimore, 1989); and John Modell, *Into One's Own: From Youth to Adulthood in the United States, 1920–1975* (Berkeley, 1989). On parental and cultural diversity, Philip J. Greven, Jr., *Spare the Child: The Religious Roots of Punishment and the Psychological Impact of Physical Abuse* (New York, 1991); on abuse itself, Elizabeth Pleck, *Domestic Tyranny: The Making Of Social Policy against Family Violence from Colonial Times to the Present* (New York, 1987). On SIDS, A. B. Bergman, *The "Discovery" of Sudden Infant Death Syndrome* (New York, 1986); M. P. Johnson and Karl Hufbauer, "Sudden Infant Death Syndrome as a Medical Research Problem since 1945," *Social Problems* 30 (1982); C. B. Norm, J. W. Eberstein, and L. C. Deeb, "Sudden Infant Death Syndrome as a Socially Determined Cause of Death," *Social Biology* 36 (1984). On sexuality, Jeffrey Moran, *Teaching Sex: The Shaping of Adolescence in the 20th Century* (Cambridge, MA, 2000). On adoption standards, Ellen Herman, "The Paradoxical Rationalization of Modern Adoption," *Journal of Social History* 36 (2002): 81–129. On envy, Susan Matt, *Keeping Up with the Joneses: Envy in American Consumer Culture, 1890–1930* (Philadelphia, 2002).

3

Discipline

THE IDEA OF THE CHILD as vulnerable had obvious implications for discipline. It was vital not to overdo, lest the parent harm a fragile psyche. Nineteenth-century advice literature had already begun a campaign against using fear to bring children into line, and attacks also targeted degrading uses of shame or excessive physical violence. These programs continued (suggesting, among other things, how slowly and unevenly the new standards were received). By the late 1920s, it was no longer necessary to point out the harm of using bogeymen to scare children, but debates about spanking and other traditional measures continued.

Concern about childish fearfulness obviously added to the pressures to reduce severe responses. Particularly with the decline of strict behaviorism, by the late 1930s, a growing expert chorus urged parents to reason with their children, explaining the boundaries of good behavior and giving positive incentives to meet proper standards.

Toilet training goals relaxed, a clear sign of parental willingness to accept nuisance in return for careful handling of children. Repression was to be avoided in teaching children not to soil themselves, even if one had to wait an extra year for children to respond to the logic of bathrooms. A host of standard 19th-century disciplinary staples, quite apart from spanking or will-breaking, were now seen as retrograde.

Fathers, in the updated view of good parenting, were no longer to be used as final disciplinary authorities. Paternal involvement with children was encouraged, but the new styles stressed friendliness—it was important to treat children as pals. And, in fact, though some fathers unquestionably maintained the older methods, in most middle-class families mothers became the chief sources of discipline. "Wait till your father gets home," the classic 19th-century threat, became less common. In part the result of a major redefinition of gender roles in parenting, the shift both reflected and contributed to an effort to be gentler with children.

Periodically, in the 1920s and then again, more consistently, from the 1960s on, new attention to child abuse also helped set limits on the most extreme forms of discipline. Again there was debate about this, and some parents and subcultures viewed as acceptable practices that the larger society came to question. At the same time, some critics felt that the attacks on abuse were too restrained, leaving too many parents free to inflict physical or psychological harm on their offspring. Still, the publicity given to abuse, and the clear effort to extend the definition to cover mental (and sexual), as well as physical, harm, signaled the growing consensus that discipline had to stay within some boundaries. Practices once seen as permissible became criminal, beyond the pale. The democratic claim that abuse knew no social boundaries drove the point home to the middle classes. Public standards, in this regard, echoed the messages being delivered in the child-rearing literature.

And, throughout the period, new expertise abounded, urging parents to reconsider their disciplinary traditions and natural impulses alike. As one guru put it in 1952, with explicit condescension: "Where professional guidance cannot be accepted . . . because of the neurotic personality of a parent, the problems become intensified."[1] Parents took this approach with some large grains of salt, but it was difficult to avoid some additional uncertainty about one's own conduct in dealing with problems of children's behavior.

The impact of expertise was heightened by the increasing isolation of many parents. Looser ties with other family members, including parents' parents, left more fathers and mothers wondering about the validity of their disciplinary choices. Suburban living allowed families to glimpse varied styles of discipline—from strict to permissive—but without full community sanction for any one style. The need for individual decision making increased, and, with it, some new uncertainty. Children, for their part, in peer networks tighter than those their parents enjoyed, eagerly reported on other, alternative disciplinary patterns that were more to their taste ("But Susie's parents let her . . . ").

From a number of angles, then, 20th-century adults, experts and parents alike, revisited the question of disciplining children. Some discussions followed from debates launched in the 19th century. Others, however, like those involving fathering, specifically challenged 19th-century conventions. It proved difficult, however, to seize on a fully acceptable 20th-century alternative, in part because the idea of children's vulnerability made almost any disciplinary move suspect. What not to do was clearer than the reverse, and parental anxiety understandably increased, given the lack of definitive resolution and the need to reexamine past practice. We can begin with the core connection to the new image of childhood, the revisiting of the role of guilt.

GUILT

Nothing suggested the rethinking of 19th-century discipline more than the growing concern about the use of guilt. Here was the central emotion deployed in up-to-date Victorian child rearing, the alternative to community shame and physical harshness alike. Children must be brought to see that bad behavior brought temporary deprivations of love, until, willing to admit their guilt, they became open to reform and a return to the family circle. A guilt-laden exile to one's room became the most widely acceptable form of punishment.

However, this tactic assumed a sturdy child, capable of standing up to emotional challenge and even to temporary suffering, and this was precisely what the new paradigm of childhood brought into question. Attacks on guilt became part of the growing warnings in the child-rearing literature about anger, jealousy, and fear. One of the new taboos in dealing with childish manifestations of these emotions or with toilet training involved making things worse by adding guilt. For example, it was thought that the angry child would become more angry (whether overtly or not) if guilt was applied. Guilt became a source of frustration that might in turn lead to lasting emotional malfunction. Up-to-date advisers were quite aware of their innovations in this area; guilt became part of a repressive Victorian past that had to be exorcised.

Guilt's potential power was recognized and addressed in essentially the same fashion as that of anger or jealousy: it should be ventilated so that it would not take hold. Children were increasingly trained to recognize guilty feelings and to express them in hopes of adult sympathy. "I am feeling guilty" became a plea for reassurance that in turn should quickly replace any intense inner experience, just as "you're making me feel guilty" was meant to force the up-to-date parent to pull back. Guilt in this sense was attacked not only because it was unpleasant but also because it could run too deep. Whereas the increasing distaste for undue shame in the early 19th-century involved an immediate if implicit quest for a substitute form of emotional enforcement, the attack on guilt was not accompanied by any move toward a clear replacement. In terms of recommended norms, the danger of severe emotional sanctions tended to preclude any systematic effort to develop alternatives for guilt. Whereas Victorians had adopted a clear, emotionally symbolic punishment to replace prior shaming—the idea of being sent to one's room, being separated from normal family affection, developing guilt to the point where one was able to apologize on the strength of the emotion—20th-century parents moved increasingly to more neutral practices.

Ruth Benedict correctly noted a move away from traditional shame and guilt in a 1946 essay: "Shame is an increasingly heavy burden . . . and guilt is less extremely felt than in earlier generations. In the United States this is interpreted as a relaxation of morals, because we do not expect shame to do the heavy work of morality. We do not harness the acute personal chagrin which accompanies shame to our fundamental system of morality."[2]

This judgment can be readily confirmed and partially explained by an examination of characteristic child-rearing literature and related child psychology texts from at least the early 1930s on. Writing for the Child Study Association of America in 1932, for example, the indomitable popularizers Dorothy Canfield Fisher and Sidonie Gruenberg wrote that it was "undesirable for a child to develop a deep sense of guilt and of failure" (the equation is of course revealing in itself). The authors admitted that children should learn to be concerned about wrong behavior, but their attempt to distinguish between such learning and the emotion of guilt was rather inchoate. A popular manual in 1934 clarified, though only in passing, that guilt had become undesirable: "Practice in controlling adverse emotions is often necessary." The authors Carl and Mildred Renz urged parents to master their own emotions in the interest of avoiding guilt in their children. When parents deal with children's sexual interest or toilet training, for example, the child should be "protected from an impression that there is anything shameful or disgusting about his misbehavior."[3]

Treatments of this sort made it clear, in fact, that guilt was being linked to other negative emotions in several senses. First, it was not constructive, being likely to cause either harmful distress or outright misbehavior in a child. Dr. Spock, for example, while not discoursing on guilt directly, warned against harsh discipline in such areas as toilet training, where punishment could damage a personality by making it durably hostile or by inducing so much generalized guilt that the child would suffer from pervasive "worrisomeness." Guilt feelings could be blamed for aggressive and even criminal behavior and could undermine confidence in much the same way that fear could. The role of guilt in anxiety was frequently cited as part of the reason why the emotion could not be viewed as positive, and the "repressed energies" resulting from guilt could induce all sorts of mischief.[4]

Further, like the more obviously negative emotions, guilt had the capacity to fester, building up in children to the extent that adult functioning would be hampered. Thus, a child made to feel guilty might suffer "a harmful effect upon his mental health as long as he lives." Guilt about sexuality received particular attention, with the related topic of toilet training running a close second. Sexual guilt laid on a child might "unfit the individual for adult conjugal relations." Far more than the campaigns against fear or anger, concern about guilt generated a direct attack on child-rearing practices of the past, when parents had used the emotion to discipline children and had created damaging inhibitions in the process; as Fischer and Gruenberg noted, "traditions of guilt and sin" needed to be rigorously overthrown.[5]

As with the negative emotions, avoidance of guilt also involved new duties for parents. Parents should help children eliminate behaviors and situations that would arouse great guilt. They should keep their own impatience in check by not expecting too much too soon (in toilet training, for instance), and they must avoid humiliating a child. Precisely because many parents had been raised amid guilt, they need to take careful emotional stock before dealing with disciplinary issues. "Unless he [the parent] can keep his own emotions under control . . . he will not be able to train his child properly."[6] Parents must come to terms with their own repressions lest they pass them on to their offspring. From these initial parental injunctions, the notion developed that an individual who induced guilt in another was in many ways a greater offender than the person whose behavior had caused the confrontation in the first place. Ironically, instillers of guilt now had much to feel guilty about, for causing emotional distress was more reprehensible than many bad actions.

Finally, and above all, guilt became a negative emotion not only because it was unpleasant (its association with anxiety conveyed this link) but also because its intensity might so easily incapacitate the sufferer. Popularizers and research psychologists alike talked of "floods" of guilt or of people "laden with their feelings of guilt." They lamented the way guilt could induce a "merciless kind of self-condemnation" and a host of related irrationalities. Guilt could paralyze thought and so prevent proper self-direction and control. Adults who had been made to feel guilty as children could be infected with feelings that they could not easily recognize and therefore could not govern.[7]

In the child-rearing manuals, guilt did not command the systematic attention that fear, anger, or jealousy did. The emotion was somewhat more abstract, and some observers wavered between the new wisdom that guilt was bad and the earlier recognition that it served some undeniable functions. Thus, a 1959 text offered the usual condemnation of guilt as a cause of frustration and anxiety but also noted, in a separate section, with no attempt to reconcile the contradiction, that the emotion was essential for society in serving as a "silent policeman." The main reason for such scattered treatments of guilt lay in the fact that commentary on guilt was diffused among more specific commentaries on sexuality, toilet training, and general disciplinary approach. Brief comments on guilt's harmfulness and deleterious intensity undergirded more specific efforts to teach parents to be patient, to "take it easy" in order to avoid making children feel guilty about perfectly natural functions and interests. Another reason that elaborate comment on the emotion itself was not judged necessary was that guilt, unlike fear or anger, was avoidable. If parents broke through the customs of the past, they could raise children free from this particular emotional distraction. Thus strategies for avoiding guilt were downplayed in favor of urging parents to gain command of their own "repressed neuroses" in the interest of raising emotionally healthier personalities in the next generation.

The larger campaign to control other negative emotions and some of the language in the comments on guilt itself suggested a sweeping, if partially implicit, attack on guilt. According to this approach, people would learn through their upbringing that inappropriate emotional expression could be condemned as immature. The warnings to parents to keep the results of their own misguided upbringings under control not only credited the possibility of rational dominance—parents could learn to behave before they distorted their own kids' personalities—but also reminded parents that their mistaken approaches to child rearing reflected an essential childishness that should embarrass any mature adult.

Several alternatives to the Victorian emphasis on guilt developed, two of which were explicitly discussed in child- rearing manuals. First, parents were urged to help children avoid guilt, not only by restraining their own emotions in situations that called for discipline but also by monitoring their children's behavior so that potentially guilt-inducing situations became unlikely. Here, attention to children's behavior could make emotionally based self-criticism less necessary in the early years of childhood. The link to the new sense of children as vulnerable was obvious.

Second, parents should help children understand appropriate behaviors by using a rational approach. The reason for patience in toilet training, for example, was that, at a certain point, after age two or three, children could be talked to about proper cleanliness. They might even, as Dr. Spock suggested, want to control their bodily processes on their own. Discipline of all sorts should make children think. Emotion should be avoided precisely because it clouded reason. Calm parents could talk to their children, who would, equally calmly, come to agree on goals— if parents did not press the goals prematurely. Ideally, then, a combination of strategy designed to avoid distressing situations and rational control would generate the good behavior families and society had a right to expect. Guilt need not enter in, and, indeed, in some formulations, no emotions of any sort were necessary to achieve propriety in word and deed.

As in the Victorian period, the role of shame in child rearing remained fairly subtle. Children were not to be taunted or exposed to the scorn of their siblings. Indeed, 20th-century parents, and even schools, moved farther from reliance on shame than the Victorians had done, reducing public humiliations in the classroom, for example. Schools that isolated misbehaving children to be ridiculed by their peers were now seen as cruel and backward. By the 1970s, laws even forbade the public posting of grades, lest children be damaged in the eyes of others.

With shame still downplayed and guilt now under attack, as well, the emphasis in child rearing, at least as conceived in the mainstream middle-class culture, shifted to rational explanation and persuasion as the proper reactions to bad behavior, supplemented by an emotionally neutral denial of privileges if necessary. Unpleasant emotions were neither to be scorned nor attacked through guilt but rather ventilated, enabling children to defuse the emotional experience through labeling and talking out. Because it dissociated emotion from action, this tactic minimized the need for formal adult response. Ventilation was the alternative to adult riposte (with its potential for harmful guilt) and to the dreaded festering that might convert a passing negative experience into an ongoing personality trait. Reliance on ventilation formed the new first stage in the complex task of disciplining oneself without arousing intense emotional impulses either as motivations for good behavior or as side effects. This strategy was supplemented, of course, by parental tactics designed to constrain opportunities for bad behavior or negative emotional experience. Both aspects imposed time-consuming new responsibilities on parents. Listening to children ventilate, and then reasoning in response, was no easy task.

Irony and complexity abounded. Irony: the anxiety about causing guilt in children formed part of the changes in standards that left many American parents feeling more guilty about their own sins of omission and commission than ever before. In no sense was guilt removed from middle-class life. Complexity: knowledge that they were not supposed to feel guilty could confuse older children when they experienced the emotion as part of growing up.

But the practical questions, as the new wisdom spread, involved the kinds of discipline that might be used to replace the old regime. For, following on the new injunctions against guilt, the list of approaches parents or teachers should NOT take expanded steadily. Obviously, they should not expose children to shame; they should not instill fear. Almost certainly, they should not spank. Child-rearing authorities did continue to debate this. They might acknowledge some need for mild physical punishment between infancy and grade school. A 1930s popularizer noted, "Spanking has its pros and cons . . . children understand it at an age when long explanations and patient reasoning only tire them . . . but it certainly should not be used after the child is old enough to feel a sense of personal outrage." And, with each passing decade, the tolerance for any kind of physical punishment diminished. But there was more: even scolding came in for attack. "Scolding is the least effective of all forms of punishment. It is likely to hurt instead of help," wrote one authority in *Parents Magazine* in 1953. Children would either ignore nagging, in which case it did no good, or they would feel hurt and diminished by it, which might cause worse behavior problems in response.[8]

The image of the child here went beyond the notion of frailty, though frailty was still part of the picture as parents were told to refrain from punishments that might damage their children's fragile psyches or somas. A strong implication that children would resent corporal punishment was present. Precisely because aggressive punishments were seen as wrong, it was easy (and possibly accurate) also to assume that children would view them in the same light and either tune them out or retaliate. And, as we will see, children did pick up these signals in developing their own new and often vigorous critique of parental discipline.

But what, then, could be done about unacceptable behavior? The new approaches to discipline were far clearer about what not to do than about what was acceptable. But there were some positive recommendations, most of which required a good bit more time and subtlety than any of the more traditional disciplinary regimes had entailed. A consensus began to emerge, though whether parents would find it entirely practical remained unclear.

THE BEHAVIORIST INTERLUDE

The behaviorist school in psychology coalesced early in the 20th century, with John Watson's first major book in 1914 a landmark in the school's formulation. The formal premises of behaviorism emphasized stimulus and response, combined with reflexes, as the basis for human and animal learning. If a rat proceeded through a maze on the basis of trial and error but was rewarded with food for a successful choice, it would learn the choice and repeat it next time around. Unsuccessful or counterproductive learning involved the same kind of connections. If a baby was left to its own devices, it would play happily with a tame animal. But if the play was associated with a loud noise (one of the few inherent fears that Watson predicated), the baby would be fearful next time it was presented with the animal, or indeed with any furry animal.

Mental illness was just a distortion of habits acquired as a result of stimulus–response learning.

Behaviorism flourished, particularly in the United States, through the 1920s, with some additional lease on life in the 1930s. It is normally treated, quite appropriately, as a development within psychology, to be explained through the increasing use of laboratory experiments, the impact of Pavlov's work on conditioned reflexes, and so on. Its mechanical qualities might more broadly be linked to contemporary developments in the industrial economy, including the increasingly machine-like treatment of workers on the assembly line.

But behaviorism also informed a generation of child-rearing advice in the United States. Watson himself wrote directly on the subject, and a variety of popularizers, including many of the early authors for *Parents Magazine*, followed in his wake. Behaviorism strongly influenced the early editions of *Infant Care*. Full-blown acceptance of Watsonianism was rare in the child-rearing domain. Watson had firm notions about avoiding the coddling of children, which led him to attack a number of maternal habits, including frequent hugging of children, and, while this strict approach had some impact, it had to be diluted at the popular level. But other behaviorist suggestions received wider play, and the explanation for this lies in the parental need for innovative approaches in discipline.

To be sure, behaviorism affected child rearing in part because of the prestige associated with psychology as a science, another example of the influence of experts, via popularization, on parental attitudes. Watson was adamant that his approach constituted the first real application of scientific observation to infants, contrasted with the approaches of earlier researchers like William James and particularly with the Freudians. But behaviorist recommendations had an impact also because, loosely translated, they seemed to promise an answer to the disciplinary dilemma that mainstream advice was already creating for parents and other adults: if I am not supposed to spank, or even scold, what's left to do when my child does something wrong?

And here a diluted behaviorism was quite clear, with certain implications that easily survived the school's decline by the later 1930s and the subsequent rise of more permissive approaches. For its adepts pushed for two key disciplinary strategies that clearly fit the modern scenario: first, emphasize rewards for good behavior, to reinforce positive learning and habit. Second, try to help infants avoid situations in which bad habits might be learned and in which, more traditionally, punishments might be administered. Environmental manipulation, more than discipline, was the new key to the behavioral kingdom.

The rewards promised for this new approach to child rearing were truly impressive. Not only would good habits be formed and crime and mental illness avoided, but children themselves would cause virtually no distress. "It is conceivable," Watson wrote, "that some day we may be able to bring up the human young through infancy and childhood without their crying or showing fear reactions" save on rare occasions. Currently, crying was almost always seen as a sign that parents had messed up: "owing to our unsatisfactory training methods in the home, we spoil the emotional makeup of each child as rapidly as the twig can be bent."[9]

Watson was vigorous in his attacks on traditional punishments, particularly spankings. "Punishment is a word which ought never to have crept into our language." Spankings were wrong for three reasons. First, they usually occurred well after the behavior problem and so created dislike of the agent of punishment, not of the misdeed. Second, they often served as an outlet for adult sadism. Third, even where appropriate, they could rarely be doled out scientifically and so set up additional negative responses, even masochism. To be sure, an immediate knuckle rap for bad behavior, such as turning on a gas jet, putting fingers in the mouth, or playing with one's genitals, could be appropriate, "provided the parent can administer the tap at once in a thoroughly objective way." But saying "don't" would be far better, in terms of limiting potentially negative responses, and in the long run we should hope "so to rearrange the environment that fewer and fewer negative reactions will have to be built into both child and adult."[10]

The behaviorist alternative to conventional discipline involved an increase in the arrangements and controls that surround the child, without the need for punitive adult intervention. Watson dreamed of an electrically wired table top that would administer a shock if a child reached for a delicate object that she might break while permitting her free access to toys or other permitted materials. Children should not suck their thumbs, but parents should not be involved in scolding or spanking; the mechanical remedy seemed obvious—coating the thumb with a bad-tasting substance or using some other physical restraint to prevent the development of a bad habit without explicit discipline. But positive stimuli loomed large, as well, in the behaviorist approach.

Want to help a child avoid jealousy? Instead of resorting to scolding about the child's hostile reaction to a sibling's receipt of a birthday present, offer a second, distracting present. It was the behaviorists who urged that treats could help a child overcome a fear of pets or strangers by gradually inducing them to come closer to the feared object until the emotion was overcome.

The idea of using manipulation in place of direct discipline, and particularly punishment, fit a transitional mood in American parenting, at least among self-appointed popularizers about parenting. Behaviorism's more mechanical features suggested alternatives to constant oversight of children, at a time when employed and family help was becoming scarcer. More broadly, the manipulative approach meshed with a belief that children were fundamentally good (Watson was at pains to argue against a belief in numerous innate dysfunctions) or at least neutral but that, at the same time, they needed a great deal of guidance. Above all, behaviorism sought directly to grapple with the need for regulating children without conventional verbal or physical discipline, now seen to be harmful, even counterproductive.

Furthermore, two features of behaviorist manipulation proved durably useful to anxious American parents. First, the idea of positive rewards to reinforce good choices rang true as an alternative to more negative reactions in an increasingly consumerist society in which providing treats gained increasing cultural sanction. Second, the possibility of mechanically manipulating the environment such that potentially unacceptable behavior simply did not occur and hence required no punishment made sense, given the growing concerns about physical dangers in the environment of the modern household and about the negative effects of reprimand. It was a behaviorist, for example, who dreamed up a new baby crib with insulated walls to protect from loud noise, within controlled temperature and humidity, and a sheet on a roller that could be removed without fuss when dampened or soiled; here was a noninterventionist, labor-saving dream. At the same time, behaviorists furthered parental introspection, the need to ask whether punitive reactions were designed to benefit the child or, more likely, represented hostile impulses in the adults themselves.

Of course, there was resistance from parents exposed to behaviorism through manuals or parent-education classes. In rural New York state, for example, one mother noted, "With one of my children punishment does seem the only way at times and I can't see that it is always a sign of faulty guidance." Or another: "I find that I do not usually have time to argue and figure out means of conquering them from within." But even somewhat conservative parents like these did work to become less punitive, to move away from traditional remedies: "Many members" of one group agreed that "talking and reasoning with a child had better results than numerous spankings in most cases."[11] Ultimately, it was this openness to reconsideration among parents, and the self-scrutiny and potential anxiety involved, that was the most important result of the behaviorist charge, not the specifics practices urged.

On the part of the new experts, at least, the hope was for an emotion-free environment for child and adult alike, in which careful arrangements would eliminate the need for punishment or for guilty introspection about what lurked behind. But specifically behaviorist popularizations did not last long, if only because they did not really lead to the promised utopia. While hostile to outright punishments, the behaviorist strictures involved a host of rules that could easily seem punitive in themselves and damaging to tender psyches. Thumb sucking and even unacceptable toilet habits or signs of infantile sexuality might not really justify the use of mechanical restraints. Behaviorists tended also to minimize inherent problems, such as fears or jealousy, that other experts, and many parents themselves, believed went deeper than mere manipulation could control. Here was where actual parents might insist on greater leeway for traditional measures, including spanking or even shaming. The promised reduction of crying, for example, simply did not happen; children's deeper anxieties still sought expression, and behaviorist devices themselves caused tearful frustration. And, finally, the emotional coolness of the typical behaviorist approach, particularly its hostility to displays of affection, simply did not catch on in a culture that remained quite sentimental about children.

PERMISSIVENESS AND DISCIPLINE

Rhoda Bacmeister captured the new disciplinary mood in her 1950 manual, *Your Child and Other People*. Avoidance of fear or pain was emphasized even more, as was the importance of bribes. It was all right to let children take some consequences "as long as they are not *too* serious." Parents should set boundaries, but they should not expect complete obedience. Children should *want* to do what they are supposed to do, and this meant suggestion and persuasion, not command. "Talk It Out with Your Child" was the title of the main chapter on discipline.[12]

The passing of the behaviorist moment had to do with more than the arrival of a new generation of experts, bent on establishing novel credentials, or with the excesses of the behaviorists themselves. By the late 1930s, concern about immigrant children was waning because immigration itself dropped down; here was a reason to rethink society's efforts to urge strict controls over wayward children. A very low birth rate reduced the need to organize mechanical constraints on children to replace the formerly available childcare help and may have inflated the scarcity value of children, as well, inducing more sympathetic coddling. A new generation of parents may have felt less need for the transitional aspects of behaviorism, the tradeoff between old-fashioned discipline and an insistence on detailed regulation. It was now easier to accept low levels of formal discipline without feeling the need for rules to compensate. Indeed, the rules themselves now seemed to contradict the larger impulse in reconsiderations of discipline.

Even one-time behaviorists, like the Harvard psychologist B. F. Skinner, who introduced the controlled crib described earlier for his second daughter, were brought to reconsider their ideas as a more permissive mood gained ground in the late 1930s and 1940s. As actual parents, the Skinners worked to cut back the number of rules that strict behaviorists had emphasized, for example regarding toilet training. Preferring neatness, they nevertheless allowed their daughters to be messy in their own rooms, rather than seeking either disciplinary or manipulative responses. The idea of avoiding the need for confrontation now went beyond the behaviorist model. The children were encouraged to follow their own interests, even when these differed from what the parents considered appropriate. Ventures in explicit discipline were soon abandoned. Intriguingly, the Skinner's younger daughter one day announced that her parents should not spank her because it only made her mad—a revealing indication of how kids themselves picked up the latest popularized expertise, in this case straight from behaviorist doctrine—and the parents quickly conceded the point.

But it was the decline in the sheer number of behavioral rules, and therefore the amount of manipulation needed, that marked the big shift from the behaviorist interlude to the advent of what was quickly dubbed permissiveness. The new expertise, soon enthroned by Dr. Spock's manual, went the behaviorists one better. Discipline was still seen as wrong. Manipulation and treats were often essential, including resorting to any device to divert a child's attention from an inappropriate reaction. But the process could be simplified further if the sheer number of targets was relaxed.

The emphasis on positive reinforcement increased, rejecting the rather dour behaviorist approach, with its doled-out treats. As a 1950s article put it, "Parents should show interest and approval when he does as he is told. Praise for some accomplishment will make most children want to repeat the same thing again and again. Praise for good behavior is generally more constructive than sharp reprimands or harping on mistakes."[13]

A final ingredient in the new disciplinary mix was an increased emphasis on the need to reason with children, to explain to them why something they had done was wrong, to listen to their explanations and emotions, but then finally to enlist their participation in avoiding the misbehavior in future. Here was a key contrast with the behaviorists, whose emphasis on mechanical responses in infancy had limited their interest in children as targets of persuasion or partners in discussion. In the wake of behaviorism, the insistence on reasoning spread widely as the desired solution to all the issues that manipulation could not conceal. As converted parents, moving from behaviorism, the Skinners spent a great deal of time discussing proper conduct with their daughters, often amid considerable storm and argument, hopeful that, ultimately at least, the desired results would emerge. Child-rearing manuals urged discussion even with children whose impulses seemed to render reasoning nearly impossible, such as those suffering from what became known as Attention Deficit Disorder. For, according to the new wisdom, shouting at such children would merely make matters worse. One had to hope that even the most incorrigible child could be calmed by parental reassurance and then led to reconsider his own lack of self-control. Until this occurred, parental worry was the main recourse. And if the child did not manage . . . ?

Here, then, was the fundamental late-20th-century formula. Avoid spanking and scolding and all the trappings of traditional discipline, including mindless requests that parental authority be obeyed. These, it was now claimed, had been proved harsh, counterproductive, hollow, or all the above. Seek to manage and manipulate the child, particularly but not exclusively the young child, so that behaviors that might require discipline would simply not occur—whether the issue was physical safety, emotional outbursts, or treatment of others. Reduce the rules, with the same ends in mind. And talk, explain, reason, listening to objections not with the intent of yielding so much as to allow the child to let off steam as a prelude to rational adjustment.

All these strictures, positive and negative alike, were compatible with the new beliefs about children's vulnerability and the potential for parental excess. They acknowledged the dangers of the external modern world and the need to find ways, through careful arrangement of the environment, to reduce the threats it posed without punishment. They blended with other disciplinary changes, such as the desires of growing numbers of fathers to be pals with their kids, rather than courts of last resort, and the concomitant effort to blend greater disciplinary obligations with the assumptions of motherhood.

ONGOING QUESTIONS

Permissiveness was in many ways a capstone of 20th-century discussions of discipline. It fully reflected all the criticisms of traditional approaches to the subject. It included some of the manipulative efforts of behaviorism as a means of avoiding confrontations, but without the mechanical regulatory apparatus. It hoped for sweet reason. But the advent of permissiveness hardly ended discussions on discipline and the concerns that accompanied them. In the first place, criticisms of permissiveness continued to complicate parental attitudes. Some parents refused to convert to permissiveness, others, partially converted, wondered whether they were undermining good character.

Furthermore, the practice of permissiveness itself harbored tensions. Three features were particularly important. First, obviously, permissiveness itself could provoke anxiety. It involved new levels of worry about traditional and spontaneous parental responses; even more than in the 19th century, the motives behind parents' reactions to their children's behavior had to be hauled out for examination (as the behaviorists themselves had emphasized). At one or more points in the first two-thirds of the 20th century, many parents actively reconsidered the disciplinary approaches their own parents had taken and found them wanting, but the corollary was some anxious monitoring as they tried to effect change in their own practices. Management and manipulation to avoid the need for discipline required considerable attention, particularly once the behaviorist fascination with mechanical restraints went out of favor. And reasoning, however laudable, had its own costs in time and attention. The fact that expert advice changed and that experts disagreed, while it provided some latitude for skeptical parents, could in itself increase uneasiness.

Second, as some historians have long noted, permissiveness had rules of its own, which it sought to get children to internalize. The rules were less numerous than those the behaviorists had urged, but they were there. They included sleeptimes and mealtimes, avoidance of dangerous household items, restraint of intense emotion, an ability to socialize well with other children, and, as we will see in the next chapter, a growing array of school achievements. The range extended from the prosaic issues of infant health and safety to some demanding goals for personal development. In this sense, the term "permissiveness" is a misnomer, for the practice never urged an anything-goes approach but rather proposed a simplification of structure so that the focus would be on rules that really mattered. When, in the wake of the 1960s student riots and counterculture, the advocates of permissiveness, like Dr. Spock, reemphasized the behavioral boundaries a bit more fully, they were clarifying (as they themselves contended), rather than changing their tune. Authority was not absent from the new model; it simply sought adherence through nonauthoritarian methods, and the result could be confusing to all parties involved.

In many ways, indeed, the permissiveness advocates (far more than their behaviorist predecessors) were urging on parents the ambitious goal not simply of making sure children adhered to some rules but of ensuring their proper attitude—which, the experts now insisted, could not be accomplished through command and punishment. The idea was to make children "into self-directing, responsible, useful persons," as Sidonie Gruenberg put it.[14] This is the reason discipline in the conventional sense would not suffice, designed as it was to stop a behavior, rather than launch a more demanding correction of outlook and a new level of agreement between child and parent. Getting a child to think and feel right, as well as to do right, represented an escalation of parental responsibilities, not a retreat from standards.

Third—and this relates both to the anxiety embedded in the new approaches to discipline and to the continued commitment to rules and goals—the advocates and implementers of permissive discipline still worried about the gap between the frail and vulnerable child and the standards to be sought in socialization. Parents told to be supportive of children while expecting adherence to certain rules could hope that guidance and reasoning, supplemented by careful environmental manipulation and a willingness not to insist on optional norms, would do the trick. They might be willing to wait through some storms and resentments. But what if rules that could not be relaxed, in the interests of the child's own safety and future wellbeing, still needed some additional enforcement?

WHEN ALL ELSE FAILED

For many parents, the obvious answer to this final quandary (and, sometimes, the answer even before the quandary arose) was to go back to older methods, including physical discipline and certainly abundant scolding. Parents varied, and American subcultures varied, in terms of their adherence to the permissive approach. It was not easy to cast off the discipline one's own parents had used, whatever one's new beliefs. Response depended as well on the age of the child. For younger children, it might be more feasible to revert to more traditional discipline than it would be with more independent teenagers, including those fully aware that many parents themselves felt that a full appeal to the older methods was already a confession of failure.

At the societal level, by the 1980s and 1990s, a fascinatingly ambiguous call arose that could in principle appeal to permissives and traditionalists alike: "just say no." In the 1980s, "just say no" was urged on teenagers and preteens as a response to the looming dangers of drink and drugs. Then, in the 1990s, premarital sex was added to the list. The campaigns seemed to have an effect in some cases—the incidence of premarital sex did go down a bit—but not in others (for example, teenagers defiantly increased their rates of tobacco smoking while the rest of the society swore off). "Just say no" could be an invitation to stricter, more traditional punishments for those who refused—even, in these behavior areas, the punishments of law. It could certainly imply guilt for those incapable of living up to the standards advocated. Or it could, in the permissive style, be an invitation also to discussion and persuasion with one's own children, a challenge and not a threat. Not surprisingly, the same authorities who intoned "just say no" also urged parents to talk with their children about sex or drugs, to allow participation and reason their role in teens' decision making. Clearly, in these behavior areas that seemed to escape acceptable controls, Americans groped for solutions that could call on old and new alike.

But there was a another option, as well, one that even more clearly sought to discipline without full disciplinary stigmata, a last resort for permissive parents backed against the wall. The idea of fining or grounding a child was an intriguing effort to answer the question about ultimate parental sanctions, while avoiding the drawbacks now associated with older disciplinary methods and the power of guilt.

The practice of fining children for misbehavior, sometimes as a direct repayment for physical damage done, developed between the world wars. Child-rearing experts described some common scenarios. A daughter is due to get her allowance, but she has overslept, neglected assigned household chores, and run across the street to gossip with a friend. So her allowance is denied. A son brings home a bad report card. "Perhaps taking away Don's allowance would be a way to get him to do his schoolwork."[15] Many experts advised against these practices, arguing that allowances were part of education in mature money management and should not be mixed up with discipline, but the practice won considerable parental attention.

Fining or not paying children reflected financial conditions new in the 20th century, and particularly the practice of allowances. The method mirrored white-collar punishments current in the wider society—a larger relationship that often has links to family discipline. But the particular appeal of fines or money denials was the potential for a visible restraint of freedom without imposing guilt. Neither party need be particularly emotional about the transaction, yet one could hope that a lesson would be learned.

Grounding—depriving a child of a desired set of enjoyments, including the freedom to go out with friends—had a similarly neutral tone. It built on the growing array of leisure activities and consumer goods children were coming to enjoy. Young children could have toys taken away for a period of time or be made to suffer without radio or television. Teenagers could be forbidden to go out on dates or other excursions. In this sense, grounding was quite similar to fines, and equally contemporary. It imposed consequences without huge emotional burdens in the hope that, the grounding period having been experienced, the child could be released to normal entertainments with a lesson learned but no painful apologies required. As Sidonie Gruenberg put it approvingly, "Such privations are 'punishment' to the child, as is a slap on his hand. But these are not intended to cause the child suffering. They are meant to associate some of the acts he is tempted to perform with a disagreeable result."[16]

In practice, of course, grounding was not necessarily so pure. The punishment was often imposed amid visible anger. It could make children feel guilty and, where peers were involved, often ashamed, in addition to denying consumer activities. But, where punishment was finally necessary, despite parents' efforts to reason, to reward, and to eliminate opportunities for misbehavior, grounding seemed to offer mothers and fathers the best available mechanism, because its official focus was denial of material privileges, as opposed to emotional or physical intrusion.

Grounding in this sense became as quintessentially expressive of 20th-century discipline as shaming and physical punishments had been in the colonial period or guilt-laden isolation in one's room had been during the 19th century. The link to the behaviorist approach was strong in that grounding constituted part of a mechanical set of consequences designed to make a child pull up short the next time the possibility of bad behavior loomed. Denial of privilege might frustrate, even anger, but it did not threaten the vulnerable underpinning of the child's psyche.

The idea of grounding built on older disciplinary techniques, such as sending children to bed early. A section on discipline in a 1927 manual by Blanton and Blanton noted that "depriving the child of something that he prizes very much, or putting him to bed, is a brief, but nevertheless an acute form of unhappiness. This form has dozens of variations and has the great advantage that it does not involve physical pain."[17] By the 1940s, grounding was also being recommended as a disciplinary mode that reduced maternal overprotection, which too often involved undue coaxing or nagging.

But it was the attack on spanking, associated with more permissive child-rearing advice in the 1940s, that really highlighted grounding's potential as a last resort. Dr. Spock was adamant in his opposition to spanking ("Some spanked children . . . feel quite justified in beating up on smaller ones. The American tradition of spanking may be one reason that there is much more violence in our country than in any other comparable nation.")[18] Rudolph Dreikurs, in a 1948 manual, similarly praised the growing abandonment of spanking and specifically urged parents to keep the child from a particularly enjoyed toy or activity as a healthier but effective alternative. After a long passage condemning discipline as a futile effort to impose adult will on children ("no amount of punishment will bring about lasting submission"), Dreikurs went on to urge that children be kept indoors for a time, "without emotional upheaval or moralistic preaching."[19] For Dorothy Baruch, also in the 1940s, grounding had the added advantage of not isolating the child, as sending him to a room did; children, even when disciplined, should not be left alone to deal with their feelings. Baruch also warned about overstrictness, particularly with teenagers; too much deprivation, of dates or use of a car, could simply increase the potential for excessive behavior once the teen regained some freedom.

Grounding became more current in the 1950s, as the range of entertainment available to children expanded. A 1957 study noted, "One of the commonest ways of producing an unpleasant experience for a child is to take away something that he values. This can be an important sanction on his behavior, especially if the object is withheld until the desired changes in his behavior have taken place." By this point, 45 percent of all mothers were using denial or threatened denial of access to television as a prime disciplinary tool. A father noted, "We depend mostly on taking away privileges," in this case for very young children. A five-year-old was thus confined to his back yard instead of being free to roam the neighborhood: "I am sure he will remember that better than a spanking."[20]

Most experts, of course, worried about even this level of deprivation, urging positive reinforcement as vastly preferable. And there were recurrent utopian hopes, reminiscent of behaviorism: "It is ideally possible to bring up a child without any question ever arising of rewards or punishment." While parents came increasingly to prefer denial of privilege to more traditional modes, because it presumably lacked the emotional overlay and would be less damaging psychologically given children's vulnerability, the uncertainty about the proper course of action when children failed to respond to reason remained the dominant feature of discipline. "How many parents," a 1959 manual admitted, "find themselves . . . [embracing] the new theories with ardent conviction, [but] are brought up short when freedom is abused, swing to excessive strictness, suffer qualms of conscience and swing back to indulgence." It was hard to feel comfortable.[21]

THE 20TH-CENTURY AMALGAM

Again, it is important to emphasize that actual American parents varied greatly in their disciplinary approaches, depending on personality and subculture. Invocations of bogeymen were pretty rare by this point, though they did crop up in some rural backwaters. Spanking did continue, even on the part of parents who felt guilty for their lapse from modernity; so did shaming and the imposition of guilt, if in less systemic ways than had been possible in earlier eras.

Nevertheless, the tendency to reconsider discipline advanced as well. Increasing numbers of parents came to feel uneasy about punishment, even when it focused on denial of privilege. As one 1950s manual noted, "At best, punishment may stop undesirable conduct. But it does not improve a child's attitude. . . . It is a stop sign, not a go sign. . . . [We do not] count on punishment to discipline our children into self-directing, responsible, useful persons."[22] Punishment might be needed, and there were certainly some approaches that were better than others in terms of their impact on vulnerable children, but it was not the main weapon in a disciplinary arsenal, and it must not be overused.

Here the other aspects of discipline, as developed through behaviorism and then several generations of experts on permissiveness, came to the fore. Parents must explain and motivate good behavior, giving reasons for what they ask of children. They should, to the greatest extent possible, maneuver their children around potential hazards, rather than create situations where they might have to command or chastise. They should provide enjoyable alternatives to bad behavior, rather than risk injunctions that might require disciplinary enforcement. They should reward good behavior extensively—here was one of the causes of the mania for providing entertainment, discussed in chapter 6. They should have some definite rules but keep them to a minimum. They should avoid do-or-die confrontation and be willing to lose a few encounters in the interest of avoiding hostility.

Not all of this, to be sure, was new. But the injunctions to invest considerable time and attention in arranging children's lives without the need for frequent punishment, and the parallel goal of shaping positive attitudes and not just acceptable behavior, represented challenges of some magnitude. It was easy for parents to tire. It was easy to fail, all the more when, as a result, some older disciplinary impulse, the scold or the slap, surfaced in response. It was easy to be unsure what tack to take, and to feel anxious in consequence.

And, as we have seen, parents were not the only learners in this new disciplinary environment. From their peers, from the media, children also picked up the signals about proper parental behavior. They became more open in expressing resentment at punishment, including any implications of guilt. "It's not fair" was a reaction that surfaced frequently, and it gave many parents pause. The sweeping injunctions of obedience that once kept such expressions submerged were no longer fashionable. Assertiveness could combine with apparent vulnerability, once the thrall of infancy was left behind, as children became more active players in the disciplinary process.

Negotiation, more than punishment, now lay at the center of socialization, given the need to deal with attitude and motivation, and not just behavior. This process might prepare children for adult life in a white-collar world in which persuasion and compromise were crucial, but it created significant demands on the parents. The demands contrasted vividly with images of parental decisiveness in the past. They imposed a strain between doing too much by imposing rules and punishments and doing too little, particularly as successive waves of experts continued to urge a review of past habits. Discipline remained essential, as even the permissives contended. But parents throughout much of the 20th century were engaged in an anxious quest to figure out how to provide this without being disciplinary.

FURTHER READING

On debates over discipline, Philip J. Greven, Jr., *Spare the Child: The Religious Roots of Punishment and the Psychological Impact of Physical Abuse* (New York, 1992). On guilt and shame, Ruth Benedict, *The Chrysanthemum and the Sword* (Boston, 1946); June Tangney, *Shame-proneness, Guilt-proneness, and Interpersonal Processes* (Kansas City, 1997); Peter N. Stearns, *Battleground of Desire: The Struggle for Self-Control in Modern America* (New York, 1999). On shifts in disciplinary advice, Kerry Buckley, *Mechanical Man: John B. Watson and the Origins of Behaviorism* (New York, 1989); Elizabeth Lomax, Jerome Kogan, and Barbara Rosenkrantz, *Science and Patterns of Child Care* (San Francisco, 1978), esp. chapter 4; Barbara Ehrenreich and Deirdre English, *For Her Own Good: 150 years of*

Experts' Advice to Women (Garden City, NY, 1978); Urie Bronfenbrenner, "The Changing American Child: A Speculative Analysis," *Journal of Social Issues* 17 (1961): 6–18; Nancy P. Weiss, "Mother, the Invention of Necessity: Dr. Benjamin Spock's Baby and Child Care," *American Quarterly* 29 (1979): 318–46. See also some relevant general studies: Robert B. Sears, Eleanor E. Maccoby, and Harry Levin, *Patterns of Child Rearing* (White Plains, NY, 1957), and Daniel R. Miller and Guy E. Swanson, *The Changing American Parent: A Study in the Detroit Area* (New York, 1958).

4

All Are above Average

Children at School

WHEN I WAS a high school freshman, my parents spent the year in England, and I went to a school that specialized in preparing boys for public school exams. Not, I admit, with its largely upper-middle-class clientele, a typical English school. I was beginning Latin and took along my high school text so I could coordinate with what I expected to have to do the following year, back home. The book was glossy, filled with pictures and stories, in English, on themes like "Mario goes to the Forum." The British text I was given was a third the size, no pictures, just lists of words and grammar to learn. My English teachers were amazed at the reluctance of my American text to force a reader into substance, at its shiny superficiality. Soon I was using just the British text, which got me ahead far faster, with the result that, when I returned home, I essentially skipped to the fourth- year class, where (being the only student in class) I simply read the *Aeneid*.

Foreign language courses in American schools remain remarkable for their unwillingness to force memorization and immersion and, as a result, for their slowness in providing students with usable language capacity. The comparison is complex: foreign language neither was nor is something Americans take too seriously (even in comparison with the parochial British). General high school populations in the United States should not be compared with elite European students. And I'm not a foreign language education expert, so my sense of American coddling may be off the mark.

Still, I believe there is a relevant point. One of the reasons we teach language with lots of sugar coating, and sometimes limited effect, is that we fear overburdening our student charges. Too much memorization or, to update my experience a bit, real immersion might strain their brains. And that, in turn, is what this chapter is partly about.

The chapter is not, I hasten to add, about American educational lag, as a consistent topic or definite conclusion. Comparisons here are truly complicated, and we are sometimes provided with apples-and-oranges contrasts that are unfair to American systems in juxtaposing our comprehensive high schools with elite secondary schools elsewhere. We also pursue goals, such as individual creativity, that work out quite well and that should be added to any full assessment. But we do have a distinctive educational system, and concerns about its impact on potentially vulnerable students form part of its distinctiveness.

The chapter focuses on concerns and commitments in relation to schooling. Other anxieties have attached to schools, including fears of strangers, violence, and drug use, and these should be factored into the parental arsenal, as well. But it is schooling itself, as a learning process, that provides some of the most central and revealing insights. The emphasis is on what parents, along with teachers and other experts, thought about children and education as the transition to a definition of childhood in terms of education was completed in the 20th century. The concentration is on the middle classes, but with recognition that other groups were involved in the process, affected by and often influencing middle-class opinions.

The early 20th century brought not only new but also fundamental shocks in parental perceptions of children and schools in the United States. This may not seem surprising. Many readers will legitimately feel that, given the distance of a hundred years, we should expect to see some fundamental problems of adjustment between past and present. Diligent readers of this book thus far, already aware of the 20th century's concerns about children's frailty, will be additionally armed.

To a historian, who tries to live partly in the past, the anguish provoked by early 20th-century schools, particularly for middle-class parents, was initially an unexpected finding. That immigrant parents felt anxious, encountering formal education for the first time and in a foreign, partly hostile culture, was predictable, and this did form part of the early 20th-century climate. But there was more.

Widespread education was not new. American kids, particularly middle-class kids, had been going to school regularly since the 1830s, except in the South. So why the early 20th century as a special point of tension, as if parents were seriously reconsidering what schools were doing to their children?

The answer is partly the host of innovations at that time, all in the context of the new ideas that promoted a sense of children's frailty. In addition to the tides of immigrant children in the schools, widespread coeducation added a new ingredient, provoking real concern about protecting boys' masculinity in view of the surge in the number of female schoolteachers in the primary grades. More important still, regular grading began to be imposed for the first time. Most 19th-century schools had operated on a loose pass-fail basis, which sometimes included considerable commingling of age groups. This now changed. Report cards emerged as standard practices, directed as much at parents as at children, from the 1920s on. This was a huge change, particularly increasing parental anxieties. School discipline also became more formal, even though random physical punishments declined. There were more rules, including enforcement of attendance and punctuality. All this occurred, further, as big city school bureaucracies increased, along with centralized direction of teachers and curricula. Children might more easily fall victim to impersonal decisions made by unseen authorities.

Schooling also expanded. Some high school education now embraced the majority of the working class for the first time, which meant that middle-class commitment to high school had to increase, as well. College attendance began to climb, but at the same time admission procedures in the best schools became more rigorous and uniform, based more clearly, if still imperfectly, on academic achievement. These were the years of the first College Board efforts, right around 1900, with the SATs (Scholastic Aptitude Tests) introduced later, in 1926.

And schooling was altered, finally, by changes in subject matter and increased expectations. Education was now not just the three Rs, but also modern history, some science, maybe even a modern language. Colleges shifted from emphasis on moral instruction to increased reliance on research-based science and social science, and the results could filter down to the better high schools.

Thus, while the early 20th century did not bring the birth of mass education in the United States (except in the South, which now began to climb on board), it did bring the birth of a modern educational experience. The resultant tensions, combined with the redefinition of childhood, become understandable.

Two other aspects of the American educational scene deserve notice as part of the general context, before we turn to the evidence of new anxieties. First, while all modern societies grapple with tensions between elite and mass education, the tensions in the United States had and still have some distinctive qualities. On the whole, before the college level at least, Americans have done better with the mass part than with distinguishing elite tracks. To be sure, early in the 20th century, new testing began to occur that was designed to assign students in secondary schools to different paths depending on presumed ability. And residential and racial segregation limited school democracy, as well. But the United States never plumped for complete separation of professionally bound and blue-collar- bound students before college, as routinely occurred in Europe and Japan. The result had many admirable features, but it also could impose anxieties on middle-class parents, worried that their kids were not appropriately challenged or recognized, just as other children, and their parents, might wonder about the relevance of their educational fare to their probable future lives. Some confusions of expectations were possible in American schools, in other words, that differed from some of the characteristic drawbacks (mainly hothouse testing and unduly rigid social divides) of other systems.

More generally still, Americans had already developed a love-hate relationship with education that was unusual, and that persists today. On the one hand, as children of the Enlightenment, Americans placed tremendous value on education. They were willing to spend a great deal of money on schools (though never enough, at least for my university). They viewed education as the great social obligation: if children had access to decent education, society had provided them with the components of success, so that, if they later failed, it was their own fault. Europeans, more convinced that certain social barriers were hard to transcend, never assumed quite so much (which is also why they supported welfare systems more readily, to compensate for social injustice). And Americans expected schools to do all sorts of things, providing lessons in driving and safety, hygiene, and temperance and sports experience that went beyond conventional education itself. Have a social problem? Install a class in the schools to teach children what to do. Training in chastity is but a recent example of a longstanding trend.

Yet Americans were also very suspicious of schools, easily believing that they were not doing their job (in part, of course, because expectations were so high). American teachers had relatively low prestige, compared to their counterparts elsewhere. Recurrent experiments tried to probe teachers' competence, but the results were not readily accepted. Laments about school quality dot the 20th century, and not just the most recent decades. Every twenty or thirty years since the 1890s, for example, Americans have learned that lots of students don't know much American history. From 1917: "Surely, a grade of 33 in 100 on the simplest and most obvious facts of American history is not a record in which any high school can take pride." From 1942: high school students are "all too ignorant of American history." From 1987: student test scores indicate that they are "at risk of being gravely handicapped upon entry into adulthood." Each probe resolutely refused to cite its predecessors, creating a sense of novel failure every generation. Reports on a new set of American history test results in 2002 again tried to create a sense that only contemporary American kids would not know that Bryan had attacked the gold standard. But this was part of the yin to the yang that was American enthusiasm for education.[1]

Still more generally, there has also been the odd American tension between loving education and being suspicious of intellectualism. This, too, shows up in parental efforts to protect children in schools—in this case, to protect them from unduly ambitious intellectual demands. The tension also applies, as many historians have noted, to the tendency to downgrade teachers even as great things are expected from schooling. "Those who can't do, teach" has been a cherished national aphorism.

This larger culture could affect perceptions of children. Schools could easily seem essential to the future (the yang part), yet be seen as failing miserably (the yin). Teachers were gatekeepers to college and social rejects. It was hard to strike a balance.

The results showed also in characteristic testing, as it began to become common in the early 20th century. American authorities, and presumably a wider public, were fairly leery of achievement tests as a measure of children and their potential. Initial College Board programs and other tracking tests emphasized aptitude, or at least tried to do so. Again, this was a contrast to testing in most industrial societies, where comprehensive achievement tests were used to track students into secondary schools and again to measure secondary outcomes and prepare for university access. The American reliance on aptitude reflected, among other things, skepticism about the reliability of schools and teachers. Children should not be victims of the incompetence of the education system. The focus on aptitude reflected the sway of expert psychologists like Lewis Terman, convinced of the power of test-based measurements. It also kept promise open for American children, who could always hope to demonstrate aptitude at the next testing stage— at least in principle. (Or, as the College Board program matured, the tests might be taken many times, on the assumption that practice makes perfect.) And the aptitude focus avoided the sheer burden of make-or-break achievement tests like the O levels in Britain or the *baccalauréat* in France, a reflection of the clear American desire to protect youngsters from too much strain.

But always there was ambivalence. Aptitude tests could in fact be prepared for; hence the proliferation of test tutoring and pressures on instructors to teach for the test. Even if tests measured raw aptitude, there was always the question of whether parents had provided good genes or done enough to ensure learning-intensive early years. Aptitude emphasis did not prevent anxiety, though it did avoid the tensions of the summative test systems of Europe or Japan.

Many Americans, in sum, had a host of conflicting thoughts about education, which easily promoted nervousness about what was happening to their children in the schools. Added to the larger concerns about childhood vulnerability and new questions about discipline, these concerns led to an array of protective or compensatory measures. Specifics changed greatly as the century progressed, but there were some impressively consistent underlying themes.

What developed was in fact a twofold response. First, and most obviously in the initial reactions, was a concern that schools threatened to overburden youngsters, exposing them to unnatural stress. Second, not entirely consistently, came a sense that parents had a responsibility for the intelligence and achievement of their offspring, that they ought to be able to ensure successful schooling. Both of these strands continued to affect parental response throughout the 20th century. But they also came together, by the 1960s, in a third current, particularly vivid in the self-esteem movement. Schools should be sufficiently gentle on students that they could do well; schools should ease up on a number of traditional practices; and they should amplify rewards so that fragile childish psyches and parental obligation would both be honored.

SCHOOL AS THREAT

The early 20th century saw the full installation of schooling as childhood's chief responsibility. Children were not consulted as this transformation was completed, which was no big surprise, and adults proved quite wary of it, which was less predictable. A number of experts, led by G. Stanley Hall, contended that children were unprepared for schooling until age eight; Hall conceded that, at most, schooling might begin earlier so long as it had no academic content. Otherwise, children's physical and mental growth might be permanently retarded because their frail constitutions would be overly burdened.

Posture concerns were the focus of one protective reaction. Beginning in the 1880s, doctors began to claim that school desks and the amount of time spent in the classroom posed an unnatural risk for students, with severe implications for posture. One physician, with the hyperbole typical of posture anxieties for several decades, claimed that school desks were causing 92 percent of all students to suffer spinal cord deviations. Another expert attacked education more generally. "For if the State compels the child to go to school, and to undergo the constant risk of developing curvature of the spine . . . universal education must be considered as at least a doubtful blessing." And it was not just the time in school: homework also compelled children to hunch over, again in unnatural activities, with disastrous effects on their vulnerable bodies.[2]

The posture anxiety was a revealing sidelight of an early moment in the larger concerns about what a commitment to schooling was doing to children. Soon, of course, by the 1910s, schools themselves were also seen as a solution, insofar as they could spearhead measurement and retraining programs that would put posture to rights again. For a decade or two, however, posture had provided both experts and ordinary parents with an outlet to express their uneasiness about whether children were up to the demands of modern schooling.

A more serious and longer-lasting attack on schools focused on homework, providing a surprising counterpart to the American enthusiasm for education in the early 20th century. Here is an intriguing sidebar in American educational history, one that historians have only recently uncovered in full. It provided a dramatic counterpart to the more heralded national enthusiasm for education and developed just as increased schooling ran afoul of the growing belief in childhood frailty.

Homework had not been a standard part of the 19th-century school experience, in part because so many children dropped out after fifth grade and so missed the exposure. High schools did set two to three hours of reading a night, which required some real adjustments in domestic chores, but again, most children were not affected. Like students with other difficulties that affected their schooling, like hyperactivity, kids who did not choose to handle the situation would just drop away, at a time when entering high school, much less completing it, was not a middle-class essential.

A full-bore encounter with homework, then, was part of the expansion and intensification of schooling around 1900, which is why reactions, though unexpected in contemporary terms, were not really surprising. With school requirements going up, children who disliked homework no longer had the easy option of dropping out. Parents quickly felt the brunt. A former Civil War hero, the father of two, lamented in the 1890s that homework tasks easily outstripped any educational value and became "the means of nervous exhaustion and agitation, highly prejudicial to body and to mind."

This combined argument—that homework did no educational good and that it sapped children's mental and physical health (an obvious corollary, perhaps indeed partly a cause, of the image of the vulnerable child)—persisted for many decades. Many parents pressed school boards to order limitations of homework, as in Boston in 1905. A doctor, Joseph Mayer Rice, took up the cudgels as part of a more general argument against "mechanical schooling" that ground children down. More important still, Edward Bok, editor of the *Ladies Home Journal*, picked up the vulnerability side of the argument, blasting the burdens on children in articles like "A National Crime at the Feet of American Parents." Bok specifically criticized the damage homework did to children's sleep, causing frightening nightmares because of overstimulation of the brain. "Is it any wonder that children have to be called over and over again in the morning, and that they at length rise unrefreshed and without appetites for their breakfasts? When are parents going to open their eyes to this fearful evil? . . . Is all the book-learning in the world worth this inevitable weakening of the physical and mental powers?" The emotional intensity of the argument is startling only if we fail to put ourselves back a century, when ideas of children's frailty ran headlong into the push for systematic schooling, creating a swirl of anxiety.[3]

From this point on, particularly through the 1950s but even beyond, experts began to debate the merits of homework, reaching no systematic conclusion. Some contended that the evidence definitely indicated that homework benefited children academically. Other studies, seemingly equally exhaustive, demonstrated that homework had no merit. The debates mirrored the more general adult uncertainties and also contributed to them. In this area, parents had no solid bank of expertise through which to resolve their own anxieties.

Buffeted by conflicting signals, from 1900 on a host of cities pondered and often regulated homework. Mother's clubs in Los Angeles, for example, worked hard to persuade schools to shape requirements to the ideas of the child study movement. Academic content in the primary years was diluted—with more attention to coloring, pasting, play skills, and naps, in a curriculum that survived into the 1930s. Early reading was downplayed, as we will see. Arithmetic was largely delayed until grade 3, and grammar instruction was abolished, making the primary grades, as one critic put it, "kindergartenized." And homework was banned entirely until the fourth grade, then doled out in fifteen- or thirty-minute intervals for in-school assignments for the rest of primary school. "The object specially in view in these changes," said the president of the school board, "has been to remove the obvious pressure which has been burdening the children." By 1901, two-thirds of American urban school districts had restricted homework; California, always in the vanguard of child protection, banned obligatory homework even in the first years of high school.

And Bok and others kept the pressure up concerning the "evil effects of home study upon the health of our pupils," thus focusing concerns about children's health on the school regime, as well as attacking homework per se.[4] Doctors continued to testify that overstimulation of the brain of the sort caused by academic work in the evening would inhibit sleep, and, of course, posture concerns entered in as well. More diffuse worries involved the impact of homework on children's other activities, including worship, and the dilution of parental authority over the child's time. Some authorities felt that homework encouraged disobedience by giving children an excuse not to do the work or church-going that their parents requested of them.

By the 1920s, eye strain and what we would today call stress were being singled out. Children needed play, and an opportunity to be out-side; schooling should nurture the whole child, not just the academic side, and it should be fun. The attacks on homework broadened into wider doubts about the link between childhood and academic en-deavor, picking up larger American uncertainties not just about child-hood but about intellectual life itself. Jay Nash, a physical education in-structor, argued that "the absence of strain is represented by the emo-tion of joy and happiness. Joy is a product of freedom and freedom is diametrically opposed to the theory of home study." Until high school, at least, homework was nothing but "legalized criminality."[5]

And homework was attacked as a burden on parents, who had their own lives to lead, unencumbered by the need to supervise their children's schooling. Even some teachers worried that parents were too ignorant to give their children guidance and that homework would become the source of more confusion than anything else. An obvious compromise was the study hall, in which children did home-work but in professionally supervised surroundings, and without the demands on afterschool hours that provoked attacks from so many different directions. Legal bans on homework endured and even ex-panded during the 1920s and 1930s; some regulations persisted into the 1960s.

By the 1940s, to be sure, while doubts lingered, advocates of home-work began to gain the upper hand. Concerns about children's educa-tional performance, heightened during the cold war, undercut most systematic anti-homework arguments, though individual parents con-tinued to worry about overburdening the vulnerable child—and them-selves. The Sputnik scare in 1957 gave an important boost to the home-work argument, and so did the international competitiveness scare of the 1980s. In that decade, the 1983 report *A Nation at Risk* contended that two of the reasons America was falling behind academically were the reduction in homework and a short school year.

Older concerns did not die, however. Many schools continued to urge caution with younger students and preferred types of homework that would entertain, not strain. (An editorial aside: one result of this policy is a continuing tendency to multiply cut-and-paste and com-puter presentation exercises through middle school, which adds immensely to the number of hours spent on homework and create stress without clearly providing real fun or educational value. Don't ask a history question; have the kid draw pictures of Columbus. But this is a parental, not an expert, observation about what kinds of homework actually end up taking the most time.)

For their part, parents, while largely accepting homework as inevitable, continued to have a battle to fight: how much should they themselves get involved? Again, as with the value of homework itself, experts provided little help. Major studies divided almost down the middle as to whether parents who assisted their kids a lot damaged the children's academic success, compared to those who supported the child's early autonomy. What was clear is that most parents, eager to help and concerned about burdens on their children, jumped in and usually felt they should be doing more than they were doing. To be sure, most child- rearing manuals, and many teachers, warned against taking on what children should do themselves: as a 1954 pamphlet suggested, "The teacher may want to recommend that the youngster who has any great amount of homework could very well be left with the responsibility for getting it done, since the way to learn to take responsibility is to have a chance to take it." But most parents, whatever their commitment to character building in principle, could not take this advice, because they either felt sorry for their kids, were annoyed at the prolonged but indirect supervision required, or both. In 2000, 58 percent of all American parents helped their children considerably. Some claimed that their children would not work otherwise: "He won't have it any other way. It's like 'If you don't sit down with me, I'm not going to do it'." Others phrased the issue in terms of obligation: "I know I should work with my children a lot more than I do. . . . They could have made straight As with a little effort—not only on their part, but on my part." A few schools, in the late decades of the twentieth century, even began to train parents on how to coach well. And it was an American president, in 1994, who urged parents to do more. Yet was "more" too much, undercutting personal discipline and later success? Parents answered variously, but it was hard to feel entirely comfortable with the process. School, home, and beliefs about stress still commingled amid continuing anxiety.[6]

OTHER SIGNS OF UNEASE

The attack on homework was the most direct expression of adults' concern about how children and modern schooling interacted. But there were other indications in the early to middle decades of the 20th century. Parent-teacher associations began to form in the early 1900s, allowing parents some access to information about the policies that affected their offspring. Thus, in the 1920s, some PTA discussions focused on how the "remote" was substituting for "local and immediate control of the environment of our children." While much anxiety focused on radio programs originating far away, the same concern could apply to school bureaucracies, as well. In general, however, PTA groups recognized the authority of teachers and did not serve as extensive sounding boards for parents' concerns about vulnerability. Many PTA activities provided frameworks for teachers to tell parents how they should raise their children in order to promote school success. Parent-teacher groups could, however, join hands, as in attempts to isolate children with disabilities who were seen as corrupting influences that endangered normal children. Here, indirectly, was a way to cooperate to reduce some of the perceived problems ordinary children might encounter in schools.

More revealing was the installation of guidance systems and their transformation, a distinctive American twist on the mass education process between the world wars. Guidance programs in the schools initially aimed at providing vocational advice to lower-end, often immigrant children, early in the century, beginning with an effort in Michigan in 1907 and one in Boston in 1908. The movement reflected a growing tendency to push some students into training tracks, but also an optimism about the relevance of education to children's future work prospects. It had little to do with childhood vulnerability. But the first programs drew the attention of psychologists, and this expert overlay helped expand the programs' missions, with tests designed not just to measure aptitudes but also to assess other traits relevant to social adjustment. More important was pressure from parents and students, often middle class, seeking assistance with personal and school-adjustment problems. By the 1920s, guidance activities were spilling over into psychological counseling and developmental concerns, dealing with children whom teachers or parents identified as troubled. By the 1940s, thanks in part to efforts by leaders like Carl Rogers, the counseling function began to eclipse the dispensing of vocational advice and assistance with job placement, and middle-class children became increasingly important targets and beneficiaries. The point was that schools had developed trained personnel with various functions that included mediation between children and the school system more generally. Guidance counselors had various roles, but providing a friendly hand, related to but not part of the educational process, was a key component.

Here was a familiar mix: ideas about children's frailty combined with parental anxieties and with aspiring experts to produce a characteristically American school function. While counselors were variously viewed, their evolution reflected a continued sense that children's adjustment to school environments was neither easy or automatic. As frontal attacks on tasks like homework declined, the interest in identifying some friendly advocates who were in the schools but separate from the classroom expanded.

Parents still stood ready to protest aspects of schooling on the grounds that they overburdened children. The revival of testing and the increased emphasis on homework during the 1990s produced an interesting backlash. By 2001, some cities, like Alexandria, Virginia, passed laws limiting the amount of homework teachers could assign (in Alexandria, an hour and a half each night). Groups of parents, for example in suburban New York, attacked standardized testing that they believed placed too much pressure on their offspring. While the dominant approach shifted, children were still seen as needing protection from school demands.

HYPERACTIVE CHILDREN

The rise of modern schooling inevitably pinpointed children who had particular difficulty in fitting in. But the modes of identification and treatment could change. The story of hyperactive children in the 20th century shows both change and continuity in parents' efforts to deal with a sneaking sense that, given children's vulnerabilities, schooling was an unnatural act.

The pinpointing of hyperactivity in children illustrates a fascinating link between medical research and popular attitudes about, and settings for, children. Until the 20th century, the issue was subsumed in the larger question of discipline and was not specifically targeted. In colonial America, Protestant clergymen often resorted to physical discipline with children who could not sit still for long church services, but, since this was seen as an expression of children's original sin and natural unruliness, it did not come in for specific comment. School situations produced similar reactions, again with use of physical discipline and shaming well into the 19th century. We have no systematic indications of how what we would now call hyperactivity affected children's work performance.

The first signs of a new concern emerged in Europe. A German children's book in the 1850s featured a character, Fidgety Phil, who was the characteristic hyperactive child, unable to sit still. By this point, the demand for better manners in children included explicit injunctions about body control, which singled out children who had difficulties in this area; more regular schooling pointed in the same direction. A truly troubled child could still be pulled out of school and either sent directly to work or (in wealthy families) given private tutoring.

Early in the 20th century, as schooling spread, new forms of testing and medical research began to redefine the issue further, again with Europe in the lead. Hyperactive children in England and Germany were seen as part of the larger group of backward or mentally deficient youngsters, to be removed from regular school and sent to special classes, where different kinds of instruction, focusing on finite tasks, could lead to improvements in learning capacity and even reintegration into regular classes. Brain researchers began to seek the nature and location of what was seen as a physical dysfunction. By the 1920s, experts began to realize that hyperactive children were often quite intelligent, and their inclusion in a generic category of backward children began to diminish. By the 1930s, when research in the United States first picked up steam, investigations into brain lesions intensified. In 1937, a study by Charles Bradley introduced the first possibility of medication, using Benzidrene.

But all of this background had little impact on most American parents and children. Already, in 1904, one researcher, Sanford Bell, had argued that childhood is nothing but motor activity, which made behavior problems in school inevitable: "one never sees a child of five devoting himself to mental things." Bell extended his argument that schooling constricted children and that restlessness was the natural result. "If anything should change in this equation, it should be school, not the child." A number of popular articles in the 1920s picked up the same theme. "It is rather that our treatment of these children is not calculated to develop the best type of adjustment of which they are capable." A number of studies did make claims about the large percentage of children who could not pay attention in school, but the implications were buried in the continued insistence on children's natural unfittedness for modern demands. A 1935 article in *Parents Magazine* noted: "At the very time when growing bodies demand movement and action, children enter school. . . . They want to run, to jump, to shout. They need such activity."[7]

Furthermore, to the extent that there were special problems, it was up to parents to bring their offspring into line. "If David is helped now in learning other methods rather than anger, of solving his problem, he will not become accustomed to using violent outbursts as a means of securing the things he wants," intoned the expert in 1935: the diffuse appeal, calling on parental guidance rather than focused discipline, was characteristic and related to the more general confusion about what parents should do if a child failed to measure up. Behavior problems, as another authority put it, were "calls for help rather than nuisances to be suppressed dictatorially." The dismissive approach extended into the 1950s. "If parents recognize and help a child's feelings as natural, helping him at the same time to control his actions, he will make progress." "A child who was not guilty of some forms of misbehavior would, if he existed, be abnormal. Misbehavior is a normal part of growing up."[8]

For more than half of the 20th century, then, American schools and parents were encouraged to recognize behavior problems associated with hyperactivity but not to apply any systematic remedies. The assumption that children were naturally troublesome in artificial settings like schools, combined with the urgent appeals for parental involvement in shaping natural emotions, seemed to cover the territory. American suspicions of schooling helped mask the problem. Assumptions about parental responsibility and the inevitability of anxiety generated the response to whatever problem was perceived.

But this situation began to change dramatically from the late 1950s on. A key innovation was the introduction of new psychostimulant medication, particularly the drug Ritalin. Now it was possible to be more candid about special problems of otherwise intelligent children and to identify them at a young age. As a *Scientific American* article put it, in 1970, "the hyperactive children's troubles had generally started at a very early age. About half of the mothers had begun to notice that their child was unusual before he was two years old." The formula did not change entirely: parents were still left with anxiety about their children. And there still could be a suspicion of schools themselves ("Parents . . . may want to consider the proposition that it is the school-room atmosphere and not the child's behavior which is pathological."). But, now, changes in attitudes, combined with the possibility of pharmaceutical redress, led to drastic changes in approach.[9]

Other factors entered the picture by the 1960s. Fewer children were being encouraged to drop out of school before completing high school. With more mothers working, parental availability to help with hyperactive children declined, and interest in finding other assistance intensified. With more children in day care facilities, opportunities to identify or investigate problems of hyperactivity at a younger age expanded. Increasing school integration in the United States exposed teachers to categories of children they might more readily define as behavior problems, and there was considerable evidence that minority boys were being singled out as unruly on the basis of teacher discomfort and stereotyping. Finally, teacher discipline was increasingly constrained by new rules: even minor physical punishments were outlawed. Children who had once been brought to attention by a slap on the hand were now described as hyperactive and given a pill, instead. And, summing up and extending the new approach, the problem gained a dramatic disease label by the 1970s: Attention Deficit Disorder (ADD).

The idea that something was wrong with one's child played on parents' old concerns once the buffering assumption that children in general found school restrictive was removed. Some parents resisted the label, insisting that their children simply had spunk that teachers should learn to accommodate. In general, however, the pressure increased to force parents to look for a special set of behavior problems in their children, as both advice literature and the general news media advertised the pervasiveness of ADD. "His mother found Jeremy hard to handle even as a baby. His teacher complained that he was hyperkinetic (overactive) and had an extremely short attention span . . . Jeremy was a 'classic case of minimal brain dysfunction.'" "Very mild brain injuries are a much more common cause of excitability than people generally realize," an expert was noting as early as 1960.[10]

Acceptance of hyperactivity as a disease category gained ground steadily, and some schools refused to let certain children attend unless they were medicated. Estimates in 1980 that 3 percent of all children suffered from ADD grew to 5 percent a decade later. Production of Ritalin soared 500 percent between 1990 and 1996. Initial requirements that a full year of behavior problems formed the basis of diagnosis were soon cut back to six months.

Popularizations of the ADD concept bolstered many parents, who could now point to a problem of brain function in explaining behaviors that used to be blamed on poor home guidance and who were not forced into unacceptable methods of discipline. Drugs were the best out. Supplementary measures, including therapy, special diets, and adult support groups, were deployed against the new scourge, but medication continued to command the greatest attention.

The 20th-century history of hyperactivity shows the pervasiveness of the sense that school and children, or at least some children, did not mix well—the constant during the entire century. Experts pressed for identification of particular children as dysfunctional. But it took a more sweeping set of factors, including available medication but also changes in schools and parental activities, to bring acceptance of the idea of disease. Particularly interesting, in this change, was the increased acceptance of limitations on traditional discipline, in school as well as at home, which made the search for other remedies truly urgent. But there was more to the change: after decades of combat, more parents had come to accept schooling as a given and were now willing to change their children accordingly. Efforts to limit the rules attached to schooling had given way to anxiety-ridden diagnosis of one's own young children, to see whether yet another disease was present. By 1990, *Redbook* was even offering a new parental quiz: "Was your child unusually active in the womb?" Even with the promise of subsequent medication, the furrow of worry about children's adaptation to school still ran deep.[11]

TAKING NEW ADJUSTMENT

For most middle-class parents, and for many in other socioeconomic groups, concern about school demands on children could coexist with substantial acceptance of the educational process. Immigrant parents, for example, might simultaneously worry about what schools did to their culture and strive for their children to excel. Middle-class parents widely accepted the idea that their children should go to school, increasingly beyond the minimum age required, agreeing, too, that it was important for them to do well. So, even while fighting aspects of schooling that they felt to be too burdensome, parents made important adaptations, as well. This led to some additional parental anxieties but also to efforts to adapt schools more subtly to student capacity, particularly after the 1930s.

It would be oversimple to posit a clear chronology in which frontal attacks on aspects of education such as homework gave way to anxieties about adjustment. We have seen, among other things, that the attack mode could resurface when school demands escalated; this continues today. But there was a shift in emphasis, and between the 1930s and the 1960s efforts to promote children's school success gained ground.

There were a number of reasons for the new priorities. By the 1930s, most parents had experienced at least some high school. Generation gaps persisted, as each new generation faced educational requirements and opportunities greater than those that had faced its parents, but the degree of unfamiliarity with schooling declined. An increasingly service-based economy made education seem more meaningful (particularly for girls, who began by the 1920s to go to school longer on average than boys). While placement in high positions still depended less on educational level in the United States than in Europe, the educational requirements for success rose steadily. The turn to mass college attendance after World War II was decisive in this transition. Even by 2001, only a minority (25 percent) of all Americans had graduated from college, but the association of middle-class identity and some college attendance became increasingly close, and this in turn put a new premium on the educational attainments that would get one into college and at least partway through. National pressures could enter in, particularly the recurrent fears after World War II that American educational lags jeopardized competition in the cold war—the Sputnik crisis of 1957—or, later, in juxtaposition with the rise of Japan, that such lags threatened our global economic standing. It became harder to emphasize the need to protect children from schools instead of working toward maximizing their opportunity to do well.

PREPARING THE SUCCESSFUL CHILD

Assimilation of schooling goals, beyond sheer attendance, encouraged parental attention to the relevant aptitudes in their children. Here, too, by the early 20th century, experts were ready to step in with claims of capacity to test the kinds of intelligence that would lead to success in school and life. Ironically, while middle-class Americans favored aptitude tests, they did not sit still out of respect for their logic. For kids might not only be tested for aptitude, they could be coached to display greater aptitude (and it turned out, as College Board critics would later point out, that "aptitude" could indeed be improved by training). So American parents played a game of anxious inquiry into their children's academic potential combined with assiduous efforts to improve that potential through a variety of adult-guided activities. Here was a crucial twist on the vulnerable child motif: children might not, without parental assistance, have the natural aptitude to meet parental expectations for school success.

Schools used aptitude tests widely in the 1920s to sort populations, often heavily immigrant, into educational tracks. One critic noted the enthusiasm as an "orgy of tabulation."[12] Middle-class parents largely accepted the tests, assuming their own children would naturally do well, but the result put pressure on these same parents to anticipate and promote good results.

Concern about possible deficiencies in young children was hardly a 20th-century invention. Many cultures urge parents to check their infants for deformities or for more subjective marks of inadequacy. Earlier in Western history, children born with a caul were viewed as possibly possessed by the devil. But the idea of explicitly evaluating intelligence, at a young age, was a product of the growing acceptance of schooling and schools goals. This gave new shape to what otherwise might seem a traditional anxiety, and it also promoted a host of parental efforts to remedy or prevent inadequacy.

The testing pressure gained ground in the 1920s, with experts like Lewis Terman claiming great precision in identifying school aptitude. As the decade wore on, testing claims were challenged, but, ironically, the claims were enhanced by other expert studies that showed that aptitude not only could be identified but could be improved.

Experts' initial hesitation about going overboard in this process periodically recalled earlier tensions between childhood and learning, based on the notion of the vulnerable child. A number of child-rearing manuals before 1930 warned against overstimulating young children, which could overwhelm any interest in early school preparation. The new concern about promoting massive amounts of sleep had similar implications. A fascinating theory, in the 1930s and 1940s, argued that premature efforts to teach children to read would damage their later capacities. Lots of kids were deliberately delayed as a result, eagerly read to by adults but not encouraged to do more themselves than look at pictures (a reason, along with sheer prosperity, that so many children's books in the United States were lavishly illustrated). Later in the 20th century, there were concerns about those parents who lined up one enriching lesson after another for their children in the dizzying quest for academic improvement. The "overprogrammed" child was the latest in a series of concerns about how children and training might not mix. The pervasive image of childhood frailty or a belief in the importance of spontaneous fun for children triggered attacks on this latter-day picture of diligence.[13]

More generally, however, the idea of helping children prepare for school success followed from the growing internalization of educational goals as part of childhood, combined with some suspicion that schools themselves might not be up to the task or might not acknowledge the special qualities of one's own child. The American propensity for testing, including the growing frequency of school tests and the heavy relevance on aptitude, have drawn legitimate attention in terms of their impact on lower-class and minority groups. They also deserve attention for their role in shaping middle-class concerns about their own kids.

Two kinds of parental anxieties reflected the growing commitment to the educational process: a desire to stimulate younger children before the age of formal schooling and, by the 1960s, the growing competitive frenzy over college admissions as a badge of parental fulfillment.

Interest in stimulating cognitive development in young children began to take new forms in the 1920s and 1930s. It built on Enlightenment beliefs that children were open to improvement through education, on earlier parental commitments to buying toys and books that could awaken a child's intellectual interests, and on kindergarten programs designed in part to promote later school success. But the 20th century added new particulars to this broader current. By the 1920s, child-rearing books and articles began to add cognitive concerns to their predominant emphasis on health, hygiene, and character. One of the reasons for the growing emphasis on the importance of sleep was the need to protect brain development, crucial in the early years. As early as 1930, popular manuals suggested that parents might wish to have young children tested to determine their IQs. Aside from formal IQ testing, pediatricians began to administer simpler procedures that generated insights into young children's probable intelligence, whether or not parents requested them. The focus on the formative qualities of the first years of life began to spill over into the area of educational attainment, as the new term "preschooler" itself implied. By the 1940s, a host of do-it-yourself manuals and articles of varying quality invited parents to get into the diagnostic game directly. Child-rearing experts, while warning against undue competitiveness and elitism, also were telling parents to get their children tested if there were any questions whether they were about living up to capacity in the early grades.

As early as the 1920s and 1930s, new standards for adoption stressed the importance of testing adoptees' intelligence to ensure a good match with middle-class parents. A Yale graduate seeking an adopted child stressed, in turn, his desire "to secure a child that will have the capabilities of making the most of a college education and all that goes with it."[14]

For it was increasingly argued, as in other aspects of child rearing, that the child's early years were crucial in preparing for school success. Schooling, in this sense, could not be left to schools alone, for the years of greatest parental responsibility were decisive in facilitating later results. Hence the anxious interest in early indications of intelligence and the growing array of school-related stimulation offered to infants and toddlers.

These currents were amplified in the 1960s and 1970s, when the commitment to schooling escalated nationwide. Books like Joan Beck's *How to Raise a Brighter Child* (1975) or Glenn Doman's *How to Multiply Your Baby's Intelligence* summed up the growing interest and sold hundreds of thousands of copies. Nationally, this interest generated programs such as Head Start, aimed at poorer families. In the middle class, the interest stimulated a growing commitment to buying things that would advance the child's intelligence from infancy on. Outfits like the Princeton- based Creative Playthings seized on parents' desire to acquire toys that would directly instill the process of self-improvement. Cribs began to be filled not just with emotionally comforting teddy bears but with eye-catching mobiles that, the experts argued, would push Jane or Johnny a bracket higher in later intelligence. Color began to factor in, as pundits urged that painting the infant's room orange had stimulating effects.

There were also lessons, and competitive nursery schools from the toddler years on. Some lessons, like dance for girls or soccer, recalled older middle-class traditions of equipping children with appropriate social graces, leisure skills, and gender identities; some embraced related goals of character building and the fostering of team skills. But the new goal of stimulation, of giving one's offspring a leg up on later studies, gained growing momentum. Music lessons began to be sold, for example, not just for their intrinsic merits but on the basis of research that suggested their role in developing intelligence.

Schooling, in this climate, was now essential, but it still was not exactly natural. It was important to offer supplementary exercises to maximize the chances of success.

The second big middle-class school commitment, building on the concern about school aptitude and its testing and enhancement, involved the post–World War II assumption that college attendance and middle-class status went hand in hand. The commitment unfolded in several stages. Post–World War II programs for veterans provided unprecedentedly wide college access. Top colleges themselves opened their doors to a wider array of applicants. Harvard's national scholarship program, for example, developed in the 1950s, was designed to make sure that Harvard had a literally national recruitment base for attracting top talent. Members of various ethnic groups began to take college attendance as a given, and at a full range of colleges, rather than purely local hothouses like the City College of New York. The conversion of many elite schools to coeducation, beginning in the 1960s, added to this thrust. By the 1960s, about half of all Americans of standard college age were entering college, and while this was admittedly a smaller percentage than the 85 percent of the population that claimed to be middle class, it marked a huge surge in the commitment to college attendance. Parents and children both participated in these new assumptions. And the trend continued; between 1974 and 1988, enrollment among white Americans of the relevant age shot up from 47 percent to 60 percent.

A decisive step in this process, and the one that converted a new pattern to a new level of anxiety, occurred in the 1960s, when the baby boom generation began competing for college access. Already, of course, the surge in attendance had strained facilities. Now, it became increasingly clear that many students could not expect to get into the level of college they had anticipated, for the top schools simply did not expand as rapidly as the demand. The blow was particularly acute for groups, like middle-class Anglo-Saxon males, that suffered not only from the results of overall crowding but from the increasingly success- ful incursions by second- and third-generation immigrants, women, African Americans, and, soon, Asian Americans.

The situation converted a well-established pecking order among institutions of higher learning to a competitive frenzy in which parents were, if anything, more involved than their offspring. It became a test of parental adequacy to do everything possible not just to make sure the child got into college but to ensure that he or she got into a good one. Multiple applications to colleges soared as parents tried to en- courage children to maximize their chance to attend a top school, while maintaining a safety school application in case the best hopes were dashed. The competitive game could be played at multiple levels, for the pecking order extended from top to bottom. Some parents and chil- dren aimed desperately at the Ivies; others, no less eager but operating in a different financial or academic context, pinned their hopes on the state's top public university. Needless to say, discussions among par- ents of college-age children routinely included carefully worded re- minders about the status factors involved, as parents gleefully noted their children's success or tried to avoid condescension when friends admitted that a second-tier state college was the best they could muster.

What was particularly interesting about this anxiety about college was that it outlasted the baby boom. Anxiety about getting into the ap- propriate college persisted in the 1970s and 1980s, when in fact admis- sion into a very good college became easier and admission to a good college was widely attainable. It remained so important to aim high that the competitive worries did not ebb. Colleges, of course, played this sit- uation to the hilt, assuring parents that their admission standards were indeed quite high and that their children's future might well depend on this particular opportunity.

To be sure, the continued increase in enrollments did create pres- sure, but college facilities were expanding, as well. A moderately tal- ented high school graduate had no real worries, and in fact almost every interested applicant could gain entrance somewhere. But the worries persisted, even escalated, nevertheless.

This was the context in which a host of supportive arrangements began to develop. Children began to prepare explicitly for entrance exams, a practice almost unheard of before the 1960s. Advanced placement programs proliferated. Officially designed to allow college-level work during secondary school, and therefore offering a potential reduction in college time and costs, most AP programs really drew attendance because parents and children believed that they would bolster competitive credentials.

With all this, there was no denying that substantial hurdles must still be faced. Parents could prod and help their offspring, but they could not finesse the entrance competition entirely, except in the shrinking number of cases where upper-class old-boy networks still ensured admission of a select group almost regardless of qualifications. The commitment, then, not just to college attendance but to competitive strivings within the rank order of the institutions involved, represented a substantial additional internalization of schooling goals. Potentially a source of pride when children did indeed shine, the process undoubtedly created even wider anxiety, often more among the parental sponsors than among their more laid-back progeny.

In this context, the proliferation of college rating publications, launched in the 1980s, fed on and in turn nourished the competitive anxiety. The idea of ranking colleges played off parental status commitments on their children's behalf and made the markers involved more concrete and public than ever before. *U.S. News and World Report*, which particularly profited from the frenzy, steadfastly refused to ease the pressure, and no major college was bold enough to refuse to participate in the ranking program.

Predictably, the college competitive anxiety deepened by the late 1990s and early 2000s when the growth of the college-age cohort—the result of the baby boom echo—really did make it harder once again to get into top colleges. Parents were described as "frantic" in the college application year. They desperately monitored children's grades, the playing time they got on the soccer field—all the components of a successful college push. Some claimed even to despair that their children would get into college at all, which was frankly ridiculous, given the number of slots available. Horror stories circulated, and expanded in the process, about National Merit Scholar kids who did not get into even less desirable but still top-tier schools. Amid the undeniably increasing competition (which will begin to lessen again by 2008), the anxiety threatened to spin out of control.

Parental anxiety mounted for yet another, perhaps more tangible reason: the burden of college costs. The United States was unique in assuming that parents were the primary source of support for college training—an assumption with which most parents agreed. To be sure, other sources were important, including government payments, but most parents, when polled, acknowledged and even welcomed primary responsibility. The commitment ran deep, and it was not entirely rational. More than half of all parents indicated that they would jeopardize their family's financial security to get their kids through college; three-quarters, in fact, went into debt. A host of parents made their job choices on the basis of anticipated or actual college costs. Interestingly—a revealing aside both on parents' commitment to college and on their desire to buffer their children—willingness to pay increased in inverse proportion to the child's test score, all other factors held constant. And the stark fact was that college costs rose precipitously, more than 80 percent faster than median family income during the 1980s. Here was a fruit of the intense commitment to college, which created relatively inelastic demand, and a further source of anxiety, as parents' sense of responsibility continued to ride high.

College anxiety escalated at yet another level—the ritual of getting kids ready to go. As colleges became more bureaucratic, yet also more committed to a quasi parental role in trying to make sure that students had fun, the list of things to do before sending Johnny or Judy off for that first year became steadily more elaborate. Parents responded in part because of their own anxiety about whether their kids were ready. Parents' commitments to accompany students on extended midsummer orientation programs expanded. The number of things to buy multiplied. In 2001, the University of Delaware sent new freshman a sheet of almost 150 "back-to-campus essentials" of which only thirty were academic supplies. While surely the inclusion of butterfly chairs, televisions, blenders, microwaves, and refrigerators would suggest to most parents that some selectivity was possible, parents were likely also to feel guilty, to feel that they had not given their student enough, that college was sufficiently daunting that compensation, as well as payment, was essential.

ABOVE-AVERAGE AVERAGES

So far this chapter has dealt with anxieties about schooling and about children's potential for achievement (and how to pay for the results). The two paths pointed in different directions, though each could elicit intense parental concern. We have also suggested a partial chronological sequencing. Understandably, the demands of modern schooling first prompted a sense of burden, particularly given the new focus on the vulnerable child. But, with time and experience, and as schooling became ever more clearly unavoidable and desirable, attention shifted to measuring and readying the child. A few throwbacks to fears about unnatural damage caused by schooling still occurred, but the dominant focus shifted. Rapid suburbanization after World War II represented in part a quest for good schools, defined in terms not only of safety and considerable homogeneity but also of solid academic standards.

Yet this is not the entire story. As achievement concerns intensified, particularly from the 1960s on, parents and other adults groped for a fuller reconciliation between an acceptance of academic goals and a concern that children might be overburdened. Without disputing the importance of academic goals directly, there was a new search for innovations that would reduce the load. Two related movements particularly captured this flavor, and both led to significant changes in the presentation of school: the self-esteem campaign and the persistent tendency toward grade inflation. Both trends sought to make it easier for schools to ensure success without forcing frontal attacks like the earlier assault on homework. These trends developed at about the same time as the formal recognition of Attention Deficit Disorder, which offered medical treatment for another set of students who could, with assistance, hope to measure up.

SELF-ESTEEM

The roots of the self-esteem movement went back to the late 19th century, where they were intertwined with larger notions of children's vulnerability and the need for adult protection and support. Most of the psychologists associated with the Child Study movement specifically discussed the concept of self-esteem as a key component in successful child rearing. Progressive era educators used the idea, as well, in seeking a supportive school environment. But it was only in the 1960s that the well- established expert theme clearly won popular and institutional backing as a way to reconcile academic commitment with parental concerns for childhood frailty and for the special value of their own children.

John Dewey and William James were among the early proponents of the psychological importance of the "self." Dewey discussed "intuition of self" in his seminal work, *Psychology*, in 1886, using knowledge of self as the talisman for knowledge gains in general. Selfhood was, in this view, essential to freedom. But it was James, in 1892, who first used the term "self-esteem" with an explicit scientific definition. A key task of socialization, in James's view, involved helping children gain the capacity to develop a "self" and, with it, the capacity to adapt to different social settings with appropriate projections of self. Self- esteem, more specifically, involved the kind of perceptions that, properly honed, were crucial to achievement and success.[15]

Popularization of psychology and the growing notion that children often needed expert help brought concerns about self- esteem to greater attention during the 1920s and 1930s. If children needed a sense of self to operate successfully, but if children were also vulnerable (and if guilt was no longer an acceptable motivational tool), it was certainly possible that special measures might be necessary to ensure that the mechanism was in working order.

But it was during the 1950s and 1960s that the connection between self-esteem and supportive school programs was fully forged. A clear symptom, as well as a cause of further awareness, was the growing spate of expert studies on the subject. Stanley Coopersmith, in 1967, identified the link between self-esteem and frailty, noting the "indications that in children domination, rejection, and severe punishment result in lowered self-esteem. Under such conditions they have fewer experiences of love and success and tend to become generally more submissive and withdrawn (though occasionally veering to the opposite extreme of aggression and domination)."[16]

While experts debated the precise relations between self-esteem and other factors—in their eyes, the subject was extremely complicated, with more funded research invariably essential—three points were clear. First and most obvious, self-esteem was vitally important to a well-adjusted, high-functioning child or adult. This was the conclusion amply prepared by previous generations of scientific writing. Second, self-esteem was crucially affected by what parents did to children. Levels of discipline, family affection, and marital stability all registered in a child's emerging concept of self-worth. Finally, self-esteem played a crucial role in school success—as Coopersmith put it, "ability and academic performance are significantly associated with feelings of personal worth."[17]

It is not easy to explain why the self-esteem movement kicked off in the post–World War II decades. Of course, it was prepared by earlier expertise and then enhanced by a new generation of studies; in part, we're back in the chicken-and-egg causation problem that 20th-century expertise routinely evokes. But if one assumes, as in previous discussions, that more is involved in explaining why the public picked up on the issue—that parents and school authorities were not merely being shepherded by the gurus—three concurrent factors come into play.

First, the American economy was shifting rapidly toward service-sector functions—sales work and middle-management coordination—in which social skills played a growing role. There is no question that middle-class parents were becoming increasingly sensitive to this transition by the 1950s. The transition meant, in turn, a growing concern with sociability—good social skills, the ability to get along with others. And the experts made a convincing case that self-esteem was in turn a crucial variable in this social equation. As one put it, "Success . . . is measured by the concern, attention, and love expressed by others. These expression of appreciation and interest are subsumed under the general terms of acceptance and popularity, while their polar opposites are termed rejected and isolation."[18] School performance and sociability became increasingly linked: both were essential for adult success, and both should be enhanced by appropriate attention to self-esteem. The self-esteem movement was directly associated with growing sensitivity to social criteria and the opinions of others, as Americans moved from a manufacturing to a service-sector economy, from entrepreneurship to organizational skills. David Riesman captured this sea change as the rise of "other-directedness," and attention to self-esteem was a vital attribute.

Second, the self-esteem emphasis played on growing uneasiness felt by many middle-class parents about the quality of family life they were offering to their children. Divorce rates were soaring by the 1950s. Women were going back to work. Surely developments of this sort must take a toll. Measuring and bolstering children's self-esteem became something of a barometer in an anxious period in American family history. Schools might be called upon to pick up the slack, and many school authorities, worried about family conditions even in suburbia, ratcheted up their commitment to protecting children's psyches. Whether wittingly or not, expert formulations about self-esteem directly played on uncertainties about the quality of family life, even in middle-class households.

Finally, the focus on self-esteem captured developments that more directly involved children. There was an obvious link, chronologically and substantively, to the more permissive disciplinary approach, after the behaviorist fling of the interwar decades and to the ongoing worries about the corrosive effects of guilt. While studies suggested that strict standards, equitably applied, might actually bolster self-esteem, a more popular conclusion was that children needed help and latitude in living up to standards, less chance to feel guilty about failure, and more opportunity to express the self in the process. The height of the baby boom also raised explicit concerns, within families and in crowded classrooms, about whether individual children were now receiving the attention they deserved; some special compensatory actions, in the form of attention to self- esteem, might be essential.

The self-esteem movement, as an adjustment between school commitments and worries about overburdening children, arose, then, at a time of significant rethinking about the preconditions of adult success, amid some lessening of confidence in the middle-class home environment, and in the presence of some very practical problems in dealing with the baby boom surge. Prepared by earlier psychological inquiry, the movement sought a new intermediation between school and child, while bolstering parental interests in providing a supportive disciplinary approach outside of school.

As early as the 1950s, enhanced discussions of self-confidence, and the need for explicit parental support, were becoming standard segments in the child-rearing manuals. Thus, Sidonie Gruenberg, in 1958: "To value his own good opinion, a child has to feel that he is a worth-while person. He has to have confidence in himself as an individual. This confidence is hard for children to develop and there are many experiences that may shake it." The approach was in interesting contrast to Gruenberg's voluminous writings in the 1930s, where the subject received little explicit comment. Now, however, the need for parents to display pride in their children gained extensive attention, with a particular plea that children be encouraged through the mistakes they made. "We must not let the mistakes and failure shatter our faith in the child . . . He needs real and lasting self-respect if he is to develop" both integrity and a durable capacity to achieve. Self-esteem, clearly, began with the home, and with a more flexible approach to discipline being urged on parents more broadly.[19]

By the 1980s, bumper stickers picked up the theme for anxiously doting parents and grandparents. Where but in the United States would one see a car proudly if vaguely announce, "I have a rising star at Mayfield elementary school?"

Application of self-esteem concepts in the schools from the 1960s onward involved a number of specific programs and a more general reorientation. Programs typically focused on the importance of providing children a wide range of activities so that they could gain a sense of achievement or mastery whatever their academic talents. Thus, many schools enhanced standard lessons with new opportunities for self-expression. History or literature courses added often-elaborate role-playing exercises to reading and discussion. Children might demonstrate skills in playing a historical character that would not come to light if they were merely called upon to recite facts about the same character. It was also crucial that most of these additional exercises were not graded, again in the interests of encouraging a sense of competence at all levels. Another set of self-esteem exercises involved a growing emphasis on "service learning." Here, students could directly contribute to the community while also building an opportunity to display an individual capacity to perform. The Challenge Program in California involved high school students in tutoring grade-schoolers, in working in a historical society, or in participating in environmental efforts. The rationale was central to the self-esteem approach: through these nonacademic activities, students would "have a reason to enjoy and a recipe for personal success."[20]

The approach was fascinating in its effort to provide alternatives to academic competitiveness and, even more, in its assumptions that school must be leavened by nonacademic exercises. Proponents argued, with apparent justification when involved students were compared with control groups, that participation in the self-esteem programs reduced discipline problems in the schools and improved academic performance itself. Why the overall achievement levels of American stu-

dents continued to raise questions, however, despite the growing uti-
lization of self-esteem activities, was less clear.

In addition to influencing specific programs, self-esteem arguments
entered into larger recommendations for teacher behavior. Thus, teachers were urged to add positive comments on all student work, in addition to (and perhaps instead of) critical observations. As with discipline,
some education authorities argued essentially that rewarding good behavior was far more useful, given children's self-esteem needs, than
castigating bad behavior. The portfolio movement, though it had a
number of justifications and though in fact it was hampered by the costs
involved, often included some self-esteem justifications, as well. Instead of being graded through conventional tests alone, students in
portfolio programs could offer a collection of different kinds of expression in the subject area, from art to computer graphics, so that various
learning styles could be accommodated with equal access to self-
esteem. And self-esteem concerns had further impact on the whole
concept of grading itself, contributing greatly to grade inflation.

Self-esteem notions and activities were often criticized, and movements to develop more rigorous testing procedures in the 1990s represented something of a counterattack. Through most of the final third of
the 20th century, however, self-esteem ideas strongly influenced many
teachers, and even some athletic coaches, while helping to reconcile
parents to the demands of schooling by providing some buffer between
academics and the psychological development of their children.

GRADE INFLATION

The development of grade inflation is one of the most fascinating chapters in American educational history in the past four decades; while it
has some modest imitations in other countries, its wide use in the
United States is distinctive. One of the reason foreign—even Cana-
dian—teaching assistants have difficulty adapting to American college
ways is that the assumption that they will grant mostly As and Bs to
their charges differs so much from their own experience.

Academics being academics, eager to probe a topic precisely and
also, in this case, more than a bit embarrassed about their own changes
in habits, there have been a host of studies debating whether grade

inflation has really occurred. It has, from the 1960s on. A 1983 study noted that 60 percent of high school grades were As and Bs, compared to less than 50 percent in 1968. By 1979, again in the high schools, among college-bound students, there were twenty-one A averages for every twenty C averages, as the number of A averages increased by about two-thirds. Between 1969 and 1981, all students, whether college-bound or not, saw the rates of largely-A performances shoot up by 15 percent. And the trend continued. Between 1987 and 1994, as SAT scores declined by about ten points, the total number of high school students receiving As jumped another 12 percent, to a total of 32 percent. Colleges followed suit. By the 1990s, prestigious colleges like the Ivies and Stanford were giving more than 60 percent of all students honors upon graduation. A notorious Yale case, in which a California junior college failure faked his credentials to gain entry, only to find he made As and Bs with ease, drove the point home.[21]

The result triggered division and soul searching. It was easy, and to some extent accurate, to assume that standards were plummeting, that young people were being indulged, and that the nation risked serious deterioration in international competition when top students, as judged by grades, failed to measure up in more objective tests. Bitter disputes raged on some college campuses between those who went with the flow, perhaps a bit uneasy but fundamentally comfortable with the more relaxed criteria, and those (often in more quantitative disciplines, where it was easy to pinpoint deficiencies) convinced that students' feet must be held to the fire. A Harvard prof blasted his colleagues, in 2001: "Professors are quite satisfied to bestow outlandishly high grades upon students. We even think those grades reflect well on us; they show how popular we are with bright students. And so we are quite satisfied with ourselves too. There is something inappropriate—almost sick—in the spectacle of mature adults showering young people with unbelievable praise. We are flattering our students in our eagerness to get their good opinion." And then the kicker: "In late life, students will forget those professors; they will remember the ones who posed a challenge."[22]

Key discussions focused on college retention. Eager-to- please administrators grew increasingly distraught about students who flunked out or who left because they were discouraged with mediocre results (for, despite inflation, many college students did receive lower grades than they had enjoyed in high school). The result was a waste, a loss in numbers, and a decline in revenue in the context of vigorous college competition *(U.S. News* ratings, among other things, punished high departure rates). So the administrators urged gentler treatment, particularly of easy- to-bruise freshmen. Yet, a handful of holdouts, often lurking in calculus classes, kept doling out the low grades. And there was some tendency, as in management schools, to increase quantitative requirements—whether necessary or not, in what might be called punitive mathematics—as a means of countering the larger inflationary trend.

Still, for all the bitter and interesting debate, there was inflation. What did it mean? A change in philosophy from viewing grades as a goad to greater effort or even as an objective measure to seeing them as a form of encouragement, for one thing—but also, in an odd way, a fuller commitment by parents and many students to schooling and to good grades, leavened with the protective desire to make sure any effort won definite reward. Here was the essential compromise, based on continued uneasiness about children and school but removed, now, from frontal opposition. I'll send my kid, I'll even supervise and help with homework, but I want a happy, ego-sustaining result.

For, along with grade inflation, older, more accented forms of indifference toward school declined. The gentleman's C progressively disappeared; Cs were no longer respectable in an age when different social groups were mixing in school, seeking more measurable success, and when schooling itself had gained greater importance. The inflated B did not necessarily represent less academic work than its counterpart two decades before, just a greater desire to receive a pleasant reward for some degree of commitment.

The key analysis must rest with causes for the change, and these have been fairly vague in studies to date. A few possibilities deserve consideration. The first, challenging but on balance distracting, involves affirmative action and desegregation. One line of argument about grade inflation seeks to explain it through the reaction of white teachers to the surge of minority students in desegregated high schools and recruitment-anxious colleges in the 1960s. To deal with underqualified students and avoid accusations of racism, the professors eased up; then, since they'd done this for the minorities, they applied the same logic to white students as well. This was supplemented by sympathy with middle-class students during the Vietnam War—the ones who claimed that a C might expose them to the draft, to battle, and to death.

There may be some truth to this explanatory line. But it is important to remember that grade inflation did not begin in colleges, where the affirmative action and antidraft sentiments ran strongest. And grade inflation applied much more to college-bound middle-class white students than to students in general, though there was some spillover.

Schools of education came under fire, for grades in education courses were higher than university averages. This reflected the prior school-teaching experience of many faculty and so really offered no explanation. School reliance on self- esteem movements, including concern about the hurtful affects of low grades, plays in here. This same impulse led to a growing array of extra-credit exercises designed to push grades up regardless of exam scores.

In the colleges, new emphasis on evaluating teaching may have contributed to the grade inflation process, another post- 1960s innovation. Teachers, it was argued, worry about bad student ratings and so grade more gently in hopes of feathering their own nests. Again, perhaps—surely this is true in some cases, for example adjunct instructors who depend on yearly reappointment for their jobs. A few colleges have recently suspended teaching evaluations as a means of fighting grade inflation. But, as a major explanation, this approach, too, has flaws. Again, the process began in high schools, where teacher evaluation of this sort is not an issue. Even in the colleges, students are remarkably generous in their ratings, and efforts to prove that tougher grades win lower marks have not borne fruit. Score this category, at most, as a contributing factor once the larger process began.

The real explanation lies, as many critics have recognized, in changes in attitudes, among teachers and parents, toward their own, middle-class kinds of kids. It relates closely to the assumption of the self-esteem movement that education must make students feel capable and empowered. Grade inflation builds on a growing adult desire to be friends with kids—the dad-as-pal approach—as well as a desire to minimize confrontation with anxious parents. Traditional grading encourages stress and competition, and a newer approach was required to create a greater sense of harmony.

As a child-development professor noted, "As soon as you get into some of the more complicated things, kids may experience failure. They may feel like they're stupid." So go easy. As another teacher, an active participant in the grade inflation process, put it, "We should not use grading to punish students. We should use it to encourage better performances. . . . A carrot is better than a stick. . . . I don't think it's grade inflation, it's grade encouragement." Or again: "It will lead to higher achievement, higher self-esteem."[23]

Parents and, by college age, children themselves actively participated in this process, badgering teachers to award higher grades so that students would feel good, so that effort would be rewarded regardless of precise quality—and, of course, so that college access would be ensured. A key component of the grade inflation shift involved the combination of the larger self-esteem assumptions, the idea that children are easily bruised and need explicit uplift, with the increased competition for access to good colleges as the baby boom generation matured in the late 1960s while the number of prestige college slots did not keep pace. College competition was enhanced, of course, not only by the size of the cohort but by conversions to coeducation (hence a reduction in openings for males) and by more interest in college attendance from some lower-class and minority groups. Many teachers acted out of a genuine concern for students' emotional health and opportunity, plus a desire to avoid hassle—to protect their own emotional independence—from the escalating quarrels with the more demanding parents and students.

The result was, unquestionably, a major change. It was accompanied by other efforts to reduce possible school stress. Teachers were banned from posting grades, lest children see others' results and have their own viewed by others; poor self-image, even humiliation, might ensue. The practice of piling graded papers outside one's office so that students could pick them up was also technically illegal, on the same grounds. In 2001, a case reached the Supreme Court in which a parent sued teachers who let grade school students mark one another's papers as an educational exercise: again, the villains were potential "embarrassment and humiliation." Ironically, students continue to insist on immediately comparing their grades in class, anyway, in blithe defiance of adults' assumptions about their vulnerability, but the assumptions themselves were intriguing.

Friendliness and persuasion increasingly replaced fear and jealousy as school motivators, and grades soared accordingly. Ideas about children's frailty that had initially persuaded many parents now spread increasingly into school systems. Here was the crucial shift that allowed many adults to abandon their open attacks on the burdens of schooling—schooling was made compatible with children's needs for support and favor. Self-esteem movements and, particularly, grade inflation squared the circle, making parents more comfortable with higher commitments to schooling despite their belief in childhood vulnerabilities. The accommodation also explained why individual parents could be so fierce in attacking teachers who did not seem to buy into the grade inflation mode, insisting that their Janes or Johnnys deserved a better shake because they tried.

Grade inflation had an interesting impact on the College Board's Advanced Placement program, designed to offer college-level work to bright high school students. Responding to parental pressure, and also to equal opportunity concerns, many schools opened their AP courses to all comers during the 1980s, and enrollments exploded. By itself, this was an interesting sign of the eagerness of mainly middle-class parents to see their children academically challenged. Many AP teachers, however, felt that one result was a dramatic increase in the number of underqualified students taking the demanding courses. And then, of course, grade inflation kicked in, with tremendous pressures on AP teachers to give high grades regardless of students' achievement. High standards were fine, as represented by Advanced Placement classes, but they must be mediated in the form of achievable good grades—the grade inflation approach in a nutshell.

The results of the various forms of grade inflation upset critics and fed a larger conservative lament about the deteriorating character of Americans. The results also challenged other educational staples. It became harder to rely on teachers' recommendations, for another set of legal changes made such letters available to the students; even without this, many teachers carried over their feel-good attitudes into the comments they sent, applying the *nihil nisi bonum* approach to the living as well as the dead. Grade-point averages became harder to interpret, though doughty admissions officers continued to argue that they remained the best single predictor of later academic success. Reliance on College Board scores (which themselves began to come out of their slump in the 1990s but still did not rise nearly as fast as school grades) increased, or at least largely continued, despite persistent criticism. Grade inflation mattered.

Other practices were reexamined. Some schools dropped the identification of particularly bright children as valedictorians or the promotion of academic awards. More common was the multiplication of identification opportunities for reasonably able kids. While a few older honor societies kept standards high, additional societies sprang up to acknowledge a wider range of youngsters, at both secondary school and college levels. The damage to the slightly less successful by naming valedictorians might be slightly obviated by having a lot of them: by 2001, some California high schools had as many as forty.

But whether this whole transformation worsened the educational process, as opposed to changing its assumptions and tone, is a more complex question, and we return to this in concluding the chapter.

VARIATIONS AND EXCEPTIONS

Approaches to children and schooling, as they developed in the 20th century, obviously permitted many variations on the part of individual parents or larger social and cultural groups. The huge range, from the idea of natural aversion to school to the embrace of hothouse promotion of academic success, permitted a host of gradations. While some parents felt perfectly comfortable intervening for a child with a hard-grading teacher, others held back, embarrassed or convinced that children might benefit from a few hard knocks. Mothers and fathers debated what approach to take; studies from the 1920s on, feeding off gender stereotypes, portrayed mothers as more eager to protect children's fragile psyches. And there were generational differences, as well, with adults' moods shifting somewhat over time. Overall, some 20th-century parents pushed their children hard toward school success, eschewing the protections of self-esteem ideas or grade inflation, while others were more indulgent.

And there were always exceptions to the general patterns. Sports and music provide two fascinating examples. For devoted children and their parents, both offered clear goals that overrode adult concerns about childhood vulnerability in a way that academic schooling never quite managed to do. The implied priorities were intriguing.

I watched two of my children commit to a serious interest in musical productions in high school. I would pick them up after rehearsals (which always ran late) and watch as the music director berated the whole cast, telling them how lazy and incompetent they were, driving them frequently to tears. And I wondered why the students put up with this kind of treatment, which they never would have tolerated from a classroom teacher. My children told me to mind my own business, that the show was the important thing and they needed to be driven.

The same thing happened with my stepson's basketball: his coaches could shout, curse, even physically intimidate, and the players found the behavior perfectly natural. Coaches could seem to be throwbacks to the era of the sturdy child, when passionate commitments could lead to what, in other settings, 20th-century parents would have regarded as abusive goading, with anger and shame were seen as valid motivators. Even a coach like Bobby Knight, long of Indiana University, could survive repeated reports of verbal harassment and physical violence against his players, because of a larger commitment to winning and because many parents harbored a sneaking suspicion that this approach was best for character growth. The oddity was that the same tolerance rarely extended to the tough, abrasive teacher.

Of course, sports coaches showed the more contemporary trends, as well. Many coaches came to pride themselves on recognizing their players' need for self-esteem and on building success through positive reinforcement. Some noted, for example, that they'd learned to clap when a player erred, as an alternative to showing displeasure. For their part, many parents, particularly when young children were involved, expected coaches to ignore aptitude in the interests of giving each child playing time and a chance to excel. Coaches or referees who stood in the Little Leaguer's way might be denounced, even physically threatened, in the sports equivalent of grade inflation.

Still, sports and music settings did demonstrate greater tolerance for behaviors that ignored children's emotional fragility and self-esteem, and in this they contrasted with more purely academic schooling. Both arenas had reasonably clear-cut standards of performance that at least by high school age could not easily be masked by invocations that every child should be able to express himself. Sports, particularly, maintained the older value of character building, which purely academic schooling had never managed to claim in the United States. And, of course, many students chose not to continue a serious interest in sports or music, whereas they could not as readily sidestep academic requirements. Still, the differences tolerated between some coaches and many teachers reflected continued adult ambiguity about what should be expected from children, and no small amount of hesitation about the validity of rigorous academic goals.

Education, one wag maintained, was, like dentistry, one of the only aspects of modern life where one really did not want to get one's money's worth, preferring instead an easier path. So, alongside many splendid educational accomplishments in the United States, grade inflation continued, maintaining the pressure for reassurance along with evaluation.

There was even an attempt, as grade inflation began and for many of the same reasons, to cushion the results of the most competitive element of the American system, the College Board exams. We have seen that many middle-class parents, and their children, internalized the importance of entry to the best available colleges, often beyond what the facts of the situation required. It was natural, in this situation, to seek some buffering. By the early 1970s, children began to be encouraged to take the dreaded SATs many times, on the assumption, usually correct, that experience would promote improved scores even on tests designed to measure aptitude. Coaching schools emerged by the 1980s—Kaplan, Princeton Review, and others—again with the same goal in mind. At some suburban sites, taking an SAT prep course became a virtual necessity for upper-middle-class kids, lest they fall behind. Practice SATs, first introduced in 1956 (and renamed in 1959) as a means of qualifying candidates for scholarship programs like the National Merit competition, quickly found favor as another way not only to obtain early measurements of ability but also for students to acquire experience. By 2000, more than two and a quarter million kids were taking the PSATs each year. None of this erased the SAT's status as a major competitive hurdle, a position difficult to alter precisely because, for so many parents and educators, they provided the rigorous measurement that qualified and justified all the inflationary cushions that parents also sought. But, if the hurdle could be softened just a bit by practice and tutoring, parents with sufficient resources were eager to oblige.

Another adjustment area was fascinating. Claims for special needs for children accelerated steadily by the later 20th century. By 2002, a quarter of all children in the Fairfax (VA) County public schools were designated special needs. This ran the gamut from Attention Deficit Disorder to particular nutritional requirements, but the percentage was nevertheless staggering, in one of the most affluent regions of the nation. The claims reflected a rich school district's sincere attempt to accommodate students; it reflected middle-class parental alertness in claiming every possible advantage for one's own children. It also reflected, on the part of parents and authorities alike, an assumption that frailty was likely, and that it legitimately commanded compensation lest schooling prove overwhelming.

CONCLUSION

Is school too hard for my kid? Did my kid do well enough? Both questions are reasonable, as parents consider contemporary schooling. Each, however, points in somewhat different directions. It's the combination that promotes parental anxiety and prompts many of the reactions that developed during the past century in the United States.

During the course of the 20th century, with many specific twists and turns, adults tried to accommodate their worries about children—their own precious cargo particularly—and schooling. It would be easy, especially in noting the eventual move toward self-esteem movements and grade inflation, to go on to the standard lament about academic decline.

The extension would be unwarranted, for several reasons. First, of course, this chapter has focused on adult, particularly parental, attitudes to children in school, and this is hardly the whole history of schooling. A host of other developments would require consideration.

More important is the basic continuity the chapter has uncovered and highlighted. Most claims of academic deterioration use some (often illusory) earlier 20th-century benchmark against post-1960s degeneration. But, in fact, parents have worried about schooling, while embracing aspects of it, for a full century. Specific accommodations to schooling have changed, but not the fundamental tension. This is one reason that studies of student achievement do not reveal the deterioration so often claimed: laments about performance gaps pervade the early 20th century as well as our own decade, and the sum total, measured over time, is complex.

Furthermore, we have been talking about an embrace of tensions, not a renunciation of standards. Parents who attacked homework may have been nervous about other aspects of schooling, but they did not request that their children not be educated. Implicit proponents of grade inflation do not usually argue that there should be no norms or differentiations. Many of the same parents who press their children's teacher for As also put their kids through rigorous sets of lessons. And they expect some strictly academic challenges, in the form, for example, of the College Board SATs, which they cannot directly finesse with the lures of grade inflation. It is a mixture of rigor and protections for self-esteem, not the latter alone, that predominate.

College itself, in the American context, represented a mixture of parental impulses by the late 20th century. The competition to get into a "good" college is behind no small amount of parental anxiety and parental coaching. But, collectively, American parents, and the larger society, are also willing to support an unusual number of colleges and college slots, making entry—somewhere—fairly ensured. We manage to have our educational cake and eat it, too, the result of a century in which parents have learned to combine commitment to schooling with protection against undue rigor.

The mixture of challenge and accommodation explains why, finally, there is no systematic evidence of academic deterioration over the century; if anything, the reverse. Comfortable gentleman's Cs probably denoted college performances that were slightly worse than those later rewarded with grade-inflated Bs. Quietly, amid the laments about student failures, achievement levels in math and even reading have actually improved. When compared to students at the same levels of selectivity internationally, American students often perform fairly competitively. Of course, one wishes that students knew more, and debates about how the educational process can work better remain quite valid. But, while 20th-century education has changed significantly, through a series of compromises between acceptance of schooling and adjustments to parental anxieties, it has not clearly deteriorated.

Confusion persists. At the beginning of the 21st century, Americans were treated to a new round of attempts to provide rigorous, presumably objective standards that would cut through the fog of teacher permissiveness and grade inflation. Standardized outcome tests became the rage as legislators attacked high schools, while rarely providing enough funding to offer examinations that probed much beyond rote memorization. A new president treated the nation to the spectacle of a gentleman-C product prodding the current generation to new heights of annually measured achievement. Did this suggest, finally, a new breakthrough against the more traditional tension between challenge and accommodation? Would schooling finally gain the upper hand over parental protectiveness? My guess is not, as middle-class protests began to surge. But the process clearly suggested how the tensions about education and childhood had yet to be fully resolved: what was less clear was whether the tensions could or should be recast.

For, along with the persistence of the tension between fearing for school's burdens and accepting school achievement, the maintenance of the basic late-20th-century deal, on the part of middle- to upper-middle-class Americans, remains most impressive. The formula, since the 1960s, has been fairly clear, if rarely fully articulated. Teach the children, but not too hard and with some attention to childhood frailties, accommodated through sympathetic grades or a bit of medication. In return, we parents accept, on behalf of our children, the almost unavoidable challenge of getting into college and in the process facing some tests that cannot be entirely cushioned. These are the exercises, separate from grade inflation, that can be prepared for but not ultimately controlled— whether the hurdle is the SATs or their slightly across-the-tracks cousins, the ACTs. We'll accept the results, consoling our kids (but sending them off to the best school possible) as necessary. This bargain established, more strident voices, like the loudest critics of the SATs who urge really different measurements and standards that, for example, tap into less familiar kinds of creative talents, win an indulgent smile but little more. For a large group of Americans, a difficult encounter with contemporary education has been managed, within the parameters shaped by assumptions of childhood vulnerability and with no small amount of anxiety about what level of achievement to prepare for, what weaknesses to cater to. The same ambiguous comfort may not apply to updating the relic of a more distant past—the subject of work.

FURTHER READING

There are lots of stimulating histories of American education: see Lawrence Cremin, *The Transformation of the School: Progressivism in American Education, 1876–1957* (New York, 1968), and David Tyack and Elizabeth Hansot, *Learning Together: A History of Coeducation in American Public Schools* (New York, 1992). Relevant recent treatments include William Cutler, *Parents and Schools: The 150-Year Struggle for Control in American Education* (Chicago, 2000), and Jerry Wilde, *An Educator's Guide to Difficult Parents* (Huntington, NY, 2000). On hyperactivity, Holly Matthews, *Fidgety Phil and Beyond: Attention Deficit Disorder* (honors thesis, College of Humanities and Social Sciences, Carnegie Mellon

University, 1998); Thomas Armstrong, "ADD: Does It Really Exist?" *Phil Delta Kappan* (Feb. 1996): 428; Mary Fowler, *NICHCY Briefing Paper: Attention Deficit/Hyperactivity Disorder* (Washington, DC, 1994); James Swanson, "More Frequent Diagnosis of Attention Deficit- Hyperactivity Disorder," *New England Journal of Medicine* 333 (1995): 1146–9. On counseling, Roger Aubrey, "Historical Development of Guidance and Counseling," *Personnel and Guidance Journal* 76 (1997): 383–91; on parental involvements, National Congress of Parents and Teachers, ed., *The Parent-Teacher Organization: Its Origins and Development* (Chicago, 1944); Margo Horn, *Before It's Too Late: The Child Guidance Movement in the United States* (Philadelphia, 1989); and the excellent Joseph Hawes, *Children between the Wars* (New York, 1997). On intellectual stimulation, Julia Wrigley, "Do Young Children Need Intellectual Stimulation? Experts' Advice to Parents, 1900–1985," *History of Education Quarterly* 29 (1989): 41–75. On college, L. C. Steelman and Brian Powell, "Sponsoring the Next Generation: Willingness to Pay for Higher Education," *American Journal of Sociology* 96 (1991): 505–29. On grade inflation, E. Levine, "Grade Inflation in Higher Education: Its Causes and Consequences," *Free Inquiry in Creative Sociology* 15 (1987); "High School Grades and Achievement: Evidence of Grade Inflation" *NAASP Bulletin* 81 (1997): 105–13; Wayne Lanning and Peggy Perkins, "Grade Inflation: A Consideration of Additional Causes," *Journal of Instructional Psychology* 22 (1979): 146–55; and Arthur Andrews, "Grade Inflation— How Great? What Are the Concerns of Parents, Educators," *NASSP Bulletin* 67 (1983). For a recent commentary that argues against college grade inflation (inconclusively) and against the idea that student performances have not improved (more persuavely), see Alfie Kohn, "The Dangerous Myth of Grade Inflation," *Chronicle of Higher Education* (Nov. 8, 2002). On homework, Harris Cooper, "Synthesis of Research on Homework," *Educational Leadership* 47 (1989): 85–91, and *The Battle over Homework: An Administrator's Guide* (Thousand Oaks, CA, 1994); and a superb historical essay, Brian Gill and Steven Schlossman, "'A Sin against Childhood': Progressive Education and the Crusade to Abolish Homework, 1897–1941," *American Journal of Education* 105 (1996): 27–66; for a contemporary reprise of the anti-homework debates, Etta Kralovec and John Buell, *The End of Homework* (Boston, 2000). On self-esteem, Stanley Coopersmith, *The Antecedents of Self-Esteem* (San Francisco, 1967); Morris Peabody, *Society and the Adolescent Self-Image* (Princeton, 1965); Jianjun Wang, Betty Greathose, and V. M. Falcinella,

"An Empirical Assessment of Self-Esteem Enhancement," *Education* 119 (1996): 99–105. On testing, D. Bray and M. J. Belcher, eds., *Issues in Student Assessment* (San Francisco, 1987); Judith Raffery, "Missing the Mark: Intelligence Testing in Los Angeles Public Schools, 1922–32," *History of Education Quarterly* 28 (1988): 73–93; A. S. Kaufman, "Intelligence Test and School Psychology" *Psychology in the Schools* 33 (2000): 748; M. M. Sokal, ed., *Psychological Testing and American Society 1870–1930* (New Brunswick, NJ, 1987); A. K. Wigdor and W. R. Garner, eds., *Ability Testing* (Washington, DC, 1982).

5

Work and Chores

Do I Have To?

WORRIES ABOUT CHILDREN'S WORK are not unique to the 20th century, but only in the most general sense. Lazy kids are not a modern invention. Traditional folklore is replete with stories about children who were not diligent, who napped when they should be working. Shepherd boys, for example, inherently unsupervised, were often regarded as deficient. "Little Boy Blue," in the nursery rhyme, let his sheep and cows ruin crops, while he was "under the haystack, fast asleep." Apprentices often goofed off or did shoddy work. While traditionally the focus may have been on boys where slacking off was concerned, girls came in for attention, too, as songs and poems about "lazy Mary" suggest.

In Western Europe and, to a degree, in colonial America, many parents shipped some of their adolescents off to other households during the early to mid-teen years to work as agricultural or domestic servants and apprentices. Up to a third of all children may have been transferred in this way before the advent of industrialization. The most obvious reason for the transfer involved household economics: families with too many children could balance resources with families that, because of infertility or aging, did not have enough children around. But scholars have speculated that farming out also made sense because it relieved parents of a disciplinary burden as their children reached a difficult age—better to have someone else do the job. And this could particularly apply to work. Some adults may have felt less compunction shaping up someone else's child than managing their own. Of course, hard knocks were still often necessary within the family. Ben Franklin's older

brother showed little compunction about trying to whip Ben into submission as a reluctant printer's apprentice, until he ultimately fled to
Philadelphia.

But, amid all these early concerns, the anxiety that became prominent in the 20th century was clearly missing, for no one questioned that
children should be working. Even lazy children contested not what
they should be doing but only how they proposed to do it. But, in the
20th century, given the new image of the vulnerable child (including the
child's need for precious sleep) and the growing pressure for children
to devote themselves to schooling, the question of whether work was
appropriate moved to center stage. This first applied (carrying over issues that had been raised initially in the 19th century) to work outside
the home but then began to attach to household chores, as well.

Indeed, the idea of the lazy child began to take on a somewhat
anachronistic tone. Of course, there were children who were better at
self-directed school work than others, and parents might also comment
on kids who were unusually reliable around the house. But laziness, as
a label, declined. Partly this reflected the growing concern about self-esteem: children should be given a more supportive context. But partly it
reflected a growing confusion about whether work performance outside the school context was a particularly relevant category for contemporary childhood. Growing numbers of parents began to contribute to
the larger social effort to withdraw children from the larger workforce,
and many increasingly took over children's chores around the house.
For their part, children, ever alert to new signals, began to question systematic work obligations, often turning work requests into a sequence
of minor but troubling conflicts.

The result may have been good: children were relieved, during the
course of the century, of some traditional tasks that many observers now
find inappropriate, from infant care to newspaper delivery. But, whatever the judgments here, there is little doubt that the result was also confusing. At the most general level, children were less than ever seen as
economic assets, and even middle-class parents who had already, by
1900, begun to think of children primarily in terms of emotional satisfaction could be troubled by this confirmation of their status as liabilities. At the more personal, daily level, there was little clear definition of
what work obligations might remain reasonable, which is where both
conflict and a dull, often inarticulate resentment could breed.

Questions about children's work took the first few decades of the 20th century to jell, despite the new image of the vulnerable child. Campaigns against formal child labor received consistent attention. Inherited from the 19th century, these campaigns gained new vigor among the flood of immigrants, with their assumptions that children should work, around 1900. There was no question, in the middle-class mind, that Other People often abused the labor capacities of their children. But the first decades of the century also saw a revived emphasis on the work ethic, which somewhat masked the larger implications of concerns about overwork. It also took some time for other social and economic developments to lead to attacks on what for a while seemed but quaint vestiges of children's former contributions, such as newspaper delivery, child care, and lawn care.

Most obviously, new levels of anxiety, particularly about one's own kids, depended on the reinforcement of the vulnerable child image, with recognition of the effort children now had to put forth in school. Individual parents surely realized that school involved labor early on, but aspects of American culture made the connections a bit more tentative, for a time, than might be imagined. The key problem was whether intellectual effort, however much of a strain, was really work. A 1931 child-rearing manual made the distinction quite clear. When boys were on farms, doing chores, they were "being educated in the real sense because [they were] mastering the forces of life. . . . [They were] gaining experiences through their muscles and nerves that were waking their intelligence. . . . It is that basis of education that is lacking in our schools today."[1] There was a difference between real work, in other words, and "the dead bones of children's book knowledge."

This distinction between schooling and "doing" never entirely disappeared, but it did fade. When parents finally acknowledged the acceptability of school homework, for example, this had obvious implications for the chores that children might be asked to do around the house. At risk of using jargon, one might say that it was at this point, around the 1940s and 1950s, that children's work in general—beyond formal child labor—became problematized. Official allegiance to a work ethic remained, but the tenor of discussion shifted. When, by the 1980s, older children began to take up a new pattern of work, it was on decidedly untraditional terms, considerably apart from customary assumptions about children's role in a family economy.

THE REFORM CRUSADE

When, soon after 1900, Ellen Key issued her famous book, *Century of the Child*, the abolition of child labor was a prominent subject. Much of the book, to be sure, focused on interventions against parental abuse. But, in Key's eyes, formal work for children, taking them away from "play and school," was itself an abuse that required legal redress. Work attacked children's physical vigor, as Key claimed that child workers were smaller and less healthy than the norm (only 8 percent were "really sound and strong"). Loss of sleep was a key problem. Work also exposed children to the moral dangers of "the street," including crime and sexual temptation.[2]

The basic arguments about child labor were not new in the early 20th century. Furthermore, most middle-class parents had long since decided that their children should not hold formal jobs. It is important not to exaggerate the anxiety that child labor discussions created among parents after 1900.

Nevertheless, the child labor reform crusades reached new fervor between 1900 and the 1930s. They fed, and were fed by, the image of the vulnerable child. And, while the bulk of reform agitation was directed at working-class, immigrant, and rural parents, the vehemence of the arguments inevitably affected middle-class thinking, as well. The arguments also raised questions about what children were for, if they were pulled out of the family economy, and how appropriate work habits could be instilled if formal jobs were forbidden. And these issues directly engaged the middle class, even though they were not entirely new.

The decades around 1900 saw the peak of child labor in the American factories and cities, in terms of absolute numbers. In 1890, about a million children between the ages of ten and fifteen (or 12 percent of the total) were gainfully employed; by 1900, the figure was 1,750,000; by 1910, the peak, almost two million such children—18 percent of the total—worked in this sense. Percentages are admittedly misleading, because they reflect the rapid growth of cities and manufacturing. Children had always worked, often quite hard, on the farms, yet this work was not captured in the official statistics. Nevertheless, it was clear that child labor was, in many ways, growing, in precisely those settings that reformers judged the worst in terms of physical and moral dangers. This was the context in which reform efforts began to build to new levels. In 1904, the National Child Labor Reform Committee took shape, backed by a number of prominent philanthropists. For the next three decades, the debate raged, often gaining massive newspaper coverage for tales of abuse. In the mid-1920s, there was even an attempt at a constitutional amendment, which did pass the Congress but failed to gain sufficient support in the states. Early New Deal measures, by 1933–1934, finally ended the most intense debate by eliminating most formal employment before the age of sixteen.

Arguments against the employment of children had many facets. For some, including the trade unions, the depressive impact on adult wages was an obvious issue. But most of the reform zeal focused on children themselves. As a speaker in the New York Assembly put it, in 1913: "To rescue . . . children under 14 years of age from nicotine poisoning [in cigar factories], from the miasma of the stock yards, and from the horrible conditions of the sweat shops is to accomplish something worth doing." Children's health was a key component of the reform argument, and vivid rhetorical and visual images of deformed and sickly children rang true amid general concerns about children's frailty. The need for schooling was another powerful plank. Even as middle-class parents debated some of the stresses that schools imposed on their own offspring, there was little doubt that some form of education was now vital and that child labor impeded it. Moral danger was another problem, again echoing earlier, Victorian rhetoric. Child workers in the cities were removed from family supervision and exposed to all the dangers associated with urban street life. Widely touted newspaper articles and state legislature debates cited the massive incidence of venereal disease among children in the factories and in street occupations such as messengers and bootblacks. "They lose their respect for parental authority . . . and become arrogant, wayward and defiant." Early marriage and degenerate offspring were other consequences of child labor, according to the reformers. "The ranks of our criminal class are being constantly recruited from the army of child laborers," a reformer claimed in 1909. These general points were driven home by repeated testimony, often from children themselves, about physical suffering, lack of schooling, and other poignant reminders of deprivation, such as the absence of any chance to celebrate birthdays.[3]

In addition to its scope and fervor, three other aspects of the child labor reform crusade stand out after 1900. First, work on the farms came under increasing attack, though urban conditions continued to provide the readiest targets. Horror stories about farm work, from the south and from migrant labor groups, made it increasingly clear that, no matter how idyllic the setting, nothing really justified the formal or informal employment of children for production. Rural child labor commanded long chapters in the new reform books and won attention from the National Child Labor Committee, as well.

> In the Midwestern beet fields children as young as seven hoe all summer. Children of five and six thin, weed, pull, top, pile and cover beets. . . . In thinning and weeding, the child crawls on his hands and knees along the rows. . . . "Jes/ like a dog," a small boy said. The other processes are more strenuous if not more tiring. It is the long continuance at these tasks hour after hour, day after day . . . that saps the vitality and warps the bodily frame.[4]

Jettisoning the idea that there were particularly noble aspects to agricultural work came hard. Even G. Stanley Hall praised farm work for its contribution to children's motor development. But the progressive extension of reform arguments to agriculture, and the vivid examples drawn in the process, helped convince growing numbers of people that formal work in general, and not just factory work, was bad for children, quite apart from the obvious impact on schooling.

The second aspect of the reform debate to win new prominence, though one that aroused heated debate, involved the rights of parents. Even in the 19th century, reformers had to contend with arguments that parents should determine whether or not their children worked, that legislation would disrupt proper family authority. These discussions continued, but focus shifted increasingly to the productive work children did directly for their parents and to the harsh discipline that sometimes accompanied this work. Reformers rarely had much compunction about arguing that society had the right to interfere with parental arrangements in these cases, for production at home could be just as dangerous to children's health and schooling as work on the street. In this context, cases instituted by children themselves against parents or stepparents, alleging abusive work, began to reach the courts, like a Wisconsin case in 1925. The Wisconsin court, focusing partly on the whipping a boy had received, noted, in its award of damages, that the child had not worked as hard as he might, which "deserved correction," but that work conditions and discipline could easily prove excessive. As one reformer put it, "Is the 'home' from which children are hurried every morning, and to which they return at night broken with weariness, the 'sacred institution' fat business men and windy professors are prating about?"[5]

Third, reform arguments sometimes contested the assumption that work of any formal sort had value for children, even if shorn of abuse. A letter to the editor of the New York *Times* in 1921 took issue with reform opponents who were warning of the dangers of idleness. "It is poor logic that assumes child idleness to be the alternative to child labor. . . . For child labor there are several substitutes: schooling is one; play, and especially supervised play, is another." Play is the real training ground for children, the author continued, providing all sorts of skills and stimuli that, along with education, will provide a better preparation for adult life than formal employment.[6]

We are, of course, talking about a debate, not a wholesale triumph of reformist principles. Big business and many agricultural interests often spoke in opposition. The idea of interfering with parents was bitterly contested. And there were many who shouted about the risks of idleness, making children "the devil's best workshop" and "destroying the initiative and self-reliance and manhood and womanhood of all the coming generations" (so argued an opponent who claimed that the whole reform movement was a Bolshevik plot). Furthermore, how far would new laws apply? A nice cartoon in the Columbus *Dispatch*, in 1925, pictured a boy resisting his farmer-father's plea to help with the wood: "I can't, it's against the law," with a daughter offering the same response to a mother's request to assist with the dishes. "The immemorial right of the parent to train his child in useful tasks, according to his own discretion is destroyed. The obligation of the child to contribute in proportion to his abilities is destroyed." The Great Depression added some further stimulus to advocates of caution, as for many families the problem became not work in excess but rather the inability of older children to find jobs and so help their parents.[7]

Furthermore, obviously, almost all the reform rhetoric was directed against Other families, not the middle class itself except insofar as its business scions were employers of children. Changes needed to come to immigrants, farmers, southerners; the middle class was already comfortable with schooling and play for its own children. There is no need to overdo the implications of three decades of renewed debate on parental anxieties within the middle class.

Yet the debate had an impact on the middle class even so. In the context of children's pricelessness and vulnerability, it raised new questions about work of any sort, and about parents' rights to enforce labor. It highlighted children's frailty and the potential for abuse. As the Ohio cartoon suggested, children themselves picked up new ideas about what kinds of activities were appropriate for them. In work, as in discipline, children participated actively in discussions of the appropriateness of work, and this influenced (and sometimes annoyed) parents, as well.

And the fact was that child labor did begin a rapid decline. By 1920, almost a million children between the ages of ten and fifteen had been removed from the roster, and only 8 percent were employed; by 1940, the figure was down to 1 percent in this age category. Farm labor dropped, as well, with more schooling for children and the progressive diminution of the farm population. What laws did not accomplish, technology and business reorganization tended to achieve. Many jobs once appropriate for children declined in salience. Urban messengers, for example, were increasingly displaced by telephones. New kinds of equipment reduced the simpler tasks in factories and agriculture. The rapid decline of maid service affected teenage girls, in part because of the appearance of new household appliances.

Parents increasingly realized the magnitude of the shift that was occurring and took other measures that both enhanced and reflected it. The advent of social security created a new generation of older parents who, by the 1940s, looked to government programs more than to family as sources of support. The birth rate also affected the change. Not only were families in all social groups cutting their birth rates by the 1920s and 1930s, in part from knowledge that children were now more an expense than an economic asset. When exceptions occurred, as with the baby boom of the late 1940s, the zeal to have children in early adulthood (most middle-class mothers were in their twenties) and to have them close together clearly demonstrated that there was no expectation that the larger broods would contribute to the family through work or have any direct role in supporting parents in later age.

It was the early 20th century, in sum, that brought the decisive separation of children from work in American society. Even in the middle class, this raised questions about children's functions and appropriate training. The contrast with adult experience widened, all the more in that some middle-class adults found their own work obligations increasing, particularly with the demands of corporate life, commuting, and a service economy. And this lifestyle too could produce questions and uncertainties as middle-class parents considered their own progeny. As a group of sober economists noted, in 1975, "neither the role of self-sacrificing adult nor the role of self-indulgent children really allows for a whole person." But the question was how, given the new beliefs about child labor, to narrow the gap. And the answer was, often, an admission of futility that acknowledged the anxiety involved but offered no solid remedies.

The implications of child labor reform and related trends were partially concealed and channeled, during the 1920s and then during the Depression, by a revival of the popularity of the work ethic in American society overall. Tom Lutz has described a cultural reaction against the kinds of concerns about overwork that had highlighted middle-class rhetoric around 1900. Various writers fulminated against idleness and boredom. Thus, a doctor, William Sadler, urged, in 1924, that the best cure for psychological stress was "Go to work." Sherwood Anderson wrote nostalgically of the joys of skilled manual labor. The *Saturday Evening Post* carried articles about work satisfactions: "When you get yourself . . . conditioned for success in your work, your work itself will become your favorite play." Obviously, this was a kind of discussion that could carry over to children. Many manuals, in the 1920s and 1930s, urged the "frequent stimulation of right incentives for ordinary daily tasks," lest a "lack of personal initiative and industry . . . create despair." And, while schools could do part of the job, parents must offer work training, as well.[8]

Enthusiasm for the work ethic, even amid the push for child labor reform, intriguingly justified one of the big urban exceptions to the new rules, an exception that affected many middle-class families directly. Having backed most new restrictions on children's work, American newspapers balked, in the 1930s, against applying the rules to themselves. Newsboys remained essential. And, as they mounted their successful counterattack, media advocates specifically appealed to the role news delivery experience could have in training children to be good workers and good businessmen. In the process, they increasingly shifted newspaper delivery to middle-class children, whose parents and who themselves often found the rhetoric appealing. Newspaper delivery, so the argument ran, offered "an invaluable service" by "providing a needed kind of part-time working experience." Arguments in favor of news delivery, and possibly other business-related exceptions, sidestepped the issue of children's vulnerability by emphasizing questions about the adequacy of schooling. As the national chairman of the Newspaper Boy Welfare committee testified in Washington, in 1933, "Surely the boy who learns business fundamentals, who meets human nature, who learns the value of business policies on dependability, honesty, courtesy and promptness is better equipped to make his way in the world than is the youngster who secures his education wholly within the four walls of a schoolroom." And, while the argument was probably meant to apply particularly to lower-class youth, many middle-class parents turned out to agree for their own youngsters, as news delivery came to be the province of boys from a higher social class. Prizes and contests, as well as training schools, stimulated boys' success ethic. The newsboy appeal rang true at a time when middle-class families were really worrying about how to combine work ethic stimulation, the long- desirable goal now receiving new levels of approval, with the fact that most job opportunities for children were disappearing. It had the added benefit of assisting in the accelerating conversion to a sales- and service-oriented economy, another transition in which the middle class was increasingly engaged.[9]

There were other potential bridges where children's work could still be justified in middle-class term. Viviana Zelizer discusses the visibility of child actors, particularly by the 1930s, where glamour and high pay could stifle parents' qualms about employment. Later in the century, modeling and certain professional sports, like girls' gymnastics and skating and tennis for both sexes, provided similar outlets, eliciting intense parental support for very hard work and formal employment. Obviously, these were situations where wide public awareness of children's work could have ramifications beyond the individuals involved. Certainly, far more parents and children were stimulated into "wannabe" efforts than ever could have made it to big-time formal jobs. Children and work still could mix.

In the long run, however, it was not newspaper delivery, child stardom, or a few other earning opportunities, such as grass cutting and baby sitting, that really played a major role in adjustment between the work ethic and contemporary children. Newspaper opportunities began to go the way of other employment categories as adult delivery services took over from the fabled newsboy, certainly by the 1980s. The same fate awaited lawn mowing, as entrepreneurial efforts increasingly went to commercial services rather than to the hardworking neighbor kid (or, sometimes, one's own kid). Changes of these sorts reflected not only inroads by technology and new business organizations but also the increasing reluctance of children themselves, and their parents, to commit to even exceptional kinds of regular employment, unless perhaps Hollywood, *Cosmo*, or Wimbledon beckoned.

But there was another channel, eagerly seized upon by commentators, and many parents, as the relevant contemporary response to appropriate work that was not, however, child labor. Household chores, all the more necessary as domestic service declined, could surely legitimately constitute a bridge between children and service, making children genuinely useful to the family if not in an earning capacity and instilling the kind of work habits that most reformers, and certainly their critics, had acknowledged even while debating the role of outright employment. Yet, the desirability of chores, too, were contested by parents and children themselves, and this ultimately continued some of the themes that had informed the child labor reform discussion in the century's first decades. In the 1920s, to most commentators, there seemed no doubt that chores did not constitute child labor and that, combined with schooling and constructive play, they could ensure the fostering of good character. But parents and children were not quite so sure, even at that point; by the 1940s, a quiet debate was in full swing, even among the experts.

CHORES

The history of household chores has not been written. Viviana Zelizer correctly notes their pivotal role in discussions of children during the child labor reform decades, and we will briefly reprise this story as part of our larger review. This larger history, admittedly, has a couple of qualifying features. First, most of us already know how it turns out: children's chores decrease. To be sure, it is terribly important, in writing about family matters, not to wax too nostalgic about the past. Children were not magic chore doers in the good old days, and there were quarrels and deficiencies in performance. But, in this case, though it must be systematically demonstrated, our common impression is correct: the number of chores has declined, the assumption that chores are a requisite childhood obligation has waned, and, yes, parents are doing (with some annoyance) household stuff they really think kids should be taking care of. The question is, in what pattern and, above all, why this has happened. (And then some may wish to ask whether we can do anything about it.) Further, while chores have declined, there is complexity to the trend, particularly over the past fifty years, and this needs attention, as well.

The second qualification on chores' history involves sources. In much of this account so far, we have relied heavily, though not exclusively, on child-rearing advice manuals. We note, of course, that not all advice is heeded and that there are many individual variations. But, in areas like assumptions about children or child discipline, popular advice does reflect social trends and patterns, so long as other evidence can be adduced about how actual parents adjusted. In the case of chores, the advice literature is interesting but substantially misleading. Popularizers, for the most part, liked chores, and urged them. But the norms they described were a departure from parent-child reality. Happily, there is other evidence, from the 1930s on, about that reality. Expert preachments remain relevant in helping to make parents feel concerned and anxious about the gap between what should be and what they found it possible to impose. They also suggest some ambiguities that help explain how the gap developed: the experts, in other words, were not as straightforward as they themselves imagined. But it's the gap itself that is really significant.

The overall dynamic was intriguing. A decline in chores was virtually inevitable, given the new demands of schooling plus the decline in the number of simple domestic tasks (thanks in part to household mechanization). But the process was exacerbated by adult concerns about children's frailty. Higher household and even lawn-care standards also played a role, making parents more impatient with children's levels of achievement. This process, often studied for its impact on housewives, seriously affected parenting, as well. Finally, while adult attitudes were crucially involved with basic trends, the decline of chores provoked parental disapproval and annoyance, as their expectations failed to keep pace with their children's actual performance.

ADVICE: WHAT OUGHT TO BE

Experts and popularizers quickly made the logical connections be-tween the decline in child labor and the need for work commitments around the house, particularly given the uncertainty about how much schooling contributed toward the development of a work ethic. But, even as their convictions paint a picture more of what might have been than of what was, their preachments are interesting for three reasons. First, of course, they were read, and parents who in practice found it dif-ficult to live up to their confident standards might experience a corre-sponding surge of anxiety or resentment. Second, experts sometimes in-troduced a few more qualifications than their official commitment to a work ethic implied, and these provide some clues about why actual parents often found the imposition of domestic work difficult. Third, the tone of advice itself did change over time—not so much in what was recommended, at least until the very end of the century, but in the growing recognition that what started out in the 1920s as self-evident truths had turned into a major domestic battleground.

Advice literature made connections between the decline of child labor and the need for chores quite early. Popular magazines in the 1890s were alerting upper-middle-class readers to the pleasures of chil-dren's work, even if just helping domestic servants. "Shelling peas on Monday because the cook is washing is to him as enchanting as count-ing pearls on a string." Working-class kids came in for even more at-tention, given the rapid decline of child labor. "It is pitiful . . . for a woman to believe that she is 'bettering' her children by . . . allowing them to think that it is degrading for them to help in the housework." Indeed, exhortation to poor and immigrant mothers to make sure their children did chores was an important theme around the turn of the cen-tury, when experts openly feared the poor habits of the working class.[10]

Directed more consistently toward the middle classes, the leading manuals of the 1920s suggested no particular problem when it seemed clear that children had time to help and needed work experience in order to prepare for constructive adulthood. Smiley and Blanton noted, in 1927, that housework helped children develop respect for family property. And there was more: "Every child should be kept from getting the impression that he, somehow, is so valuable to society that it must perform for him the various menial acts of his environment. This train-ing should be presented not as 'helping mother' but as a way in which 'baby can pull his own weight in the boat.'" Feagre and Anderson added that chores from the toddler stage on were crucially linked to the development of self-reliance. "The growing child should never, of course, be subjected to heavy, routine work; drudgery in childhood does not lead to a happy attitude toward work later. But the assignment of small regular duties should begin very early, while the child's interest in helping is keen." It was revealing, in fact, that most attention went to early childhood, when parents might hesitate about imposing a burden. The association of older children with chores was so obvious, in principle, that it scarcely warranted discussion.[11]

At most, parents might need a bit of advice about whether to pay their kids for work, and here a few revealing ambiguities surfaced. Most authorities at this point urged a clear separation between allowances, intended as training in money management, and the work that should be assumed as part of family obligation. Smiley and Blanton acknowledged that payment for special jobs was all right, but: "it is quite unwise . . . to pay him for everything that he does. . . . He must be taught to work for the approval of his parents. . . . A pat, a kiss, a smile, a complimentary word—these, as well as gifts, should be used for rewarding a child for desirable conduct." But the notion of gifts introduced some ambivalence, and Smiley and Blanton compounded this by adding, without explanation, "It is all right to reward him with candy, toys, or money for doing certain chores—especially unpleasant ones, such as taking out the ashes or helping with the dishes." But if something as routine as dishwashing needed special motivation, where was the inherent work ethic or family obligation? It's tempting to suggest that, even as early as the 1920s, the sense of children as vulnerable, so that work of any sort might be too unpleasant or demanding, plus a growing belief on the part of adults that housework was inherently unfulfilling, were leading to contradictions barely concealed by the formal rhetoric.[12]

And there was a second set of concerns that began to surface more clearly in the 1930s, perhaps because work itself began to be rethought in the throes of the Depression. A White House Conference on Child Health and Protection subcommittee, in 1931, strongly recommended that "less emphasis be placed on the amount of assistance rendered and more on the educational values [to the child] of the responsibilities involved in the performance of household tasks." Here, clearly, it was what the child learned, not what he or she did, that mattered. Amey

Watson, a home economics expert, admitted that "for a busy mother . . . it is far easier to do the job herself than to stop to teach a child to do it; but if she has the long-range point of view and is thinking of the character development of the child, the work should be planned so that . . . the mother . . . can have enough leisure to stop and teach the child." And more conventional child labor concerns intruded, as well. Parents were warned to "take great care not to overburden the child with responsibility . . . lest the weight of it should crush him instead of developing a greater strength." And *Parents Magazine* added, obscurely, that one should "never give . . . children cause to suspect us of making use of them to save ourselves work."[13]

Early 20th-century advice, then, suggested more than met the eye. Work was indeed vital; about this there was no expert dispute. But unpleasant work and childhood might not go together. Arguments emphasized character development more than the need to help the family. And anxieties about children's frailty added another caveat. A conscientious parent might well be excused for wondering what chores were really acceptable.

New divergences opened up in the 1940s and 1950s. This is the point, of course, at which greater permissiveness entered into child-rearing advice, so one might expect some rethinking. This is the point, also, where growing acceptance of school commitments might have affected attitudes toward chores, though this connection was implicit at best in the advice materials.

In fact, three tacks developed. First, some of the most popular authorities returned to an unambiguous commitment to chores as vital to children's training and their place in the family. Second, another set of authorities began to translate some of the permissiveness concerns into more elaborate instructions for parents about how to implement chores, extending some of the uncertainties that had opened up in the 1920s and 1930s. And, finally, a growing number of manuals, still committed to chores, began to recognize that parents found it really difficult to implement their advice and as a result needed sympathy and assistance. Disagreements between the first two approaches added to parental confusions, contributing to the more complex realities that the third approach began to pick up.

Dr. Spock, so flexible in some matters, was adamant on the subject of chores. "How do children learn to perform various duties? By their very nature, they start out feeling that dressing themselves, brushing their teeth, sweeping, and putting things away are exciting and grown-up things to do. If their parents succeed in keeping on good terms with them as they grow older, they will enjoy going on errands, carrying packages, and raking the lawn, because they still want to have a part in important jobs and to please their mother and father." Spock went on to list things kids could do from age two on, like emptying wastebaskets. By age seven or eight, children can really lighten the parental load, "carrying out genuinely useful jobs each day." Spock admitted that no one can bring up children to be "cooperative all the time," but "if we realize that children want to be helpful, we are less likely to make household tasks sound like unpleasant duties or to assign them when we're irritable." Spock did remind parents of a need for patience so that chores were not associated with nagging ("that kills all pride in a job"), and he noted that tasks that family members could do together made work more fun. But the basic responsibility was clear, and parent need not hesitate in imposing it. "Participation in the work of the home is good for the child's soul and provides a basis for the very soundest kind of companionship with parents." Children must do their share, and feel they are doing so.[14]

Spock went on to list a wide range of appropriate jobs, associated with cleaning, helping with younger kids, meal preparation, and lawn care. Later editions added some strictures specifically for adolescents, possibly reflecting a recognition of the difficulty of eliciting their cooperation. "Adolescents should have serious obligations in helping their families—by doing regular chores and special additional jobs. This benefits them by giving them a sense of dignity, participation, responsibility, and happiness, as well as helping the parents." He weakened this only by admitting "you can't enforce these rules"—but parents had the right to express their principles. Another addition was a growing conviction that boys and girls should be given "basically the same tasks, just as I think it's wise for men and women to share in the same occupations, at home and outside." There should be no discrimination, and boys can do as much cleaning, girls as much lawn work, as their sibling counterparts.[15]

Growing concerns about psychological development could provide another basis for renewed insistence on the importance of chores. Frances Wickes, writing from a Jungian perspective, emphasized that regular chores were vital to inhibit neurosis. Household work prevents children from developing "tendencies toward self-aggrandizement" by promoting "a proper share in the family responsibilities." David Levy, writing in 1943 from a less theoretical vantage point but with general concern about maternal overprotectiveness, warned that allowing evasion of chores promoted "infantilization" and "prevention of social maturity." Mothers must insist that children do their work.[16]

Sidonie Gruenberg, in the 1950s, was a bit less strident but aimed in the same directions. A good parent should be able to convince kids that, "in a family, everybody does some of the work." Pay should not enter in, though she recognized that some families did offer wages and that knowledge of this might raise some discussions in other, better-organized households. (Her advice, interestingly, included specific reference to the fact that mothers, also, did not get paid.) Parents must guide children in good work habits, including time management and the ability to see long-term rewards from work that, in the short run, does not seem to yield much benefit. And praise was vital, so that children would take satisfaction in even the most trivial tasks. Gruenberg admitted that some household chores were "not much fun." But this was true of a good bit of adult work, as well. "Our children can be made to understand that many tasks, some disagreeable, are necessary to keep up our homes, and indeed our whole everyday life. We want to see our children do their work faithfully and well, and also to take real satisfaction in it as useful and worthy." Parents can help children see the joys of a job well done, like a trim lawn or a tidy stack of ironing, so that children can learn to enjoy even monotonous work. Of course, work must be scaled to capacity, and parents must help make sure that children do not become resentful. But, on the whole, Gruenberg, like Spock, plumped solidly for the importance of participating in family tasks and gaining valuable character training in the process.[17]

But there was a final aside that suggested how praise for chores could slide over into a more complicated stance related to the wider currents of permissiveness. "Getting their boys and girls to do their work is only part of the parents' task," Gruenberg wrote. "They want, *if possible*, to get them also to like it, or, at least, to take for granted that certain chores are their own, that they accept them as their responsibility."[18]

Permissiveness added at least two concerns to the process of assigning and enforcing chores. First, children's voices must be heard. Both personal development and family harmony would be damaged by an authoritarian approach. This did not mean that chores should be abandoned, but the process of implementation became more complex, and some parents might, against the experts' advice, decide that the game was not worth the candle. Second, even as chores were done, children's attitudes must be right. Getting children to like the work was at least as important as getting the work accomplished. Here, as in discipline more generally, the advocates of permissiveness intensified the demands on parents, essentially by arguing that work, magically, should be fun.

Agnes Benedict and Adele Franklin dealt with the first issue, on children's voices, in 1951, and, while their approach was unusually elaborate, it picked up a theme that was increasingly common in the child-rearing literature. The process of assigning chores required planning and consultation; it was not just a matter of results. Benedict and Franklin argued that a formal family council could delegate chores in a way that would inspire children to work. "By and large the government of most homes in this country is hopelessly out of step with the times, for it is little more than old-fashioned despotism. Children are assigned chores and told when and how to do them. . . . [In a democratic family council] all matters that concern the family group should be thrashed out [including] the assignment of chores." Once a family council was in place, children still might grumble and forget their chores, needing to be reminded, "But they do far less of this, and"—somewhat obscurely—"what they do has less the quality of bickering, of avoidance of responsibility."[19]

The broader idea that children should enjoy their work and that work should be fun picked up not only on the tide of permissiveness but on new commitments to play and leisure that are discussed more fully in the next chapter. A number of manuals began to be peppered with ways in which parents might help children see work as a game. Mothers might play hide-and-seek with the laundry. Fathers might encourage sons to mow lawns in imaginative zigzag patterns. The process, not the efficiency or even the quality of the result, was now crucial. But it was easier to suggest the goal than to provide very convincing stratagems for its realization, particularly for children expected to do chores on a regular basis. At a time when many suburban parents were deciding that housework was not in fact very enjoyable, the injunction to be concerned with children's positive attitudes toward chores could add to the burdens of the whole subject.

The idea of making a game of work invariably involved parental participation—for example, in a joyous, vaguely competitive picking up of toys, rather than assigning a job to a child alone. It also took imagination to continually come up with different ploys—"you will have to be more ingenious." All this could increase an uneasy feeling that the chores weren't worth the trouble. Certainly, the injunctions to parents potentially widened the range of children's own responses to the assignment of chores, and this, too, could complicate parental implementation.[20]

At an extreme, some advocates of permissiveness came close to saying that insistence on chores was too risky for children's psyches. Bruno Bettelheim, writing of exceptionally disturbed children, advised against assigning chores to them. His treatment program involved exposing children to a garden but insisting on no particular work—they should do what they like, including nothing at all. More generally: "We try to prevent the expenditure of emotional and physical energy that would go into picking up toys or making beds. This energy the child needs for more important tasks. . . . We prefer him to save all his emotional energy for the task of relating himself to other persons. . . . [An advanced child] may be asked to help with sorting out his laundry or making his bed, but only when the task is performed with and never for an adult. . . ." Here, clearly, work has become a burden, not a source of constructive socialization, and the purposes of healthy childhood had been defined away from this kind of responsibility. Some parents, dealing even with relatively normal children but with the tenets of permissiveness and an awareness of the increasing school requirements in mind, might reach somewhat similar conclusions.[21]

But the most typical advice from the 1940s on operated neither with work-ethic simplicities of the Spockian sort or with the let's-make-work-fun demands of extreme permissiveness. Rather, the characteristic stance involved a recognition that some chores should be insisted upon but that the process had become very difficult and required some special strategies. Rudolf Dreikurs, writing from the late 1940s on, railed against permissiveness run amuck. "Dependent children . . . give a great deal of trouble. . . . The more capable the mother, the more she tends to assign to herself all the domestic duties and responsibilities, the more likely will her children become dependent. You should never do anything for a child that he can do for himself. If he is used to being catered to and waited on, then this procedure must be stopped . . . never should you relieve him of any obligation." Parents should refuse to cater to a lazy child by doing his chores for him—"this would never aid him in meeting his problems." But Dreikurs also recognized the parents must not "urge or exhort him to work." The result was a clear dilemma. In one passage, seeking escape, Dreikurs suggested a Spock-like optimism: "Children should be drawn at an early age into active participation in domestic life. This promotes their social interest and their capacity for cooperation. . . . But"—drifting away from optimism—"if you make brusque and impatient demands for his help, you arouse an antipathy toward work." The whole situation was dreadfully difficult, and on the whole Dreikurs was much more successful in telling parents that they were not doing it right than in extricating them from the dilemma.[22]

Dorothy Baruch, also writing late in the 1940s, moved a bit further toward offering solutions. She recognized the reasonableness of parental expectations that, as they matured, children should become more dependable in doing a range of activities such as garbage removal, lawn mowing, dishwashing, cleaning, taking care of pets, car washing, and child care. But she also recognized that these very expectations produced a host of recurrent domestic irritants. The problem—and here the new permissiveness shone through—centered on parental strategy. Too many parents took a "do this, do that" approach, insisting on controlling the timing and the results of the work. "They expect results like a grownup's. But they treat like a child." The solution: assign children the work, and don't back off from this. But give them latitude on when and how the work is done. Don't stand around—the idea of sharing, so important to Spock, here become counterproductive. Offer lavish praise when the whole thing is over, and, within reason, accept the results you get. Cater to children's needs for self-esteem and latitude. And, finally, let them complain; don't assume that because they start a fight over a particular chore they won't actually do it. One mother let her son write a song to express his feelings: "You make me do things I don't want to do. I hate to do things. I hate you." The result? The kid actually did the work assigned, while gleefully mouthing off. Finally, for older children, Baruch urged parents to recognize that adolescents, because of the demands of their physical growth, actually were often short of energy, so that what might seem laziness actually warranted a certain amount of tolerance.[23]

For Baruch and hosts of successors, the subject of chores became a matter of intelligent, flexible tactics, in which parents should invest both energy and patience, while not insisting on terribly demanding standards and while allowing a certain amount of grumbling. The tension was recognized, in contrast to the earlier, more optimistic strain. "Perhaps one of the most difficult areas of conflict between parents and children is in teaching children to take on the responsibilities of keeping their rooms clean and assuming a share in household chores." In this situation, too much rhapsodizing over instilling a work ethic or demonstrating the joys of labor yielded to considerations of strategy, in what was now seen as a crucial power struggle that parents might easily lose.[24]

A good bit of ink was spilled about how to impose some consequences while not provoking a power struggle. Don't: assume that you can get a child to pick her clothes up by telling her you won't wash them while also going on about how inconvenient her behavior is and how important it is to be clean. The child will see that the parent really has some clear goals in mind—her having clean clothes to wear to school—and, resenting this, won't pick up, thus calling the parent's bluff. For the child in this scenario correctly expects that the mother will do the wash in the end. Do: calmly say that clothes not in the hamper won't be washed and ironed, and then follow through, so that the child converts the issue into what she could do, rather than what the parent wants her to do. It is even worth wasting some money by letting some clothes or toys be ruined because of the disorder to gain the desired result. So, the experts urged, there were methods parents could use to win, but the methods took "time and patience" and, sometimes, some funds.[25]

The shift toward tactical admonitions, while it confronted the fact of the conflict over chores, had one further consequence: the need to be sparing in imposing requirements. Few of the popularizers in the second half of the century explicitly recognized how short their list of essential chores was becoming, but the implicit trend was obvious. What was worth enforcing, with all the strategic patience that could be mustered, came to focus increasingly around minimal arrangements for the child and his living space, rather than wider assignments for the family. Elaborate negotiations might be essential even here. Thomas Gordon, writing about "parent effectiveness training" in 1970, discussed a number of conflicts over chores. While his introductory exordium urged parents to make sure their children understood they had obligations around the house, lest they end up thinking the world owed them a living, his detailed stratagems suggested tremendous complexity, with no set standards involved at all, only negotiation. Not only should parents not order their children to do jobs; they also should avoid implicit criticism about problems like messiness. Try to make your own feelings clear, instead, and then let children rebut. A good parent stresses how badly she feels about having "my clean living room" messed up as soon as a kid comes home from school. The kid replies: "You're too fussy." The good parent says, "That may be true; I'll think about that," while going on to repeat that she still feels upset right now about the living room. The hope was that, having exchanged feelings, the child would modify his behavior—but it was unclear who'd pick the mess up if the modification didn't occur. And the importance of letting children participate in decisions about who would do what, for example during housecleaning on Saturday mornings, continued to loom large. Sometimes, swapping tasks so that the child could do something of greater interest (like cooking a meal once a week instead of cleaning her own room) would prove constructive. It was also vital to let kids do their work on their own schedule, recognizing that they might have other tasks, like schoolwork, of which parents were not fully aware. And, sometimes, Gordon's treatise implicitly suggested, it was a triumph simply to get a child to sit in front of the TV on Saturday morning so that the parent could clean the house, in what the book termed an "area of acceptance" in negotiation that sidestepped the question of chore obligations altogether.[26]

By the 1970s, in fact, many manuals approached chores through a case-study approach that presented specific problems and solutions without massive generalizations. John and Helen Krumboltz, in 1972, scattered chore issues throughout their book, without systematic comment on what chores were for. A mother learned to praise a child for putting his toys away when the father came home, but in the child's presence, rather than simply thanking the child; the more public comment proved effective. A family set up a chore chart, with children checking off when they'd finished their assignments so that neither parent was singly responsible for reminders; additionally, when all children had a perfect record all week, the parents would take the family out to dinner, thus helping involve the children themselves in mutual admonitions. Other cases showed how children could be motivated by permission to move on to higher tasks: the boy who mowed the lawn might be allowed to build a rock garden, the six-year-old given the treat of spraying window cleaner on the window. But there were few general principles here, just one instance after another as parents groped for ad hoc solutions to particular domestic dilemmas. And, as Langdon and Stout noted, in the 1950s, "be prepared to give necessary reminders but take means to cut them down."[27]

Two other common admonitions informed the wearily realistic approach that came to predominate, in the field of children's chores, from the 1950s on. First, parents must be reminded that they had to invest time in teaching children how to do things, as well as in mustering the patience to manipulate the situation. Case after case highlighted parents who simply found it easiest to do things themselves. The experts, quite consistently, emphasized the shortsightedness of the approach, as parents trapped themselves in unending obligations and felt resentful in the process. But, because the new realism could hardly paint a picture of massive work contributions or steadily growing dependability on children's part, the rewards of putting in the time were not as clear as might be imagined. To be sure, a few exhortations about the work ethic and character development could accompany the recommendation that parents help ready children for chores, but the brighter images of the earlier 20th century, of self-reliant children and cohesive families, were harder to come by.

Second, all the manuals noted the need for parents to expect periodic declines in children's performance. Children who did a chore well for a while might slack off. The freshness of a new assignment could not be sustained. Children might grow accustomed to praise and lose their motivation. And all this might occur well before the further woes of adolescence, with the distraction of peers and leisure, more school work, and new kinds of sleep demands.

Small wonder that a few writers, by the 1990s, urged that the whole mess be bypassed by eliminating chore expectations of any sort. Thus, the novelist Jane Smiley, in a *Harper's* magazine article, in 1995, disputed the whole assumption of chores, while bragging that her "daughters have led a life of almost tropical idleness, much to their benefit." Her reasoning was that chores did not in fact develop work habits but rather taught children alienation, in that they always got the least appealing jobs and never learned that work that one wanted to do is not really labor at all. "It's good for a teenager to suddenly decide that the bathtub is so disgusting she'd better clean it herself. I admit that for the parent, this can involve years of waiting. But if she doesn't want to wait, she can always spend her time dusting." "Good work is not the work we assign children, but the work they want to do, whether it's reading in bed . . . or cleaning their rooms or practicing the flute." This was a maverick view, of course—Smiley noted that most of her Midwestern neighbors continued to believe in some of the older merits of chores in teaching work, or at least responsibility, and family togetherness. But it did cap a long period in which writing about chores tended to lose sight of the larger subject of chores' function in favor of ad hoc exploration of tactics in an area rife with problems and disputes.[28]

For, clearly, what had begun, in the first third of the century, as an opportunity to maintain children's commitment to work in an age of disappearing formal employment had degenerated into a drive to instill a resigned routine. Chores remained on the agenda, but their range had diminished, and their purpose had become more symbolic than real. Experts still encouraged certain expectations in this area, while also recognizing that parents maintained some expectations on their own that required strategic guidance. But chores had not helped keep the beacon of work alive, as some of advocates had hoped. And they often served more to challenge family cohesion than to support it. Most of the expert admonitions and case studies came to revolve not around socialization so much as around an effort to reconcile a residual parental commitment to chores with the task of maintaining some semblance of family harmony.

Yet, the enthusiasm for chores did not die out, as witness the continued popularity of Dr. Spock's manual. In the mid-1990s, the American Academy of Pediatrics praised chores as "an essential part of learning that life requires work, not just play." And Anthony Wolf's brilliantly titled manual *Get Out of My Life, But First Could You Drive Me and Cheryl to the Mall* urged the assigning of chores, especially on weekends, even at the cost of a bit of adolescent sleep. Advice givers had divided on their recommended approaches, and defenders of chores unquestionably were under attack, but a real commitment to the value of chores did not yield entirely to a concern for tactics.[29]

BENEATH THE SURFACE: SOME CHANGE FACTORS

Why and how did the context for chores change during the 20th century? The child-rearing literature suggests not only key patterns of change, and the confusions attached, but also some of the causes.

The same concerns about children's vulnerability that led to attacks on formal child labor could also apply to uncertainties about chores on the part of experts and parents alike. There was a consistent fear of overburdening children with physical tasks and responsibility beyond their capacity. Parents, particularly, also cited anxieties about the potential for accidents. Growing numbers of chores around the house and yard involved machinery, and the dangers could be quite real. Many parents preferred to assume the risks themselves or to pass them on to adult employees—such as a lawn service—rather than to expose their children. Germ anxiety might affect other chore assignments, such as bathroom cleaning. Concerns about children's sleep clearly affected parents' willingness to wake their darlings to get some housework done. Finally, some parents, even loving ones, might question their children's competence, as confidence in children in some ways diminished. One mother, in the 1920s, cited her daughter's "awkwardness and unreliability" as the reason she did not entrust her with housework, fostering what could obviously turn out to be a vicious circle. The fact was that it was no longer essential, in most urban homes, for kids to do domestic chores, and some parents opted out.[30]

Just as in the workplace, the range of potential jobs in the home shrank, whether for good or ill. Reduced birthrates and the practice of having children closer together cut the possibility of using children to care for siblings. Ongoing urbanization reduced the availability of farm chores. Urban children had at most 75 percent of the chore assignments of their rural counterparts even early in the century. Changes in heating systems virtually eliminated a large work category for boys in dealing with wood, coal, and ashes. The availability of new household equipment might be offset by higher standards for home maintenance, but certainly after World War II the advent of dishwashing machines, automatic washers and driers, and a growing array of prepared or fast-food meals greatly diminished the chores previously available for girls. The steady reduction of sewing, both to prepare and to repair clothing, was a crucial development for mothers and, through them, their daughters. The child-rearing manuals, in increasingly focusing on picking up rooms and laundry, leavened by a bit of dish stacking and lawn mowing, implicitly revealed the shrinkage of possibilities, which in turn helps explain why the discussion of the larger socialization functions of chores dwindled.

More subtle changes also entered in. Reduced birthrates meant that parents had to expect that children would provide chore service during only a part of the parents' adult life. It became less possible to think of some jobs as things that children would always be around to do. Some adults reacted by assuming that they might as well do the work themselves, since the presence of kids was transient; others became open to the use of commercial services to handle housecleaning or car washing or lawns, services that would be around after the children left home. More important still, in the changes in family structure, was the decline of sibling chains that could help in child training. As early as the 1920s, many mothers simply felt they were too busy to teach a youngster how, for example, to dry dishes; the sentiment may not have been novel at all, but what was newly missing was an older daughter ready to step into the breach. Finally, the valuation of many domestic jobs decreased, which meant that both parents and children might be bothered about the menial status they carried. It was not easy to insist that precious children do work that adults themselves were trying to flee. And there is every indication that the distaste for housework was growing as early as the 1920s, as evidenced, for example, in the Lynds' classical study of "Middletown," though this factor probably accelerated after World War II. It was a 1920s housewife who commented that she wouldn't compel her daughter to do anything around the house. "I figure a woman's job is a lifetime job in the home . . . it's a long time for a woman, so why start them too young. That's how I feel."[31]

There is also the question of rising standards, particularly in chores that related to hygiene. A Midwestern woman insisted that she did the dishes, rather than ask her children: "I'd rather wash them than see my children wash them and put them away dirty." Some fastidious suburban men felt the same about standards of lawn care or gardening or car washing. Again, kids just might not measure up.[32]

It's tempting also to speculate about the ongoing impact of a modern time sense in differentiating parents and children, particularly when it came to chores. More and more adults, including women, had long experience of clock-based assignments, as a result of school and work experience. Children's work pace could seem infuriatingly slow in this context. A midcentury mother reports on her efforts to teach her daughter to go out to pick up the evening paper, an assignment simply designed to teach responsibility. "I mean I could do it so much faster myself, it drives me mad sometimes." As the actual pace of adult work accelerated with increased commuting distance, the growth in the number of mothers in the labor force, and, by the 1980s, the increase in the number of hours on the job, the sheer press of time almost certainly became more of a factor.[33]

These developments help explain not only the growing confusion about chores but also the extent to which many adults, as the case studies reflected, seemed to begrudge children adequate training time. The chores were no longer seen as interesting work by any of the parties involved, their range had diminished, and adults had to expect to do the work after the children left home, anyway. Why, then, take the time to explain?

It is also probable that, with greater commitments to peers and to schooling, and with the rising leisure interests discussed in the following chapter, children themselves became more recalcitrant, thus fueling their parents' uncertainties about what kinds of chores were appropriate. The level of contestation reflected in the child-rearing manuals emanated partly from parents' own hesitations and from the mixed signals sent by the experts, but it takes two to tango, and children themselves were directly involved, as well. And there is also the impact of steadily increasing consumerism. With each passing decade, households seemed crammed with more stuff, children's rooms were packed with growing profusions of toys and clothes, undergirding the rising focus on simply putting things away and arguing about messiness.

Yet, the idea of chores did not disappear. Full renunciations of the sort Jane Smiley recommended in favor of a childhood defined in completely different terms were unusual. Chores clearly receded as a core definition of childhood, but not as a source of concern. Even as parents and, in their wake, experts deemphasized chores, dissatisfaction and confusion about their utility remained.

AND WHAT WAS: CHORE TRENDS

Work that children did in and around the home diminished. We all know this. The child-rearing literature reflects the trends. This section briefly fills in some detail. Obviously, precision is difficult. The data come from different sources and are rarely exactly comparable, and there is some disagreement at points over precise levels. Despite a certain fuzziness around the edges, the patterns are fascinating. Their impact is all the greater precisely because the amount of change outstripped the formulations by the child-rearing experts and by many parents themselves. We return, briefly, to the resultant frustration after the trends themselves are outlined.

The most precise snapshot over time involves not just chores themselves but also disputes about them. The classic study of Middletown (Muncie, Indiana), in 1924, briefly replicated in 1977, paid considerable attention to arguments between parents and teenagers. While in both studies the most frequent subject of parent-child dispute involved nights out, the frequency of arguments about chores was at only a moderate level in the 1920s, whereas for both boys and girls it had increased considerably fifty years later. The gender pattern was interesting, also: girls quarreled more than boys in 1924, doubtless because they had far more duties assigned; in 1977 (despite modest gender differences we must still discuss), the level of contention had evened out for boys and girls, by even as it greatly intensified for both sexes. By 1977, 45 percent of all boys and 46 percent of all girls reported quarrels over chores, up from 19 percent and 26 percent a half-century before, putting this category in second place among arguments overall. Interestingly, concerns about nagging—regardless of subject—went down dramatically, suggesting that the chores category had become somewhat atypical in the larger pattern of parent-teenage interactions. Girls, particularly, stopped buying into parental commitments about the quality of cooking or cleanliness. The rate of increase in arguments over work was remarkable, giving precision to the general sense conveyed in the child-rearing literature over the same period. Older children were finding chores inappropriate, while many parents retained a rather desperate belief that they must draw a line in the sand lest children's participation in household responsibilities slip away entirely.[34]

The most obvious trend during the first six decades of the 20th century was a dramatic decline in chore time. Structural changes account for much of the transformation, but there was active, if implicit, parental choice, as well.

The continued erosion of rural life (America was still half- rural in 1920) almost automatically cut chores. All relevant studies show children's chore levels in cities running between 25 and 50 percent lower than in the countryside, partly because of greater school commitments but even more because there were simply fewer appropriate tasks available. The differential still applied in the 1980s, and it goes far to explain patterns over time.

The rapid decline in the birth rate by the 1920s automatically reduced child care responsibilities for older children. The shift was particularly marked for immigrant families, and for girls generally. We will see that girls continued to have more domestic chores than boys, even at the end of the century, but the differential declined, partly because boys at some ages were more drawn in to family responsibilities but above all because there was less for girls to do (and/or less willingness to do it).

The general expansion of the middle class, however diffuse, generated more parental uncertainty about the suitability of chores. Postwar prosperity and suburbanization increased the number of families in which chores generated parental confusion, for throughout the century, according to all available data, the number of chores in middle-class families was about 60 to 70 percent of the number in working-class households. (A similar difference was found in white and African American families.) Middle-class families, with more equipment and, sometimes, more outside help in the form of cleaning or lawn services had less need for children's help, and they imposed fewer demands. This means that, at some point in the 20th century, many upwardly-mobile parents of working-class or immigrant (or rural) background found themselves with kids who were doing far less than they themselves had done as children. And, while they might welcome the greater freedom for childhood, they might also wonder about the results. Hence, among other things, more arguments.

Increasing household technology usually impacted children's household work disproportionately. Ruth Cowan's marvelous study of housewives in the first half of the century shows that each new piece of equipment (e.g., vacuum cleaners) elevated standards of cleanliness so that women actually spent no less time at their tasks. But a subset of this commitment involved women's taking over work that children had previously done (partly, no doubt, to do it better, partly to demonstrate maternal caring).

Only a minority of established middle-class families in the first half of the century reported (through adult recollections) a countercurrent, where children were asked to take on some new jobs to replace the vanishing servant class. The recollections of most middle-class people, and certainly those of new entrants to the class, ran the other way. Chores were decreasing in number.

By the 1950s, in fact, many parents were reporting difficulty in thinking up things for kids to do. One of the real issues, for parents and children alike, derived from the sense that there was relatively little importance to what children could accomplish around the house. Only 7 percent of all families, in one study, tried to insist that young children do anything at all. Fifty-four percent had either no tasks for young children or were just "thinking about it"; 35 percent tried to identify one or two small regular jobs, but enforced even the picking up of toys irregularly. Only 9 percent of all parents described themselves as rigorous.

At this point and beyond, for children of all ages, only fairly minor chores were imposed systematically, focused primarily on setting and clearing the dinner table and shoveling snow where relevant. By the 1980s, 40 percent of all children were reported as helping to cook or take care of the yard once a week. Help with laundry (mainly by girls) was also sporadic. For many children, the most common assignments, aside from brief help at mealtimes, involved work on their own stuff, particularly cleaning their rooms, rather than activities of wider family benefit. More than 80 percent of children over six were supposed to help at least in cleaning their rooms, though fulfillment was often another matter.

And there were some fascinating differentials, at least by the 1970s and 1980s, in addition to the peculiarities of the urban and suburban middle class. Single mothers won some extra help from children, even boys. But if the mother remarried, children's—particularly boys'—household contributions plummeted. The shift in some ways is unsurprising; it expresses a lack of real commitment to chores and, sometimes, a resentment against the male newcomers. But the reversal of tradition is also striking, for historically stepparents were associated with more arduous work routines for children, not less. Clearly, stepparents themselves, in the new family regime, became wary of demanding very much. Another tidbit: while children with full-time working mothers pitched in a bit more than average before adolescence, the level of chores in families where the mother worked part-time was actually lower than in two-parent families. One might speculate that mothers (disproportionately middle class) in this work category felt guilty about their dual roles and worked harder at home to compensate.

None of this is intended to suggest that chores had disappeared. Indeed, a key point is that certain expectations, if diminishing, continued. Kids did provide some family labor, in some estimates about 12–13 percent of the household total. (But the specifically middle-class percentage was lower, from 8 to 11 percent.) Kids did pitch in a bit more where the need was clear, as with single parents or working mothers in two-parent households, though the differences were not, on average, massive. Actual time put in proved the subject of some scholarly dispute in the decades after the 1950s, with several studies suggesting about six hours a week in middle-class families, others only two to three (with girls, again, contributing about 50 percent more than boys). But there was no clear trend, after the big reductions of the century's first half, toward further decline—just toward continuing arguments. Some studies indeed suggested a modest increase in the 1970s, in response to working mothers, followed by a drop in the 1980s.

Furthermore, there was variety, even within the middle class. The optional quality of chores now increased the range of choice. Highly educated parents, with strong school expectations, were far softer on chores than the average. While most parents agreed that some chores were essential, middle-class parents rarely insisted that they mattered very much to family functioning. Their concern, more diffuse, involved training children in good habits and a sense of responsibility, and, while this was ample motivation to generate recurrent arguments about chore level, it hardly justified the imposition of rigorous requirements. Very few parents in the middle class rejected children who did not do their chores. And some, like Jane Smiley, if less articulately, simply dropped any sense that chores mattered at all, though this group was a minority.

And there was a final, fascinating change: the age balance among children compelled to chores shifted steadily. In 1976, 41 percent of all high school seniors said they worked almost every day at home. By 1999, the figure had dropped to 24 percent. In the late 1960s, working-class families where the mother was employed reported that teenagers put in two hours a day, far more than their younger siblings. This was decidedly *not* the pattern twenty to thirty years later. Families with teenage children saw the number of chores go down and parental domestic work go up. The prime age for chores shifted to grade school. By the 1980s, while chores for all children between three and eleven rose, those for children nine to twelve dropped by 40 percent, suggesting that the immunity to chores was shifting downward. The most competent children were bowing out, their parents pulling back from more than the occasional complaint. Even parents seeking a neighborhood babysitter found the age range shrinking steadily to a window of about eighteen months between the time the sitter was old enough to be considered capable and the time she no longer was interested.

A few classic battlegrounds emerged. Responsibility for cleaning one's room, one of the few chores still systematically on the books, proved more and more difficult to enforce, and many parents simply gave up or, very occasionally, risked children's wrath by doing themselves. The increasing availability of separate bathrooms for kids created another choice about whether to insist on cleaning or whether to ignore the mess with distaste. Saturday mornings were another frequent flash point, particularly with teenagers. The decline in daily chores reflected the demands of schoolwork, plus an increasing tendency, on the part of working parents, to put off most tasks until the weekend. But family collaboration on Saturday chores increasingly fell victim to children's adamant insistence, by age thirteen or fourteen, on sleeping away most of the morning, with the grudging acquiescence of their parents.

It was hard to know what to do. While few parents elevated the chores problem to crisis level, there was a varying sense of dissatisfaction. At one end, flexibility: "There's just so much to do [with schoolwork and lessons] that I don't want to fight about it"—this in response to evidence that the kids involved did not know how to use either can openers or vacuum cleaners; at the other end, frustration: "I would change that if I could. But I'm not sure how." Chores remained a minor but persistent battleground, the fruit of the growing clash between expectation and reality that had emerged by midcentury.[35]

The disputes unquestionably involved a sense of lack of reciprocity, as when parents took care of the Saturday chores while the kids were sleeping in (sometimes, even, concerned about being quiet so as not to disturb the darlings). But there was more. Overwhelmingly, after World War I at least, and to a degree before, parents looked to chores not primarily in terms of work service but as contributors to and talismans of good character. If parents had lost the ability to impose chores, was this not another sign of a failure in values, a breakdown in the considerable responsibility of raising children right in a dissolute age?

Scholars have repeatedly debated the role of chores. Some have found no correlation, or even an inverse correlation, between chore requirements and family solidarity—perhaps in part because about half of all parents who require chores continue in a bossy, authoritarian mode. Lawrence Kohlberg, for example, writing in the 1960s, disputed the idea that cleaning activities, done at parental behest, played an positive role in children's moral development. But most parents, like most child-rearing advisers, continued to think otherwise, at least vaguely. They focused particularly on the role of chores in expressing and encouraging responsibility ("I think it helps them grow into responsible adults"; "It builds their responsibility"). In a century when concerns about character continued to run strong, it was hard to abandon chores entirely, even as they became more difficult to identify and enforce. Concerns about family solidarity—another key 20th-century theme—ran a close second in promoting a continued commitment to chores—"they become part of the family that way." Yet, these responses fell short of any traditional capacity to identify the family as a real working unit, or to see chores as really necessary to the unit, rather than as contributing to the socialization of the child. And here, clearly, was where some ambivalence could come in, when it came time to move from principles to actually winning one of the arguments with kids about what to do and when to do it. This, in turn, was where chores as a source of family tension, often rivaling or even surpassing husband-wife debates about who should do what, seemed to become a permanent fixture in parental life.[36]

For the actual pattern of children's chores ran against not only parental expectations but parental domestic activity, as well. We have already noted that, before 1950, mother's work often replaced that of children, particularly when supported by new technology and higher cleaning standards. The same pattern of increasing women's work at home continued into the 1960s and 1970s, even when the mother had a job, at least part-time. To be sure, women's housework did decline a bit by the 1980s. But, while chores by preteen children picked up the slack a bit, at least briefly, contributions by husbands were even more significant and, intriguingly, often replaced children's work from yet another angle. One of the reasons working women found less relief in their husband's contributions than they wanted and expected, in fact, involved the decline in children's contributions under dad's unintentional mantle. Hence, although formal parental discussion focused on character, the ongoing clash between chore trends and actual adult labor took on a dimension of resentment, as well.

LATER DEVELOPMENTS

Two trends, beginning in the 1970s, added to the complex 20th- century history of children, parents, and work.

First, the ever-growing commitment of many mothers to work outside the home and the further rise in single-parent families, increased the possibility that children might be asked to do things around the house. Latchkey kids, for example, might need to start dinner or maintain other activities until the parent got home. David Elkind describes one such case, involving "Janet." Janet's mother leaves for work an hour before Janet needs to get to school, and the girl has to make sure her sister has breakfast and to get both sister and self off to school. Then she has some housecleaning tasks when she gets home and barely has time for her own schoolwork. Elkind points to this kind of case as severe contemporary stress.[37]

Unquestionably, such cases became more common after the 1970s. But what is really remarkable, given the rise of single parents and working mothers, is that the overall level of chores did not go up, according to all available evidence. There was some significant impact on younger kids, but this was balanced by the continued decline in commitment to chores by older children. Parents—even single mothers—worked hard to avoid a real redefinition. They went to great lengths to prepare meals before they themselves left the house, requiring a child at most to dish stew up from a hotpot. Weekends became times for frenzied parental activities, cleaning the house with at most an hour or two of help from a younger child. Stress may have existed for children, given parents' absence and mental preoccupation, but the actual chore level reflected parental guilt, rather than parental imposition. The need to protect children from work obligations largely survived the huge change in maternal activities. We have seen that husbands, when present, more than kids, became the swing labor force, however inadequately.

The second trend, in contrast, was quite real. A growing number of teenagers, from age sixteen on, began working part-time and during summers, mainly in sales jobs and at fast-food restaurants. The trend built on the rapid rise of these activities in the larger economy, as well as the growing commitment of adult women to other kinds of jobs. Older teenagers became the next group of choice. It is important to note that some of this work in essence replaced farm and factory work, both of which continued to decline as sources of youth employment for older teenagers. Between 1940 and 1980, the number of teenagers working part-time and full-time in sales and service (mainly fast-food) work jumped from 14 percent to 57 percent of the total age group.

Much of this new employment involved teens from working- class and minority families, some of whom had left school entirely. But middle-class kids were drawn in, often in summers and, increasingly, on a part-time basis during the school year. Predictably, the trend spurred considerable debate, which reprised some of the 20th century's earlier themes about child labor. On the pro side, many adults argued that work of this sort gave children a welcome taste of the real world and cut their sense of isolation from adult concerns. The fact that only older teenagers were involved was another plus: the new trends did not disrupt the solutions that had been reached regarding younger children (which meant also, of course, that lingering concerns about these children's work habits and commitments persisted full force). On the con side, many alarmists pointed to high rates of accidents. They also correctly noted that most of the jobs involved were tedious and low-paying—indeed, often outright exploitative—and did not necessarily offer much preparation for the real work conditions middle-class teenagers would face later on. Job stability was another crucial issue. Teenagers were often first fired or could not find the work they sought. This problem affected primarily minority youth and school-leavers, where the rate of unemployment often reached crisis levels. But middle- class kids might have some problems finding work, as well, even in summers, particularly in trough periods like the early 1990s—another limitation on the impact of the new patterns.

Obviously, new work commitments cut the time and interest teenagers had for household chores, but that bus had long since left the station, and the change did not come in for much comment. Privately, the gap between teenagers' willingness to work elsewhere and their resolute avoidance of work at home could increase parental annoyance. The gap between adult domestic obligations and teenage participation widened still further in the 1990s, leaving many parents to feel they were staffing a hotel in which teenagers passed some nights en route to their own work, school, or leisure activity.

Overt parental anxiety focused on two related issues. First, there was the question of work's impact on schoolwork. Unquestionably, some teenagers worked to the detriment of their grades, and particularly their ability to do homework. Many family arguments centered on this tension, and adults did not always win.

The most pervasive new anxiety, however, focused on what kids did with their earnings. For this new commitment to work was not, for the most part, a revival of contributions to a family economy. Teenagers themselves sought the work in order to increase their own earnings and independence. At most, some might commit a portion of their earnings to savings for college. But a good bit of the motivation to work involved enhancements of lifestyle, sometimes including a car, at other times a stereo, even a vacation with friends. Parents often disapproved of these expenditures as frivolous and wished they had the gumption to control teens' earnings and the acquisitive desires. As one mother put it, "I would like to have my son give me the money and let me dole it out. But I'm afraid to say that, because that tells him that somebody is governing his spending. . . . You can't do that." The issue involved the decline of parental authority, sometimes dressed up as a desire to teach adolescents about personal responsibility and decision making. But it also involved a tremendous sense that children deserved high levels of consumption and fun, and that parents could only welcome their contributions to the process—a nexus discussed in the following chapter.[38]

The new work trends had mixed results. Many middle-class children did not participate, or worked only in summer, in which case the work issues remained as they had previously been defined. Others worked with a real interest in saving for college. Here, parental anxiety did not necessarily increase, particularly because most such adolescent workers saw no impact of work on grades. The same motivation applied to jobs and schoolwork alike. The real issues concerned the earners-for-lifestyle, where grades might well be affected and where parental disapproval, whether or not expressed in open dispute, could fester—along with some appreciation that the children involved were at least showing a degree of willingness to work.

CONCLUSION

A definitive solution to the question of children's work in contemporary society had not emerged by the end of the 20th century. The century had seen huge changes in practices and attitudes. A clear gap opened between what most adults, parents and experts alike, thought should be happening and what actually happened. It was a situation ripe for recurrent annoyance, with both parents and children feeling put upon. Traditional patterns died, a huge change in family history when not only jobs but household chores are taken into account. At the century's end, furthered by economic changes, teenagers experimented with some new formulas. But for most children before the age of sixteen, and for many older adolescents, as well, the level of work and work preparation remained a great question mark, with parents and children alike unsure of appropriate standards. While some middleclass parents simply wiped work off the slates for their children, in favor of school and self-expression, a larger number wondered, lamented a bit—and argued repeatedly with their progeny.

Work changes, of course, related to play. It is hardly a secret that, during the 20th century as a whole, children's playtime increased as worktime went down. Here could be another source of parental worry or resentment. When children came home tired from play, eager to sleep until Saturday noon, through the standard chores period, the clash was overt. But certain kinds of play could also be seen as a surrogate for work, so the trade-off was more complicated than appearances might suggest. Parents had an obvious stake in the play process, and they often benefited from it, sharing new pleasures with their offspring. This could compensate for the obvious decline in shared work. But play generated its own anxieties, precisely because its importance increased. Even parents who managed to adjust complacently to nonworking, play-oriented children developed some new concerns.

FURTHER READING

There are a number of useful studies and evaluations of children's work, but no real history of chores (until the present chapter). The following materials are particularly helpful. In addition to Zelizer's *Pricing the Priceless Child* (see ch. 1), see M. David Stern, "How Children Used to Work," *Law and Contemporary Problems* 39 (1975): 93–117; Helen Witmer and Ruth Kotinsky, eds., *Personality in the Making: The Fact-Finding Report of the Midcentury White House Conference on Children and Youth* (Washington, 1952); William Stephens, *Our Children Should Be Working* (New York,1979); Ruth S. Cowan, *More Work for Mother* (New York, 1989); Barbara Ehrenreich and Deirdra English, *For Their Own Good: 150*

Year of Experts' Advice to Women (New York, 1989); Stephanie Coontz, *The Way We Really Are: Coming to Terms with America's Changing Families* (New York, 1997); Elliot Medrich et al., *Serious Business of Growing Up: A Study of Children's Lives outside School* (New York, 1982). On child labor reform, Walter Trattner, *Crusade for the Children: A History of the National Child Labor Committee and Child Labor Reform in America* (Chicago, 1970). On the work ethic, Tom Lutz, "'Sweat or Die': The Hedonization of the Work Ethic in the 1920s," *American Literary History* 8 (1996): 259–83; Todd Postol, "Creating the American Newspaper Boy: Middle-Class Route Service and Juvenile Salesmanship in the Great Depression," *Journal of Social History* 31 (1997): 327–47.

On actual trends in chores: Frances Goldscheider and Linda Waite, *New Families, No Families? The Transformation of the American Home* (Berkeley, 1991); see also Naomi Gerstel and H. E. Gross, eds., *Families and Work* (Philadelphia, 1987), especially Lynn White and D. B. Brinkerhoff, "Children's Work in the Family," pp. 204–18, which correctly notes the absence of many sociological studies. See also Theodore Caplow and others, *Middletown Families: Fifty Years of Change and Continuity* (Minneapolis, 1982); Lynn White and David Brinkerhoff, "Children's Work in the Family: Its Significance and Meaning," *Journal of Marriage and the Family* (1981): 789–98; Sampson Blair, "Children's Participation in Household Labor," *Journal of Youth and Adolescence* 21 (1992): 241–58; Scott Coltrane, "Research on Household Labor," *Journal of Marriage and the Family* 62 (2000): 1208–33; Robert Sears, Eleanor Maccoby, and Harry Levin, *Patterns of Child Rearing* (Evanston, IL, 1957); R. Hill, *Family Development in Three Generations* (Cambridge, MA, 1970); Sandra Hofferth and John Sandberg, "How American Children Use Their Time," *Journal of Marriage and the Family* 63 (2001); John Robinson and Geoffrey Godbey, *Time for Life: The Surprising Ways American Use Their Time* (University Park, PA, 1999); Frances Cogle and Grace Tasker , "Children and Housework," *Family Relations* (July 1982): 395–99; Janice Hodges and Jeanne Barrett, "Working Women and the Division of Household Tasks" *Monthly Labor Review* 95 (April 1972): 9–14.

On recent trends, David Elkind, *The Hurried Child: Growing Up Too Fast Too Soon* (New York, 1988); Ellen Greenberger and Laurence Steinberg, *When Teenagers Work* (1986); and Shirley Soman, *Let's Stop Destroying Our Children* (New York, 1974).

6

I'm Bored

The Two Faces of Entertainment

PARENTS' OBLIGATION to keep children entertained intensified fairly steadily in the 20th century. The amount of entertainment specifically available for children increased massively, a major facet of the burgeoning consumer society. Entertainment standards went up accordingly: if it was easy to give children fun, then surely parents and other adults must keep up the pace. Advertisers rang the message endlessly: buy this, take them there, and you'll know from their joy that you're a really good parent. Often, the sense of responsibility for providing fun seemed to outstrip the activities that were regularly available.

Obligations increased at times, also, because of new parental guilts. If I am forcing all this schooling on my kids, and if schooling is not really natural, surely I owe them an extra-good time in compensation. If I as a mother am going out to work, leaving my kids in a way my own mother did not do, I'd better make sure they're entertained when I get home. Or even: if I, as a new-fashioned dad in the 1920s or 1970s (the type kept getting reinvented) know that I owe my kids attention but have to go on a business trip, I must be super-fun next weekend. Or, obviously: if we're getting divorced, so consumed with our own disputes that the kids have to take second place, we have to be sure to provide pleasure in repayment.

Obligations increased, finally, because in some ways kids found it harder to entertain themselves than had been true in the past, and not only because of the intrusion of more school discipline. Given the dangers of city life and the isolation of the suburbs, more and more families found themselves in situations where children had trouble organizing activities on their own outside the home. The decline of large families reduced the availability of sibling playmates. Again, parents had to think about taking up the slack.

The idea of the entertainable child bore some relationship, clearly, to the vulnerable child, with fun helping to cover up children's deeper demons. It certainly followed from the idea of the precious child, owed more because of his or her scarcity value in a low-birth-rate society. Schooling entered in, and not only because of concerns about its burdens. We will see how entertaining young children became part of the need to stimulate creativity and intelligence as part of the preparation for school—but this also meant entertaining them in the right way. We have noted, in the previous chapter, how changes in attitudes about children's work were also involved in the entertainment revolution, as parents increasingly were told that they should help make work fun. Work and play changes were almost inseparable by midcentury. One reason children's chores declined was to make room for fun, as the parental entertainment quota grew.

Two kinds of anxieties developed around children's entertainment, and this chapter explores both. First, parents worried deeply, if not always effectively, about their degree of control over the entertainment their children received, and about the appropriateness of the entertainment offered. Second, parents worried deeply, if not always effectively, about whether their children were being entertained enough, about whether they were falling into boredom. Here is where the parent-as-impresario entered full force.

The two facets of parental entertainment anxiety were not always compatible. It was easier to be assured that children were being entertained if one could erase worries about the source and quality of entertainment, and vice versa. Trying to operate on both fronts could easily up the worry ante, creating some genuine parental frenzy to keep children amused, but in the right, not the easy, way.

Not all was gloom, of course. While parents in every age and every society have had fun with kids, opportunities expanded in the 20th century. Certainly, there was every encouragement in the new culture to share enjoyments with children. Many parents appreciated children's sense of wonder and spontaneity and sought to benefit from these qualities in their own recreational lives. Here was a key component of the idea of the precious child. But it could be challenging to draw a line between sharing pleasure, taking advantage of children to enjoy amusements that might otherwise seem too childish for contemporary adults, and feeling that one was on another parental treadmill, toting up the fun occasions that one had provided and wondering whether they were adequate.

The two major anxieties about children's entertainment developed at a somewhat different pace within the 20th century. Concerns about monitoring the source and quality of children's toys and leisure activities go back into the late 19th century, as capitalist consumerism began to spread its tentacles to the American young. The idea of entertaining children as a responsibility, and particularly the power of the obligation to prevent boredom, surfaced gradually during the 1920s but emerged full force only in the 1940s and 1950s, when it became an integral part of what the sociologist Martha Wolfenstein perceptively dubbed the advent of a new fun morality. It was during the second half of the century, then, along with the new commitments to schooling and the changes in attitudes to work, that parents faced the dilemma of needing to provide children with pleasure while also fretting about the tawdriness of one commercial offering after another.

The main goal of this chapter is to grapple with the two anxieties about entertainment and about their uneasy relationship. But, because both anxieties were largely novel, bearing even less relationship to past parental concerns than work, discipline or schooling entailed, a bit of background is in order. In entertainment, the 20th century emerged in stark contrast to the past; while this is hardly surprising, understanding its applicability to the world of parenting needs preparation.

CONSUMERISM AND CHILDREN

Modern consumerism was born in the 18th century, with Britain in the lead. A growing interest in material possessions and the process of acquisition spread quickly to the United States, and it represents a fascinating change in human values. By the mid-19th century, shopping and the lure of goods were enhanced by the advent of the department store, a French innovation that, again, quickly spread across the Atlantic. Interest focused on clothing and household furnishings, including tableware, initially. But leisure activities were soon drawn in, with new forms of commercial entertainment, including the circus and popular concerts, as well as professional sports and vaudeville soon after the Civil War. By the end of the century, the United States was gaining a lead in consumerist forms, pioneering, for example, in the establishment of professional advertising agencies and, soon, producing the most commercial movies.

All of this has a rich and intriguing history, but, for our purposes, the main thing to note, beyond the existing and steady acceleration of modern consumerism, is that children were involved only very selectively until right around 1900. Respectable parents bought things for children, primarily in the interests of improving their social graces and of offering educational enhancement, not primarily for entertainment— granting that the line can be a fine one. A new industry of children's books emerged at the end of the 18th century, but the focus was on literacy skills and moral uplift. Children might enjoy the reading, but this was not the main point. Toys had a similar purpose in training. Girls, for example, were given dolls to train for motherhood, even in the 1870s acquiring mourning clothes and coffins to learn how to handle death and bereavement. Boys obtained some sports items and toy soldiers with gender socialization purposes in mind. Home furnishings included the requisite piano, to improve girls' social graces and to provide family recreation. Choosing clothing, of course, required attention to children's proper appearance, again with primary emphasis on respectable attire for social occasions and church. Parents filtered all these major items. They certainly might expect, at least hope for, their children's satisfaction, but the idea of an obligation to provide fun was simply not explicit. Family vacations approached this new sense of obligation, with upper-middle-class mothers taking the children to a rural or seaside location, but there were no explicit projects for children involved, just a new setting in which the kids presumably could find ways to entertain themselves. And this really is the main point: Victorian families, for all their seriousness, were not anti-enjoyment. They just did not connect specially child-centered consumerism to the enjoyment process in any elaborate way.

Revealingly, one of the main 19th-century injunctions about toys involved the insistence that children use them to share, rather than become attached to any particular item as a source of personal meaning. In Louisa May Alcott's *Little Women*, the March girls give away some of their possessions and even accept their destruction in order to minimize their emotional attachment. Again, there was no implication here that children should not have fun. But the source was not in commercial items, and parental obligation lay not in consumerism but rather in moral control.

This situation began to change rapidly around the 1890s. Increased obsession by middle-class adults with their own consumerism, amid increasingly alluring advertisements and new products that included bicycles and, soon, automobiles, set a context for the greater involvement of children. Holiday spending, particularly on commercial Christmas gifts, escalated, and the child focus here was important. The new practice of giving children allowances, while it was predicated on a need to train them in money management, including savings, had obvious consumerist implications, setting up a situation where children could decide on some of their own small purchases, with parental encouragement.

A crucial shift involved consumer items for very young children. Soft, cuddly toys, like the teddy bear, appeared in American markets for the first time. They were widely appealing at a time when parents were trying to facilitate new sleeping arrangements for babies and also to guard against unduly fervent emotional attachments to mothers. The decline in paid help for young children also opened the door to the use of toys as surrogate entertainment. American manufacturers of soft toys soon displaced more expensive European imports as the local market expanded. To be sure, there was brief criticism. Commentators worried about the encouragement of fantasy life and consumer commitments as children grew up. "Why foster a craving for novelty and variety that life cannot satisfy?" A minister blasted teddy bears as substitute objects of affection that corrupted the maternal instinct. But, amid growing concern for the vulnerable child, other arguments prevailed. Cuddly dolls "may have robbed childhood of one of its terrors"—the fear of animals. An article from 1914 captured the point: "Children's affections have come to center around toys with which they have lived and played," and linking dolls to the emotions of very young children was absolutely fine in this setting. This new consumer practice both reflected and encouraged further commitments to the use of commercial toys to provide childhood pleasure.[1]

Soon, of course, child-rearing authorities were advocating the use of toys to counter a variety of childhood problems. The jealous child should receive separate gifts on a sibling's birthday, to prevent further tension and emotional damage. The fearful child should be induced into a darkened room or near a stranger by placing a desired consumer item near the source of concern. Doing right by children increasingly meant surrounding them with store-bought goods, from which presumably they would derive both entertainment and meaning.

Even concerns about undue materialism tended to be countered by more materialism, just otherwise organized. By the 1920s, a number of critics worried about children who could not entertain themselves without "outside stimulus," who would become shallow adults who "turn . . . complacently to bridge and golf, movies and radio, gossip and endless rushing from one amusement to the next." What was the solution? Different kinds of toys, purchased under parental supervision. Hobbies, like carpentry or stamp collecting, would develop inner resources. Experts urged special playrooms, which could be filled with creative stimuli that the children would also enjoy. These also would be rooms in which adults did not have to pick up after their offspring, thus sidestepping the growing problem of getting children to do regular work around the house. Backyard play sets also came into popularity in this period, again as a clearly consumerist alternative to consumerism away from home. Play in this context could be extremely useful to children's socialization, and, of course, it could be conducted safely under family supervision. But it must derive from a parental commitment not just to worthy goals but to genuine fun. As the nursery school educator Elizabeth Cleveland put it, in the 1920s, parents have to infuse family activities with some "attractiveness, instead of a wishy-washy, negative, colorless ideal of deadly, dull goodness. . . . [If] our stimulation is to compete with Satan's . . . we must provide legitimate thrills." Even eating, another expert urged, should be dressed up, by calling spinach dishes "Babe Ruth's Home Plate" or "Mary Pickford's Beauty Compound." Home should become an entertainment center of sorts.[2]

This level of family consumerism involved two crucial assumptions. First, of course, parental obligations had expanded and now required the organization of consumer-based purchases and activities that could compete with the more dangerous corner store or neighborhood movie house. The only way to fight undesirable consumerism was to become responsible for more desirable consumerism, and the effort could be draining for parent and child alike. As early as 1931, one critic, Ruth Frankel, noted that "the modern child, with his days set into a patterned program, goes docilely from one prescribed class to another, takes up art and music and French and dancing . . . until there is hardly a minute left." Eventually, Frankel argued, such overprogrammed children became jaded and turned "desperately to the corner movie in an effort to escape ennui." But, ideally, and this was the second assumption, the playful parent also learned to consult children themselves, and not simply to prescribe for them. In some visions, children themselves, properly heeded, could become the source for a healthier consumerism. Ernest Calkins thus claimed that "the average child is far more original, unhackneyed, interesting than the average grown-up . . . [who] has been beaten into the stereotyped pattern by our mechanical civilization." But listening to children had its own demands: what if the childish voice simply argued for more commercial fare as the source of fun?[3]

By the 1920s, explicit consumer advertisements to children were becoming commonplace. Even earlier, reading matter had been sold directly to children, featuring tough-guy detectives and a good bit of violence for boys. Comic strips, though not exclusively for children, provided another site around which advertising could be based. Radio shows, by the 1920s and 1930s, greatly expanded the potential for reaching a young audience with commercial pitches that, among other things, began urged auditors to become "the first kid on your block" to have one. Some ads directly appealed to children with small amounts of spending money to take to the corner store. Others, for bigger ticket items, subtly or unsubtly urged children to press their parents to get them this or that.

In the space of a few decades, children and middle-class parents alike had become wedded to a life of consumerism. This changed the definition of children's activities. It opened children to a host of influences from a larger commercial world. It pushed parents to redefine their own obligations to children and to assume responsibility for children's fun. As one parent noted hopefully, "the family that plays together stays together."[4]

BOREDOM

Ultimately, new commitments to entertain children would become commitments to banish boredom. And, ultimately, these commitments would give children a new source of claims on parents and other adults.

But this turn was completed only toward midcentury, and before we get to this juncture another bit of background is essential.

Like consumerism, boredom was born in the 18th century. The word "boring" in its mood-related signification first came into usage in the 1750s, and the noun "boredom" became common only in the 19th century. These innovations raise fascinating historical questions about whether and how people experienced what we call boredom in previous periods, and some scholars have argued that other concepts, like melancholy, did the job in part. But the creation of a new word both reflected and encouraged a more common realization that one was not having fun and that having fun was both appropriate and desirable. The advent of boredom as a concept reflected a growing concern about individual personality, part of a new set of manners that would help make respectable individuals more pleasing to others, and a growing separation between work and leisure that helped generate a further sense that leisure, at least, should be fun. Not specifically tied to the new forms of consumerism also developing in the later 18th century, it surely reflected their influence.

Like consumerism, however, boredom was not initially linked to children, who, as far as most adults were concerned, could be bored aplenty as long as they were learning and doing the right things. The idea of boredom certainly encompassed a sense that being interested and entertained was desirable and that people had an obligation to avoid being boring—both parts of the 20th- century formula ultimately applied to parent-child relations. But, intriguingly, the idea was long focused primarily on the potential bor-er, not the bor-ee, and applied to children only to the extent that, as they neared adulthood, they (particularly females) needed advice on how to be interesting. Children, in all this, need not apply, for they were not particularly relevant as causes of boredom and did not enter in as victims of the state. Pictures of children enduring long sermons or rote lessons at school before and during the 19th century suggest the strong potential for boredom, but there was no specific application of the term. The child-rearing literature, not interested in entertainment issues anyway except to ensure moral guidance, avoided comment on bored children.

What was emphasized was the need not to be boring, particularly in conversations, as part of good manners and, for women, appropriate courtship strategy. Etiquette books, as a result, served as the locus of discussion. Thus, Anna Richardson, in 1925: "All this information should be kept in mind to introduce into general conversation, but it should not be used to bore people with knowledge which may be new and interesting to you, but old, or a matter of indifference, to them." Specific topics were singled out for their boredom potential: Richardson noted sickness, clothing, and servants. A bit earlier, in 1859, feminism made the list, as well: "And none make poorer livings than those who waste their time, and bore their friends, by writing and lecturing upon the equality of the sexes, and what they call 'Women's Rights.'" Money matters were also taboo for women, as was much discussion of the wonders of one's children. Men were singled out less, but they, too, were advised not to focus too much on themselves ("I will not talk about Myself for more than thirty minutes, then reduce it to twenty five . . . and so on to the irreducible minimum.") Laughing at one's own jokes was also discouraged, as in a 1936 essay for men.[5]

This advice was supplemented, by the 1920s, as a transition began to suggest movement away simply from personal character, in two ways. First, girls were increasingly given advice about how to draw boys out, to make them feel less boring and more interesting. Adults were also given advice about how to get away from bores: for example, the quick passoff, "Have you met Miss Smith?" Emily Post added, in 1940, that "to be bored is a bad personal habit," but this still kept boredom as a largely personal trait. Finally, the frequency of discussions of boredom increased, suggesting growing uneasiness with boredom—as in a 1922 *Reader's Digest* article, "To Bore or Not to Bore."[6]

But it was only after World War II that a full breakthrough occurred, and it involved two facets. First, being bored began to be much more important than doing the boring. Claiming boredom was now a major, justifiable complaint, whether the occasion involved a boring individual or, increasingly common, a more systematically stifling situation. Second, boredom began to shift to children, which meant, when combined with the first shift, that responsibility for avoiding or pulling children out of boredom became a significant parental charge. The bored child became something else to worry about, and the fault lay outside the child himself.

We must return to this shift in boredom, and the related anxiety, after retracing the dominant entertainment anxieties of the first half of the century. But a teaser: in 1954, Frank Richardson wrote a book on *How to Get Along with Children*. It contains a quietly striking passage. A mother asked, "How can I keep our son and daughter from showing boredom when their father tells one of his favorite jokes before company?" And the answer is: this is a common source of family tension, and it's dad's fault. If we remember how important it is "to treat our children 'like folks,' it will not be asking too much of Dad that he limit himself to two or three recitals of his best yarns. . . . To be sure, this may mean that Dad will have to hunt up some fresh jokes. . . . But [he] can stand it. And it will relieve the rest of the family of a painful strain." Here, obviously, children are now particularly important candidates for boredom, and their boredom is significant (a serious strain)—and their claims to be appropriately entertained have pride of place. The situation was surely not novel, for parents have doubtless bored their children for centuries. But the notion that this is a problem and that parents, not children, have to make the resultant adjustments is truly revolutionary. The question is—and we will get back to it shortly—why did this little upheaval occur? Why this new gloss on an already interesting modern state of mind?[7]

TRYING TO KEEP CONTROL OF ENTERTAINMENT

The most familiar 20th-century parental anxiety about entertainment involves a long series of commercial manipulators, eager to interest children and to draw them or their parents to spend, for pleasures deemed of limited value or positively noxious. What's intriguing is how early in the century this battle began, and how it recurred despite one failure after another. We build here on existing historical work, particularly the intriguing account by Steven Starker, while adding further facets and a wider sense of context.

We have already noted how the extension of modern consumerism to children raised concerns about drawing youngsters into dubious locations and into equally dubious taste. As early as the 1890s, modern toys were criticized for being too slick: as one critic put it, "the more imagination and cleverness the inventor has put into the toy, the less room there is for the child's imagination and creativity." Anxiety about family cohesion was another frequent complaint, as toys and recreations drew children outside parental control and outside the home. Particularly by the 1920s, there was widespread concern about the development of shallow, consumerist adults and therefore about the kinds of children who seemed headed in that direction.

Concern about the sources of children's consumption and play involved three main factors. First was the issue of control itself. At a time when parents' ability to influence their children was yielding ground to outside experts, to schools, and even to their children's peers, the desire to maintain at least some authority was paramount. When the issue was relatively young children, for whose development parents were feeling increased responsibility, this motivation became especially important.

Second, and most obvious, parents objected to commercial motives in children's entertainment because they so often pandered to children's weak sides. At a time when beliefs in children's vulnerability and frailty were growing, there was declining confidence that young people, by themselves, could resist the blandishments of commercial purveyors of sick humor, violence, or sexuality. This aspect of the dispute over children's entertainment showed up particularly in the frequent adult belief (not always supported by facts) that children would act out the images they clearly enjoyed, becoming, for example, more violent when they saw violence in a comic strip.

The third factor in the dispute over control of entertainment was less obvious, but it followed from the other changes occurring in 20th-century childhood. For many adults, play, at its best, was taking on a number of new functions that were in fact extremely serious. For appropriate play was now a vital component of preparation for and success in school. Give your child music lessons, so the experts in the 1990s argued, not because music was fun (though they might have believed this) but because studies showed that appreciation of classical music enhanced school performance. Play must also make up for the decline in work as a way to teach children how to apply themselves. The rise of adult promotion of hobbies was directly predicated on the notion that play could in essence be work. The young stamp collectors would be learning geography—good for school—but also patience, care, and other good work qualities. Play was also vital for gender guidance, now that gender-specific work training was declining. Most obviously with sports for boys, play took on important socialization roles in the eyes of mothers and fathers alike. These uses of play were not brand new, of course, but their significance increased as other parent-directed activities declined.

The seriousness of play emerged very early in the century. It showed in the debates over monitored playrooms versus free play outside. It showed in a growing number of treatises by play "experts" eager to teach parents about the difference between good play and bad. Toys, for example, were good if they stimulated imagination, physical and mental abilities, and good social habits. But mechanical toys that had no useful purposes but could only be wound up to go "serve only to stimulate a desire for novelty and breed boredom and restlessness." Play, in sum, required discipline and choice. There were huge differences between good play and bad.[8]

Actual parents, of course, took the most severe formulations with the necessary grain of salt. Few believed that every toy or every movie had to have a higher purpose—particularly when some experts were also urging that parents and children should have fun. But the existence of play advice related to many parents' own sense that play did have functions in school preparation and work replacement. And this sense, added to parents' concerns about authority and commercialism, could frequently lead to quiet battles over who and what should guide children's entertainment. Simply the struggle to make sure that books and reading retained a place in children's play, as other media opportunities came to compete, could occasion no small amount of anxiety.

The range of consumer items that came in for anguished comment was impressive. By the early 21st century, as adults grappled with porn sites on the Web and other menaces, the historical memory of past campaigns was distressingly dim, but in fact this strand of parental anxiety has a distinguished, if not usually very effective, ancestry.

KEEPING CHILDREN PURE

Even before rumblings about toys surfaced, around 1900, a crusading spirit had developed over the kinds of reading matter that began to be made available to children by the 1870s and 1880s. The material reflected steady improvements in publishing, which permitted cheaper products (such as the interestingly named "penny dreadful" in Britain) aimed at a growing working-class readership. Many of the products that ultimately reached children were at first designed for newly literate adults, an important audience in terms of the widening range of entertainment. It also affected commentary, which frequently combined sincere concern about child protection with a somewhat elitist snobbery about taste. The new fare, as it reached children, depended on their having some independent spending money, via child labor wages or, increasingly for the middle class, allowances. And it reflected an earnest desire to make a buck on the part of a growing array of commercial publishers.

Anthony Comstock, famous for his use of postal regulations to regulate the dissemination of birth control information in the 1870s, helped get the anxiety ball rolling, concerning the cheap novels that began to find their ways into the hands of children, mainly boys. Dime novels featured Wild West themes or tough-talking detectives, and levels of violent action were high, by the standards of the times. Comstock and other concerned citizens blasted both the lack of literary merit and the immorality of these new series, highlighting their corrupting potential for the ill educated and for children. A New York Assembly bill proposed to prohibit their sale to anyone under sixteen years of age. Comstock's New York Society for the Suppression of Vice, formed in 1872, gave wide publicity to moral and legal attacks on the producers and sellers of dime novels. Comstock urged parents: "Let your newsdealer feel that, in just proportion as he prunes his stock of that which is violent, your interest in his welfare increases and your patronage becomes more constant." While not technically illegal, because they were not obscene, dime novels began to fall under the same moral cloud, and parents' responsibility to keep children away from them was strongly emphasized.[9]

Whatever one thinks of the precise contours of the purity crusades and their mixed motives, it is important to realize that, where children and the media were concerned, parents were confronting a new problem, as with work and schooling, at the turn of the century. Of course, in the most general sense, worries about children being led astray were not new. Strangers and local degenerates had posed threats before. But new media and commercialized toys, reaching out directly to children, were far more pervasive than the Pied Pipers of old. They suggested a need for a new kind of monitoring, which is why, among the fiercest advocates, concern so often spilled over into appeals for outright regulation or proscription.

Changes in ideas about fear were also crucial. In earlier times, parents had accepted violence in stories told to children—in fairy tales, for example, like the bloody versions of Cinderella's retaliation against her stepsisters, which Disney had to clean up in the 1950s—because they thought instilling fear was useful. Of course, these stories were told orally, under community control, so the context was different, as well.

But, by 1900, concerns about violence were beginning to reflect parents' belief in children's vulnerability, as the frequent comments about overexcitement and excessive stimulation suggest. (Unfortunately, of course, as the subsequent century would demonstrate, large numbers of kids did not agree, and either did not feel put off or positively enjoyed the titillation and the violence offered to them in ever larger doses.)

Concern about protecting middle-class children from street-life recreation also emerged by the late 19th century and extended for several decades. Experts warmed about working-class children who hung around night spots and urged a protective reaction. Jane Addams, for example, wrote of the "overstimulation" of children's senses in the modern city. A Chicago pediatrician, in 1912, insisted that parents should apply the "principle of regularity" to their children's entertainment habits: "For countless ages the young of all animals have naturally slept and rested at night. They have not been careering around cities."[10] Boys' clubs and other organized activities were designed to assist parents in this aspect of recreation regulation, as were recurrent waves of curfew restrictions. The idea of curfews specifically aimed at children was new, having first surfaced in the 1880s. Working-class youth were the main targets here, of course, but the effort and certainly the anxieties could spill over to the middle class, as well. In Chicago, a discussion about a curfew ordinance, in 1920, drew a general lesson, insisting that "parents [should] provide their children with clean entertainment and interests in their own homes," lest criminal connections emerge. While this particular curfew was passed, the nighttime recreational tensions continued. By 2001, 80 percent of all American cities with population of more than thirty-thousand had juvenile curfew restrictions, with adult anxieties to match.

The advent of newspaper comic strips in the 1890s triggered the next prolonged salvo. Regular comic strips surfaced in the 1890s, again with a mixed audience in mind. Full-fledged comic supplements emerged around 1910. The menace seemed acute, and whole range of popular articles sounded the alarm. Mary Pedrik, in *Good Housekeeping*, found the comics "a carpet of hideous caricatures, crude art, and poverty of invention, perverted humor, obvious vulgarity, and the crudest coloring . . . which makes for lawlessness, debauched fancy, irreverence." Comics were seen as threatening law, family, and adult authority. *The Outlook* went further still: "We are permitting the vulgariza-

tion of our children on a great scale. . . . We are teaching them lawlessness; we are cultivating lack of reverence in them; we are doing everything we can, by cheapening life, to destroy the American homes of the
future." Psychological damage was invoked: as the *Independent* noted,
in 1907, comics created the "pathological effect of the nervous erethism,
which results from the cultivation of the imagination to a high degree."
Again emphasizing children's frailty, more than the conventional Victorian concern about bad adult example, the author specifically noted
the dangers to mental health. *The Ladies Home Journal* dismissed comics
as "A Crime Against American Children," and a number of newspapers
did indeed pull back.[11]

Themes of violence and hostility to authority formed the greatest
problem. A prominent opponent, Gershom Legman, noted how, in
comic strips, "both father and husband can be thoroughly beaten up,
harassed, humiliated and degraded daily." In 1911, a League for Improvement of the Children's Comic Supplement formed, though without much effect. By 1944, more than two-thirds of all children regularly read comic strips, and half of all adults joined in. But this did not
mean that adult comfort had been achieved, even among some of the
readers.[12]

Movies and radio were next on the list, chronologically. Radio, particularly, quickly reached widely into homes and into children's use of
time and attention. Programming for children became a fact of life during the 1930s, mainly around adventure themes, with shows like *Buck
Rogers, Eno Crime Clues,* and *Jack Armstrong,* but children could and did
listen to presumably adult fare, as well. Criticisms of radio emerged as
quickly as the shows themselves, initially primarily on grounds of taste
and excessive advertising. By 1933, parents and teachers were being
drawn in, as attention turned to radio's impact on children. Most of the
popular shows were dismissed: as an article in the *Nation* noted, in 1933,
"What the parents rated poor and very poor the little savages almost invariably set down as their favorite entertainment." Once again, violence
headed the list of problems. A 1933 article in *Scribner's,* called "The
Children's Hour of Crime," blasted radio for presenting to children
"every form of crime known to man." "I should like to postpone my
children's knowledge of how to rob a bank, scuttle a ship, shoot a sher-
iff, the emotional effects of romantic infidelity, jungle hazards, and the
horrors of the drug habit for a few more years at least." Various teachers and school organizations became particularly vigorous opponents

of children's radio. By the 1940s and 1950s, sober child development studies could routinely claim that "few writers deny" that radio has a "profound effect" on children, with fears, tensions and nervous habits—including sleep disruption—a result at least for some.[13]

But proposals to boycott products or otherwise regulate them made little headway, despite the real adult dismay. As one of the concerned groups noted, in discussing the gap between anxiety and effectiveness, "Radio seems to find parents more helpless than did the funnies. . . . It cannot be locked out or the children locked in to escape it."[14]

Periodic promises by the networks to clean up their act were hollow. A 1938 article claimed that radio was breeding "a race of neurotic impressionables" through daily doses of terror. "Radio has resumed its daily task of cultivating our children's morals—with blood and thunder effects." And, while loud laments later died down in favor of other targets, the concern persisted. A physicist, Lee De Forest, excoriated radio, in 1947, for debasing his children's musical taste, demeaning intelligent conversation, and making children "psychopathic" with its nighttime fare.[15]

Movies were a clear menace, as well, and here sexuality, as well as violence and bad taste, quickly drew attention. The impact on children warranted slightly less comment than with early radio, if only because the corruption wreaked on adults was more obvious and because some children could be kept away from the movie houses. Initial problems were strongly noted, though the emphasis on working-class attendance may have diluted "respectable" parents' worries for a time. Nevertheless, the potential threat to morality was obvious, and movies were compared to dime novels, yet "ten times more poisonous and hurtful to the character." There was no question that children were widely attending films, with admission prices at a nickel. The vividness of movies encouraged worries not just about morals in general but about impacts on specific behavior. The head of a New York mission for wayward women argued, in 1914, that westerns caused boys to run away from home, while films about Indians prompted children to tie their playmates to stakes and light bonfires.[16]

Jane Addams, in 1909, claimed broader psychological damage when poor children were exposed to dream worlds that would leave them unsuited for reality. She also worried about children stealing money to gain admission to theaters and suggested that both delinquency and neurosis might result from films. A 1909 conference discussed movies' potential to "sap the mental and moral strength" of young people. One survey claimed that at least 40 percent of all movies were totally unfit for children. Children themselves, pressed by reformers, made it clear that their tastes ran to action. A twelve-year old boy at Hull House noted, "Things has got ter have some hustle. I don't say it's right, but people likes to see fights, 'n' fellows getting hurt, 'n' love makin', 'n' robbers, and all that stuff." Before World War I, a number of cities passed laws against movie attendance by minors, though few had any impact. Scientific claims about the promotion of delinquency multiplied between the wars. Specific examples were adduced, like the eleven-year-old boy from a good home who stole regularly, in order to see movies, and finally had to be jailed. Again, parent and teacher groups joined in. The National Congress of Mothers and Parent-Teachers Associations featured an article titled "Solving the Moving Picture Problem," in 1924. Films were "too exciting and emotionally stimulating for the younger child"; "movies are making the children emotionally unstable and very nervous." Studies, in the 1930s, found that delinquents like movies better than reading (unlike Boy and Girl Scouts, whose movie viewing was the lowest). Two prominent sociologists made the links clear, in 1933, with a book titled *Movies, Delinquency and Crime*, which claimed that a substantial minority of delinquents were spurred by movies, including girls who had sexual relations after being aroused by a film. The child at the movies "loses ordinary control of his feelings, his actions, and his thoughts."[17]

Also in the 1930s, the Payne Fund launched what turned out to be a steady series of scientific efforts to examine the link between media—in this case, movies—and disturbed child behavior, and the results were widely publicized and popularized. Again, child development experts took the movies' potential for damage as common knowledge by the 1940s, talking about eye strain and loss of sleep but also about "detrimental effects on health and conduct." The claim that delinquents were disproportionately interested in movies was passed along without any attention to which predilection came first. The need for adult restrictions, including banning movies altogether for the "high-strung" child, seemed obvious.[18]

Anxieties about the media took a new turn in the early 1950s, initially with the great comic book crusade, round two. Several factors promoted this intensification. Parents' worries about losing control over children, particularly teenagers, were increasing, with some justification. Delinquency seemed to be rising, and, although perceptions undoubtedly raced ahead of reality, there may have been some real shift. Even cold war anxieties may have fanned the flames. Most important of all, the media themselves began to change, particularly when a series of court rulings widened First Amendment protections. Decisions against local censorship in the 1950s—what one historian has labeled the "repeal of reticence"—set a context in which previously proscribed novels, plus new entries such as *Playboy*, could hit the newsstands, and in which Hollywood could begin to introduce greater license in language and imagery. And, even before the major rulings, changes in many genres, such as the advent of comic strip superheroes bent on violence, however just their cause, inevitably heightened already acute sensibilities. Even as adult concerns mounted, comic publishers introduced ever more graphic sequences to their readers, particularly around gore and aggression.

In 1954, the psychologist Frederic Wertham issued a dramatic book, *Seduction of the Innocent*, that held comic books responsible for a variety of ills among children. He blasted superhero comics for their racism, for all were white. He condemned homosexuality, noting that Robin, Batman's "boy wonder," was often posed with his tights-clad legs provocatively spread. But, above all, he attacked violence and the direct contributions of comic books to a menacing tide of juvenile delinquency. Wertham did not stand alone. From the late 1940s on, a new generation of critics condemned crime comics for their "emphasis on murder, mayhem, sex and glorification of crime." American children, another writer noted, "take their daily lethal dose of crime and cruelty, torture and terror as regularly as their daily vitamin-enriched breakfast food." A number of cities once again initiated actions to ban the sale of violent comics.[19]

But Wertham went a step further, in adducing a host of specific cases that linked comics to criminal behavior. All sorts of comics—"jungle" romance (a particular danger to girls, in promoting sexualized expectations), as well as crime—came under his purview. A *Collier's* article, publicizing his views, featured a large photo showing two children jabbing a third with a fountain pen "hypodermic," claiming this was a direct re-enactment of a crime comic scene. Wertham cited a murder by a thirteen-year- old Chicago boy, who "reads all the crime comic books hc can get hold of." And he asserted, more sweepingly: "comic book reading was a distinct influencing factor in the case of every single delinquent or disturbed child we studied." He also claimed, without evidence, that 75 percent of all parents opposed crime comics. Wertham's work not only was widely disseminated but also became part of a sweeping congressional inquiry on delinquency sponsored, and widely publicized, by Senator Estes Kefauver. Wertham summed up: crime comics "create a readiness for temptation"; they "suggest criminal or sexually abnormal ideas"; they "suggest the forms a delinquent impulse may take and supply details of technique"; and "they may tip the scales toward maladjustment or delinquency." It was absolutely imperative that parents take this menace seriously.[20]

Wertham's descriptions of crime comics were both dramatic and, to jaded 21st-century eyes, surprisingly contemporary. He noted one story, from 1950, in which twelve of thirty-seven pictures showed near-rape scenes. One depicted "the girl falling over, her breast prominent, her skirt thrown up to reveal black net panties, the 'attacker' a black, shadowed figure looming over her." "What is wrong with the prevailing ethics and educators and psychologists that they have silently permitted this kind of thing year after year, and that after I had drawn attention to it some of them still continued to defend it as helping children to learn about life and 'get rid of their pent-up aggression?' . . . When I saw children getting into trouble and getting sent wholesale to reformatories, I felt that I had to go on with this tedious work." And, while Wertham called for regulation, ultimately the default responsibility went to parents. "Someday parents will realize that comic books are not a necessary evil. . . ." Wertham ended a revised edition of his work with a story drawn from a clinic, as a mother discussed the repeated legal confrontations with her delinquent son, now headed for a reformatory. "'It must be my fault. . . . I heard that in the lectures, and the judge said it, too. It's the parents' fault that the children do something wrong. Maybe when he was very young—'" And while Wertham consoled her, citing the huge influences working against her, the impression was clear. Parents were the last line of defense. "'Tell me again,'" she said slowly and hesitantly. "'Tell me again that it isn't my fault.'"[21]

The story after the comic book phase becomes increasingly familiar, because so many Americans have lived through much of it. The advent of openly sold pornographic magazines, led by *Playboy*, prompted great concern, their lurid covers initially readily available to children's eyes.

Here, two decades of protests ultimately forced withdrawal of the magazines from places like supermarkets and the addition of plain brown wrappers over the material on the newsstands. But young purchasers could easily circumvent these barriers, so the problem remained.

Television quickly became a prime enemy, as Wertham himself began to note in the 1950s. As always, part of the problem involved taste and the medium's impact on education, as TV was decried as a "vast wasteland." Ubiquitous sales pitches added to the degradation. A great deal of the criticism focused on the passivity of TV watching and on its inhibition of critical response, as fantasy and reality blurred for youthful viewers. But the corruption issue quickly became prominent, as well. The 1950s brought a spate of westerns to television, and, while they observed the rule that gunshots and death should not be shown in the same moment, and while black-and-white TV limited the potential for gore, the violence quotient was already high. Crime shows, once on radio and designed for kids, were quickly transferred to television, as well. A federal official, in 1961, sounded positively Wertham-like as he recounted "blood and thunder, mayhem, violence, sadism, murder . . . gangsters, more violence. . . ." The popular press quickly called on parents to regulate their children's viewing with great care; the entertainment responsibilities multiplied simply because the media became more omnipresent. The Saturday Review of Literature, as early as 1949, intoned that television shows were taking over from the comics as "prime movers in juvenile misconduct and delinquency." A 1950 study suggested that the assiduous viewer could see three thousand murders a week on standard shows. TV seemed to be promoting "a craving for violence and fantasy among children." Polls of middle-class parents indicated wide concern, along with periodic efforts at boycott either of the whole medium or of selected types of shows. The downward spiral seemed endless.[22]

Critics of the critics quite rightly noted the potential for hysteria in the various warnings and the sublime lack of historical perspective. Coming at the tail end of the comic book crusades, it was striking that the crisis was presented as brand new, the contrast with idyllic childhood innocence before television unsullied by historical data. The sheer volume of warnings and inquiries was staggering. A spate of federal studies, some of them launched in the wake of the 1960s protests, others sponsored by the U. S. Surgeon General, kept parents aware of the link between television and severe misbehavior. While the 1969 Surgeon General's report did admit that findings were "preliminary and tentative" and noted that only some children were affected, it went on to state "a causal relationship between viewing violence on television and aggressive behavior." Anxious parents might be excused for forgetting the scholarly caveats. A 1982 report confirmed the behavioral linkage, and by this point the Christian revival and a more puritanical feminist surge added to the chorus. Television was faulted not simply for youth violence but also for promoting sexual license, drug use, erosion of respect for authority, and declining school performance.[23]

And yet the range of offending media refused to stop growing. The 1980s brought cable television, and a vast increase in the amount of violence and sexuality available to viewers, thanks to late-night movies and explicit pornography channels. Concerned citizens were quick to mobilize, through groups such as Morality in Media, but the problems hardly abated. Video stores filled with pornographic material, as well as violent films, and, while some organized distinct "adult sections," most of the major outlets mingled the offerings indiscriminately.

Movies became steadily more explicit. Ratings systems reflected adults' anxieties about exposure of young children to unsuitable material, but they actually stimulated interest among middle- and high-school youth, eager to find ways to get into R- rated fare. Summers were filled with youth exploitation movies, an intriguing number of them R-rated with the knowledge that kids would find a way to gain admission, anyway. The tremendous increase in graphic violence, thanks to computer-aided materials, was the most obvious objectionable component, along with humor that was sophomoric in large part because it was singlemindedly aimed at sophomores. But sexuality intensified, as well. Movies that deliberately combined sexually provocative costumes with violence against young women directly recalled the comic book materials Wertham had described two generations before.

Rock music created yet another venue. Youth music had drawn criticism before, for its adulation of stars like Frank Sinatra and for its presumed bad taste, but it had not previously loomed as a widespread source of corruption except for some of the dance styles involved. Now, with its incessant beat and suggestive lyrics, music presented an ongoing menace. Youth music seemed directly linked to drug use, sexuality, and violence. A host of adult groups, some of them headed by politically prominent people like the wife of then-Senator Al Gore, campaigned for regulation, seeking as well to shame manufacturers into greater decency (an appealing strategy that has never made much headway in contemporary society). The introduction of MTV in 1981 brought music, lyrics, and graphic visual imagery together, with scenes of sexual temptation, aggression, and bondage sent directly into children's rooms on television. Medical authorities again warned that "children are being bombarded with messages of violence and sexuality that are very confusing and suggest easy ways out of complex problems." The national Coalition on Television Violence studied the number of violent acts or threats in music videos.[24]

Video games began to emerge in the 1970s, and adult concern developed instantly. At first, the critiques focused on players' addiction and passivity, both enemies to social development and attention to schoolwork. Local efforts to regulate games reflected the new worry but had little effect. By the 1980s, violence added to the anxiety. The Harvard psychologist Alvin Poussaint warned that games were teaching children that violence was acceptable. Parents in 1983 responded to a survey by claiming that "no other toy in recent memory has caused them so much perplexity, ambivalence and soul-searching." As before, stories multiplied about direct linkages between the games and real-life violence, with children moving from video games to murderous attacks on other children, stimulated by the violence in the game they had been playing and by their inability to separate image from reality. Even new board games, like Dungeons and Dragons (1970s–1980s) seemed to confirm the violence link. The psychiatrist Thomas Radecki bluntly stated that "the game causes young men to kill themselves and others." Growing concern about teenage suicides and violent attacks within schools seemed to confirm these kinds of linkages, as reality, adult anxiety, and expert warnings coalesced once more.[25]

Then finally—except that there never really seemed to be any finally—the spread of the Internet in the 1990s added yet another media component that was difficult if not impossible to control. A large minority of Americans worried greatly about the implications of Internet access for children, and more than 80 percent expressed at least some anxiety, a relatively high figure in international studies when levels of usage are taken into account. Pornographic materials and invitations were a focus of concern. So were chat rooms, which 73 percent of all American adults rated as problematic where children were involved. Here, of course, was the ultimate fear of strangers, now translated into a domestic medium. Predictably, given the Internet's potential but also the way this kind of anxiety fits into a much longer experience, the levels of expressed concern were dramatically higher than were the rates of actual contact with objectionable content. Appeals for regulation and manufacturer self-discipline were rampant—interestingly, while a majority of all Americans preferred to rely on personal responsibility to control the Internet, a majority of American parents opted for regulatory help. A vast majority also—in direct conflict with their children—preferred that chatrooms be open to outside monitoring. The Internet raised again a tremendous new field for parental responsibility. The issues were somewhat more complicated than with comic books or music videos, for the Internet had undisputed educational merit. But it also elevated concerns about control over children's media fare to new heights, and, at the simplest level, it added a new bead to what had clearly become a long string of 20th-century parental worries. There was no reason to believe that the 21st century was going to get any better in this regard.[26]

ASSESSMENT

The rich history of parental and adult anxieties about children and the new media suggests several conclusions. First, parental concerns had little overall impact against the power of technological innovation and the sheer size of the children's media market. The shock level of children's fare continued to intensify. Each new generation of adults was fighting more explicit fare than its predecessor. Media representations that once seemed horrific came to seem tame, almost idyllic, when measured against the targets of a later decade. Media producers were unscrupulous. Children themselves were demanding, in best consumer fashion, constantly seeking innovations that would distinguish them from the tameness of the previous cohort. And the market was huge. By 2001, girls between the ages of ten and nineteen directly spent $75 billion a year in the United States, not counting other purchases that they could obtain by influencing their parents. The chances to sell directly to children, or to use children's fare for advertisements, became steadily less resistible.

In this context, the few gains registered by morality crusaders were paltry indeed. A handful of products were at least temporarily withdrawn. More commonly, media producers, from movies to comics to

Internet providers, offered some kind of ratings system that at least provided parents with limited information about program content and that, at most, might actually lead to prohibitions on sales to certain age categories. Obviously, the results of these systems, measured against the ever more graphic content, were meager at best. While some parents might draw comfort from their ability to forbid Jane or Johnny to attend a particular movie, still more found their responsibilities escalating as it proved difficult to keep Jane or Johnny away or when the same movie popped up on a cable channel six months later.

Second, though there is room for debate here, the impressive length of the contemporary history of parental concerns has not been matched by comparable increases in youth degeneracy. There have, to be sure, been some changes in youth sexuality, undoubtedly to some degree because of media presentations. The lessons on violence are more complex. Simple fighting has probably declined. Even in the 1990s, despite some horrific school incidents—all the more appalling to middle-class parents because they were perpetrated largely by middle-class white males—overall rates of school violence dropped. Most children were not deeply affected by what they heard and saw in the media. This does not preclude the possibility that a few were, and it was possible to argue that these few justified the massive concern, even regulation. But there was a clear gap between the jeremiads of each successive wave of experts and the actual impact of the media—which means that, intentionally or not, a large number of experts were actually exploiting their audience of parents, trying to create a level of frantic concern that, to date (it could always theoretically get worse next time), the facts did not warrant.

There was also, however innocently, a stubborn nostalgia within the cautionary expertise that replaced accuracy with fervor. An idealized past was constantly invoked or implied that had never really existed. Marie Winn, for example, lamenting the fate of "Children without Childhood," pinned the blame on the 1960s, when childish innocence was so obviously undermined. But we have seen that observers in the 1950s had been convinced that innocence was being lost to comics, TV, and radio and that the age of purity was back in the 1920s—a point the critics of the 1920s would themselves have disputed. The history lesson is not merely academic. The lack of perspective was part of a movement designed to convince each generation of parents that theirs was a particularly troubled moment, that it was they who risked letting the true value of childhood disintegrate.

Third, the sheer pace of media innovation, combined with well-meaning or exploitative laments and warning from experts, greatly increased parents' sense of anxious responsibility. Believing that children were emotionally vulnerable and incapable of resisting evil lures, parents found it hard not to worry. In fact, as we discuss later in the chapter, most parents took the direst claims with a grain of salt, preferring their own judgment, often with some confidence in their kids' good sense, to the vagaries of a rating system. It was revealing that, even when explicit control devices were provided, such as V-chips to regulate television channels, most American parents declined to use them. Polling percentages in reaction to the Internet suggested a tripartite division that probably applied to earlier threats, as well: a minority was deeply concerned, eager to embrace regulation and full of dire forebodings about impact on children; another, smaller minority was cavalierly unconcerned; and a majority expressed a more intermediate level of worry, watchful but not desperate.

Yet, even with these grains of salt, the anxiety was there. It was impossible not to wonder whether maybe the experts were right. There was always a parent down the block who seemed to be extracautious, extraresponsible, regulating television viewing hours or systematically keeping the kids away from movie fare that was not robustly PG. Maybe I should tell them to stop with the Play Station or to get some fresh air, the way the experts, and Mrs. Johnson down the street, suggested. Maybe I should be more rigorous. For many parents, a certain ambivalence set in—substantial indulgence much of the time and occasional anxiety-fueled outbursts against the kids' listening or viewing habits. And, even in the indulgence mode, perhaps particularly in the indulgence mode, it was hard not to worry at least a bit.

Fourth, whatever the accommodations in practice—despite the fact that most parents were not as anxious as the self-appointed moral guardians—the facts of modern media created an automatic gap between children's and parents' taste that inevitably complicated relationships. Each generation had preferences and levels of tolerance that differed from those the parents have grown up with. This pattern prevailed during the whole century, not just at the end; such was the ineluctable dynamic of media fare. The gap could be managed. It could be cushioned by humor (though, even here, parents had to be careful not to offend, for children did not find their tastes amusing at all). One of the obvious purposes of each successive media wave, from the children's standpoint, was precisely to provide identity and shock value in contrast with parental tastes, that allowed differentiation. Feeling outright anxiety about the results of children's entertainment preferences, parents worried about their lack of control and about barriers to communication.

Yet this was not the whole story. Indeed, this part of the story, particularly the gap between anxiety and enforcement, cannot be understood without the second main component in the contemporary entertainment relationship between parent and child. The need to monitor was challenging enough, as media spun beyond parental authority. The responsibility to entertain, to make sure children were having fun, added to the challenge. Beginning clearly in the 1920s and reaching full articulation in the 1950s, it became important to make sure that children were not bored—a task at least as difficult as trying to make sure that they were not being led astray.

THE LEISURE ETHIC

While the full conversion to what the sociologist Martha Wolfenstein dubbed "fun morality" occurred only in the 1950s, delayed by depression and war, the seeds were clearly planted in the 1920s. It was in the 1920s, for example, that the "play for all" movement developed in the schools, designed to make sure that all children had access to enjoyable activities like sports. While girls were confined to their own sports, with protective rules, the change was actually particularly great for their gender. It was in the 1920s also that, eager to improve family life and particularly to lure fathers into renewed contact with children, the YMCA set up its "Indian Princesses" and "Indian Braves" programs for daughters and sons, respectively. The central concept involved group efforts to help fathers learn to play with the kids, to create a fundamental bond that, in a mother-dominated age, could reintegrate fathers beyond the margins of their children's lives. Parents who could play with their children, so the argument ran, were vital to compensate for the disruptions that urban living caused in family life. And the motto was "friends forever."

A new valuation of fun spilled over into recommendations about dealing with infants. Approaches to masturbation shifted in the advice literature, during the 1920s and 1930s, from regulation and punishment to distraction. To be sure, the anxiety about masturbation itself declined, but this was less significant than the change in methods for coping with infants' impulses. Instead of trying to restrict access, parents should make sure that babies had other things to entertain them. "The baby will not spend much time handling his genitals if he has other interesting things to do." "See that he has a toy to play with and he will not need to use his body as a plaything." Thumbsucking, another previously disciplinary problem, was viewed similarly. A child provided with a suitable range of distractions won't thumbsuck too long—"other interests" will take the place of the disagreeable habit. In practice, of course, this meant a growing use of pacifiers, a modest parental bow to the new plea to keep children happy.[27]

As permissiveness replaced behaviorism, crying was another infant territory that was recharted. Parents should respond to children's cries, but, while checking for physical problems was part of the process, a new awareness of entertainment needs also surfaced strongly. As the 1945 edition of *Infant Care* put it, "A baby sometimes cries because he wants a little more attention. He probably needs a little extra attention under some circumstances just as he sometimes needs a little extra food and water."[28] It was also during these decades that the desire to prevent envy without repression created new recommendations about providing abundant toys and entertainment.

Again, the decades before World War II were transitional. Behaviorists had warned against play that was overstimulating; a father, trying to fit in a romp after work, might cause a "nervous disturbance" that would upset sleep. Childhood could still seem to be serious business, indeed, where character formation and training in work held center stage. As a 1927 author put it, "Mere coddling by making everything easy and pleasant does not build character which can face reality confidently . . . he must build from himself something which gives him fun and satisfaction to do things which would otherwise be a hardship; and equally to refrain at times from conduct which he prefers. . . . The pleasure in overcoming is a genuine and possibly natural pleasure; nevertheless, it needs help and cultivation from without"—in the form of discipline and endurance, and through the valuation of social rather than personal good. And there was a recurrent lament, even from play-friendly authorities, about the excess of goods in modern consumer society. From 1955: "Our modern American children usually have plenty of things to play with, and, provided there are not too many toys and materials, this is a good thing. Surfeiting children with toys, of course, is just as bad as giving them too much of anything else or as depriving them entirely of things to play with."[29]

On balance, however, the pendulum swung steadily toward the importance of play and the responsibility of parents to help provide it. And play, in turn, increasingly came to mean entertainment, at least in part. As a New York *Times* commentator put it, in 1950, "Youngsters today need television for their morale as much as they need fresh air and sunshine for their health." Indulgence was essential at once to keep children happy and to socialize them properly, for an entertained child becomes less demanding, rather than more. Play became part of the child's daily interaction with the parent. "Play and singing make both mother and baby enjoy the routine of life." And, as we have already seen with the make-work-a-game impulse, the corollary was an obligation on the parent's part. "Daily tasks can be done with a little play . . . thrown in." Parents, in turn, were increasingly rated not for their ability to discipline or promote morality but for their good humor and their willingness to keep children amused.[30]

By the 1930s, popular magazines were explicitly urging the importance of training children for leisure. Since "the best recreation in the world is that which contributes to the development of the individual," it was essential to "prepare for leisure . . . in youth." *Collier's* magazine advised parents to "teach your children how to employ their free time fruitfully as well as to work competently and you will add measurably to their chances of happiness." An article in *The Survey* predicted "that the problem of the future will be lessened if attention is focused upon helping youth to form habits in the use of leisure that will carry over into their mature years." Here, obviously, the emphasis was on self-improving leisure, as writers tried to square the circle between a change in American habits and the importance of character, but the cultivation of a major new facet of childhood was significant even with these constraints.[31]

Correspondingly, the definition of a good child shifted, and there was an increasing emphasis on interesting hobbies and a personality demonstrated in part through leisure and fun. Being work-driven child, by 1950, was not enough. Children were expected to have unique talents and "personal magnetism," to be capable, among other things, of talking about their recreations in an interesting way. Applications, including applications for college, broadened to include the need to discuss "extracurricular" activities—which in turn increasingly converted these activities into compulsory agenda of leisure performances in which parental involvement might be essential. Even schoolwork, as Wolfenstein noted, began to incorporate an increasing play element. Textbooks began, by the 1950s, to tout their fun-giving capacity. Thus, a grade-school arithmetic book was called "Range Riders," with a picture of a mounted cowboy on the cover and a subtitle, "Adventures in Numbers." And, sure enough, the problems within were built around horses and cowboys. The scope of the play imperative is obvious: learning should be fun. Less obvious was the implication that the math teacher, like the parent, was now obligated to put on a show.[32]

WHY FUN, AND WHY PARENTAL RESPONSIBILITY?

The emergence of a growing commitment to entertaining children was not, of course, a complete turnaround. Martha Wolfenstein, in her discussion of "fun morality," suggested a stark contrast with earlier, restrictive traditions. It was true that the strictest behaviorists had argued strongly against embellishing childhood with much parental attention, but there is no indication that many parents or popularizers went this far. Certainly, Victorian traditions, though fearful of certain childish impulses, had countenanced childish play and had assumed that parents, particularly mothers, would participate to some degree. So there is no need to seek explanations for some reversal in human nature, parent division.

There was real change, however, both in the extent to which childhood was now associated with enjoyment and in the extent to which parents were held responsible for providing it. Four or five factors combined to produce the change. The rise of explicit, often worried attention to play followed from the changing imagery of childhood, from urbanization and suburbanization, from the decline of work and from the growing, though often grudging, accommodation to the imperatives of schooling. Growing habituation of adults to consumer and leisure values completed the mix.

The growing belief that children were vulnerable, while also cherished, produced some sense that the difficulties and fears of childhood should be compensated by pleasure. Now that a sleepless or anxious child was no longer seen to be at fault and subject to punishment, the idea of providing some joy was, if not inevitable, at least a logical outcome. All the more when the parent slipped and briefly criticized the child; a playful outing might erase the mutual guilt.

This general point was quickly supplemented by a growing belief that children needed play but could not find it spontaneously but safely in the increasingly urban conditions of American life. The dangers of the commercial media had a role here in promoting the need for salutary play alternatives, but there was more. By the 1920s, a number of child-rearing manuals drew a distinction between rural life, in which children could find opportunities to play spontaneously, and urban constraints, where issues of space, safety, and physical health increased the demands on parents. As Irene Seipt noted, in 1955, "If you live in the country or on a farm, it is a very simple matter for children to find things to play with outdoors. In city and suburban areas, try to provide some outdoor toys or equipment which will keep your child and the neighborhood children happily occupied out in the fresh air and sunshine." It was vitally important, at the least, to provide a safe place to play, even when it was assumed that children could then take care of themselves—"Here they can play in complete safety and freedom. . . . Here they should be permitted to keep their priceless collections of boards, boxes, discarded sacks, kitchen utensils and the like, which mean so much to them." And it was not hard, particularly when surrounded by the growing profusions of a consumer society, to assume that more was due, including far more elaborate, parentally sponsored toys. The challenge was, on the whole, intensified with the spread of suburbanization, particularly after World War II. The suburban movement responded in part to a desire to have play spaces for children in the form of spacious yards, one of the goals cited by the play experts in the 1920s as an antidote to excessive urbanism. But suburban yards were often isolated, limiting the capacity of children to join in the kind of spontaneous cohorts that had earlier formed in small-town America. At the least, parental responsibility for driving children to more organized play sites could feed the sense of a wider obligation to provide entertainment.[33]

Parental obligations increased for one other structural reason, though this was not often noted explicitly: the decline in the number of siblings and, often, increased tensions between those siblings who did coexist. The extent to which brothers and sisters helped entertain packs of siblings, even in the urban upper middle class, as late as the 1890s, is quite striking, as various memoirs and diaries suggest. But, with smaller, tenser cohorts, and also with the increasing emphasis on the importance of strict age-grading in play, this alternative declined. The need to provide play, often in part to distract a rivalrous pair, grew accordingly.

The impulse toward greater parental responsibility was heightened in turn by two assumptions about children's proclivities in the modern world: first, that, when underentertained, they could get into unprecedented trouble, and, second, and more important, that appropriate entertainment was vital to educational development and ultimate school success. In both these categories, children could not in fact take care of themselves, even in their own space, but required explicit adult provision.

The delinquency argument cropped up with increasing frequency as public fears grew, from the 1920s into the 1950s and beyond. Dreikurs posed the problem in alarmist tones, in a 1968 offering: a group of teenagers destroyed power lines in a Midwestern city, offering as an alibi "They were 'bored' and didn't know what to do about it." The manual drove the point further: "At this point, no home in America can be considered exempt. No parent today can safely feel that none of his children might become one of these vandals." Providing entertainment could be a crusade against children's propensities for evil. And, even if this fear was dismissed as extremist, the broader point, that parentally provided play was vital to children's psychological health, to their ability to cope with otherwise festering emotions, was widely accepted, in the popular literature, from the 1920s on. Seipt again: "We can learn a great deal about our children through watching their play. Indeed, psychiatrists and educators have developed so-called 'play therapy,' which often helps children to attain a better emotional balance and an improved attitude toward the world around them." The point here was twofold: children needed play, and parents were actively responsible for providing and monitoring that play.[34]

Play, in fact, became a contemporary equivalent for work, preventing the kind of idleness that the devil could find, in the form of crime or of psychological imbalance. With children's work declining, parentally sponsored entertainment stepped in to take up the slack.

Delinquency arguments, picked up by ordinary parents, figured strongly in the growing support for the rapid expansion of Little League baseball in the 1950s—in turn a substantial commitment of parental time in the days before soccer moms. Little League teams had 11,800 participants in 1949, 334,300 by 1958, and more than a million by 1964. Several factors entered in, including white-collar fathers' delight at finding a new way to bond with their sons, and there was a great deal of blatant commercial sponsorship. But parents' growing delinquency fears were central. As one parent—also an FBI agent—put it, baseball helped boys stay clean "by channeling the efforts . . . into wholesome recreation rather than mischievousness and acts of vandalism." Parentally sponsored baseball was also preventative against sexual crimes, another 1950s fear that experts pinned on an "unwholesome family and social atmosphere" and in which, as a leading psychotherapist put it, "the fault lies with the parents." In reaction, Little League fathers not only took their sons to practices and games and ardently cheered them on but also spent vast amounts of time building ballfields and otherwise devoting themselves to this new target for parenting.[35]

The schooling message was even more strident in justifying new responsibilities for leisure. Of course, many parents doubtless believed that their entertainment obligation stemmed in part from the burdens that contemporary schooling placed on children, particularly given Americans' ambivalence about intellectual endeavor and the sense that schooling might overwhelm frail children. But the official connection, and one that clearly struck home as well, involved the importance of play in stimulating learning, exploration, and creativity. This was a theme that had been sounded in the first wave of consumerism, around 1800, when middle-class parents began buying specific books and toys for their children's educational benefit, and by the 1920s it began to expand greatly, with increasing attention to the now-crucial early years. "Children learn through play. . . . Very early in a baby's life, play is something he enjoys. Parents can enjoy their children's play. You can take advantage of your child's interest and delight in play by gently directing it so that it can count in his development." Play, in other words, was natural but needed guidance to pay off, a characteristic waffling that highlighted children's and parental responsibility alike. Another manual, by Langdon and Stout, featured the same amalgam: "Play is natural to all children. It is the way in which they get acquainted with the world around them. Even if your child has a physical handicap it is still natural for him to play." But this comment was preceded by a twelve-page chapter that told parents how to organize children's play, with detailed lists of appropriate items and activities to make sure that all the functions of play could be carried forward: healthy exercise, creativity, motor skills, inquiry, social play to teach interaction with others. Therefore, parental obligations were several: to provide "a variety of toys with which to carry on his (the child's) interests," changing with every new developmental stage; to organize play to make sure that children could encounter new situations and other people ("making sure he carried out . . . [his] interests in different ways at different times") and, finally, to use play as a family bond, participating in it actively. Particularly because of its crucial developmental role, arranging play was a basic parental function, "providing for it as one provides for eating, sleeping, and all the other family doings."[36]

A double-edged quality could emerge when school readiness was added to the functions of children's play. There was a more than sneaking suspicion that schooling could be dull, which could prompt some parents to seek compensatory entertainment in the off-hours as their contribution to making the burdens of childhood more endurable. But there was a suspicion, as well, that the child who did not take to schooling had somehow been ill prepared by parents. One expert sought to dismiss parents' wishful thinking that a child turned off to school was too smart: "It [lack of interest] usually occurs because a child is noncreative in using opportunities which are almost always available in a well-conceived school situation." And this most likely meant that the child had not been sufficiently stimulated before he even got to school.[37]

All this—the worries about urbanism, psychological adjustment, and learning readiness—accumulated during decades in which adults themselves were enjoying increased opportunities for commercial entertainment, making it natural for them to seek to share some of their interests with their children and to believe that successful adulthood now included the capacity to enjoy oneself and to project a personality with active leisure interests. Wolfenstein suggested that fun morality involved obligations—"obligatoriness"—in the adult world, beyond provision for children: adults who lacked a recreational life might well wonder, in a consumerist culture, what was wrong with them. A growing emphasis on having a "pleasing personality"—another general cultural current that began in the 1920s on—included the capacity to present interesting avocations, as well as the ability (particularly on women's part) to encourage others to display versatility in their own self-presentation. Amy Vanderbilt put the point clearly, in her 1950s etiquette book: "people are always at their best . . . talking about themselves and their interests," and the capacity has to be honed early by an appropriate range of leisure activities. If adults were to begin to measure themselves by play—as they were now encouraged to do in job and school applications—it was imperative that they train their children appropriately. The growing commitment to children's entertainment reflected not only a desire to share the fruits of family prosperity but also to share the burden of measuring up to a new standard. As the rueful question "Are we having fun yet?" implied, there were both goals and measurements that adults could easily apply to their children and to their assessment of their own adequacy as parents. As consumerism exploded, advertisers and sales outlets were only too ready to make sure parents were aware that this or that new product or entertainment form was an essential component of a happy, well- adjusted childhood.[38]

And there was a final factor, impossible to quantify but very real: as parents became more engaged in adult social activities, as in the 1920s; as mothers went out to work, as in the 1950s and 1960s; or as parents became more likely to divorce, the guilt element clearly enhanced parents' desire to entertain in compensation. Because children were seen as needing fun for so many reasons, and because the lures of general commercialism were so great, guilt easily factored into the redefinition of good parenting.

THE TRANSFORMATION OF BOREDOM

Along with the heightened anxiety about children's psychological well-being and school success, the growing commitment to keeping children entertained was the clearest addition to parental burdens after 1945. The real revolution in attitudes toward boredom captured the shift.

Quite simply, boredom increasingly mutated, after the late 1940s, from being an attribute of personality that needed attention to being an inflicted state that demanded correction by others. The importance of boredom increased in this process, along with its growing association with childhood. Children were easily bored, and, while the condition might lead to an impoverished personality in later life, the responsibility for dealing with it did not lie with children themselves. Rather, parents and schools were at fault, and it was with them that the remedy must be sought.

Parents and popularizing experts alike began raising the question of boredom explicitly. The contrast with child-rearing manuals earlier in the century was striking. The traditional manual mentioned boredom not at all. The only exception, in a 1928 offering, really proved the rule, in that bored children were "usually those who are over-stimulated and over-corrected"; while parents were asked to "modify the underlying cause," the correction would not clearly involve a higher quotient of entertainment.

Not so the commentary of the 1950s. A 1952 manual, by James Hymes, commented elaborately on the convenient excuse of blaming someone else for a child's boredom—it's the school, or too much television, or even the child himself. Not so: almost certainly, parents are at fault. "This soul-searching is the last thing we come to, yet each of us is a part of the environment children live it. Each of us makes children act the way they do." So the child who whined and moaned, whether at home or at school, now became a commentary on parental adequacy.[39]

There were a number of corollaries. The boredom-with-learning situation was one. "My five-year-old doesn't seem to take an interest. . . . Does this mean he is less intelligent than most children? How can I arouse his interest?" "There are many reasons besides lack of intelligence. . . . Is it possible that he does not feel sure of your interest, that you seem to him too busy and preoccupied with his small affairs? Surely you must have noticed some things which arouse his interest."[40]

A child's boredom when sick now came in for explicit comment—the situation was not new, but the need for discussion was indicative of the new parental range. "All the while that Mother was trying to get her work done that insistent little voice kept calling, 'Mommy, I haven't got something to do.'" And then the followup—a list of things that parents could do to entertain their bedridden children.

Or the rainy day: "Six-year-old Ellen, facing a long rainy Saturday, asked her mother plaintively, 'What shall I do.'" And the mother, concerned about unsuitable television fare, but needing to tend to two smaller children, had to take on an extra entertainment task. Again, the dutiful manual writer went on to list of series of activities parents could help arrange to answer the rainy-day plea.[41]

Dr. Spock, to be sure, was a bit less tolerant, criticizing a whining child for pestering about something to do "when she herself could easily have found remedies for these small needs." But Spock was also eager to make sure that children were interested in their own activities, at school or at home, and to this extent raised the ante for parental self-scrutiny.[42]

Comments on children's boredom could, of course, range farther afield; they might reflect even more clearly not only the anxiety about the mind-numbing aspects of some of the most commercial entertainments for kids but also adults' own concern that life had become too prosaic. "What is wrong with so many men and women of today? Why are they so afraid of time in which there is nothing to do? Why do they go to the pictures so often? Why do they play cards night after night? . . . Surely it is, in most cases, because of the poverty of their inner life; because they have found no channel into which they can pour their whole personality, thereby satisfying a natural emotional need." The problem was part of modern life, but it began in childhood, which meant in turn an added need for parents and schools "to enable each child to discover himself, to gain that self-confidence which comes through his finding out his particular ability." The attack on boredom here related directly to the concern for school success. As a 1951 book stated, "Interests come about both directly and indirectly through schooling and special training . . . and through having an opportunity to follow through on things that catch the child's attention." Boredom and achievement did not mix.[43]

By the 1960s and 1970s, scholarly studies of children's boredom followed on the heels of parental and popularizer concerns. Schools came under new scrutiny. Debate continued over whether bright children were bored in school, and, if so, whether the result contributed to delinquency or drug taking. Boredom among children in poor or minority families received special attention and was blamed for their behavior problems and school tensions. Even here, however, children themselves were not its fault but rather the combination of family and school approaches that failed to engage. Boredom was a social ailment, but the remedies lay mainly with individual adults.

Most obviously, the transformation of boredom and the related escalation of public discussion created a situation in which parents and children alike found the state a reasonable measure of a child's welfare. Childhood had not necessarily become more boring overall, but in one sense it clearly had, as the capacity to label boredom, and to judge accordingly, automatically escalated the evaluation. A few settings, like school (sometimes) or automobile rides, became particular targets for children's boredom claims, but the random half-day with nothing planned or the off time when there was "nothing on TV" could be

equally provocative. Boredom and childhood became widely associated, and not only in schools—and the result, in turn, was a clear challenge to parents. A 2001 cartoon, in a typical case, shows a family reaching a lakeside vacation cabin where the mother had spent her summers
as a child. She's delighted, but the kids immediately notice that there's
no television, no special activities. The oldest child immediately notes,
"I'm bored," while the youngest starts crying; the husband joins the pa-
rade, asking how many days they will have to commit: the mother,
who'd decided on the whole plan, in the name of quality family time, is
clearly at fault for an unacceptable lack of real entertainment.[44] Boredom was bad, a legitimate source of concern about an idle half-day and,
in the longer haul, harmful to a child's development; children had the
right and the ability to judge when they were bored; and someone, most
likely a parent, often a mother, should clearly respond. It was as simple
as that.

INTENSIFICATIONS IN THE BATTLE AGAINST BOREDOM

The steady upsurge in children's consumerism, including recreations, is
hardly a new historical finding. All of us, regardless of our age, have
lived the change, whether our point of reference is the 1930s or the
1980s. A few reminders nevertheless drive the theme home. The need to
keep children entertained and, often, to buy things or services in order
to do so is a fruit not only of growing marketing aimed at children but
also of growing parental commitment to the provision of fun. There is
no reason to debate which came first, the commercialism or the redefinition of parenting: they symbiotically intertwine.

Take some simple activities, like birthday parties or eating. Into the
1950s, children's birthday parties (a 19th- century innovation) were
usually self-contained, with friends invited (often too many) to enjoy
homemade games and dessert. By the 1960s, it was increasingly realized that the parties risked being boring, to both honoree and guests. So
a variety of commercial or nonprofit-but-for-fee supplements arose,
from the lure of cheap games and pizza and massive noise, as at Chuck
E Cheese, to the strange joys of laser tag, to group attendance at amusement parks and museums. The trend toward enhancing parties with
special entertainment was obvious. The burdens on parents increased
in the process, at least in terms of finance and transportation.

Or eating: the rise of frequent family dining out began in the 1950s, with the proliferation of pizza parlors and the decision by McDonald's to convert fast-food operations to family fare. The role of kids and the importance of their definitions of enjoyable eating increased accordingly. But there was more: for young children, eating must also be associated with additional sources of fun, with the provision of playgrounds and an endless series of tie-in products and games, usually based on movie fare. By 2001, more than a third of all the toys distributed to children, mostly at the low end, were given out at fast-food restaurants. Without question, commercialism ran rampant as entertainment moguls realized that an item featured in one place, such as a movie theater, could sell goods at a fast-food emporium, and vice versa. But another factor was the driving need to provide fun, for which eating itself might not suffice.[45]

Car trips, a classic site for boredom, were embellished by the 1980s with specific products to keep kids entertained, including more elaborate games, portable CD players, and video systems.

The same evolution applied to vacations. For the middle and upper classes, the idea of a family vacation went well back into the 19th century. Characteristically, mother and children packed off to the countryside or seaside, with fathers visiting on the weekends or for other shorter stints away from work. The goal was family solidarity and a relief from the urban environment. Children's pleasure was part of the package, and at some resorts the development of boardwalk activities, copied from England, added explicit entertainments. Often, however, and particularly in lakeside or mountain resorts or cabins, the contrived entertainment aspect was modest or nonexistent: the main point was to provide a distinctive, healthy setting in which children could devise their own amusements. A strong emphasis on vacations as a source of improvement, certainly to health but often to knowledge, as well, with trips to nature or historical sites, also diluted the attention to children's fun.

This changed after World War II. Growing prosperity enabled more Americans to take vacations, though the nation never converted to the extensive vacation ethic that began to emerge in Western Europe. Taking the family along provided one of the key justifications for time off in a society in which a rigorous work ethic remained deeply entrenched. But taking the family along increasingly involved more than just having the children on the trip, it meant targeting sites that had explicit entertainments for children, that indeed often placed children's entertainments at the center of the whole experience. The Disney complexes, first in California, then in Florida, became the nation's number one vacation destination, which meant in turn that children's entertainment had become the most salient criterion in choosing a vacation spot. The Disney parks were quickly supplemented by other theme parks, which built an earlier American innovation, the amusement park, into a vacation experience, and by the complexes organized by movie studios, both in Florida and California. Families could now spend days surrounded by childlike, some would say childish, rides and exhibits, with a dual predicate: first, that kids deserved elaborate commercial entertainment, rather than providing their own fun, and, second, that these goals were preeminent in family vacation decisions. And the commitments continued to accelerate. By 1999, 309 million Americans attended theme parks, an increase of 22 percent in the 1990s alone, with the middle class in the lead.

Other adult roles as they related to children changed at this time. Grandparents, no longer likely to reside within a household full of young children, became increasingly known for their entertainment value, bringing gifts and relating to children by taking them to more entertainments than busy parents could often manage. Grandparenting was not a matter of fun alone, but the linkage became increasingly common. *Parents Magazine*, between the 1920s and the 1970s, clearly suggests the transition from grandparents as sources of multigenerational wisdom to grandparents as playmates.

Fathers, who had begun to emphasize being pals with their children in the 1920s, often upped the ante. During visitations after divorce, fathers frequently were consumed with their need to provide fun and games as an expression both of their own guilt at not being around more often and of the larger belief in this aspect of contemporary responsibility. Trips to ballgames, amusement parks, and movies combined with gifts of toys and snacks as father-impresarios tried to cram pleasures into a weekend that the father-pal of their imagination would spread over a month. Quite commonly, even apart from divorce, fathers began to be rated the more entertaining parent by children themselves. But the style was catching, and many a divorced woman found herself trying to compensate by providing a regular diet of entertainment treats.

Parents acceded to a growing array of children's perceived leisure needs in the final decades of the 20th century. They increased allowances so that children could attend the summer glut of films directed explicitly at childish tastes. They bought a growing array of toys. In some cases, they admitted children into decisions about family purchases that had leisure implications, such as the type of car selected. Christmases became ever more elaborate rituals of consumer profusion, with the bulk of attention and expense usually devoted to making sure the children were abundantly provided for. In 1997, the average child received gifts worth $365 for Christmas; this figure rose to $900 in affluent areas, with grandparents often rivaling parents for display. The varied array of opportunities reflected not just growing prosperity but the growing desire to meet a major criterion of contemporary parenthood.[46]

ANOMALIES AND ACCOMMODATIONS

The commitment to organize children's leisure and to provide fun helps explain two of the ironies of anxious parenting mentioned earlier: driving and diets.

The anxious focus on children's frailty could have provoked a tough stance toward teenage driving, with demanding license tests and training requirements. In fact, of course, the United States was notoriously lenient, compared, for example, to Western Europe. Kids were expected to learn to drive easily and early, and, with rare exceptions, they did so, despite their relatively high accident rates. American affluence made provision of driving opportunities, and sometimes personal cars, seem logical. Poor public transportation in the suburbs augmented the need. Driving was part of ensuring older children's access to pleasure and entertainment. Restriction simply would have been too difficult, given the assumption that access to entertainment outside the home was virtually a birthright. The result was a period of immense ambivalence for many parents. Children's licensed driving provided welcome relief from the chauffeuring obligations of contemporary parenthood. But it also occasioned tremendous anxiety, at least for many months, as parents checked nervously on their children's safe return from the latest encounter with the highways.

The failure to do much about children's eating habits, even as evidence of childhood obesity mounted in the last three decades of the 20th century, was slightly more complex, but it, too, reflected the overweening commitment to children's pleasure. The fact was that middle-class parents, despite growing concern about adult weight patterns from the 1890s on, did surprisingly little to restrict children's intake. Nor, until the 1970s, did experts prod them very much. Medical and insurance advice was filled with comments about weight gains in adults, and diet programs blossomed by the 1920s. But attention to children's overeating was almost nonexistent for decades, and, when it did emerge, in the 1970s, parents paid it little heed. Again, the contrast with Western Europe was intriguing. In France, experts and many parents operated from the assumption that children did not choose foods wisely on their own; careful training in eating habits, portions, and times was essential. Snacking was discouraged, as even Euro Disney would discover to its fiscal dismay when it first opened its doors. And, in Europe, obesity problems in childhood were indeed uncommon.

There were two primary reasons, both operating in a commercial context in which purveyors of junk foods eagerly and directly solicited a childhood audience, that overeating was not widely recognized as a childhood problem in the United States. First, American parents continued to focus their attention on the underweight child long after this ceased to represent the predominant problem. Anxiety about eating there was, but it took on more traditional targets. Plumpness, in babies and children, continued to be associated with good health. The Depression, with its images of emaciated children, encouraged this focus, as did news of starving children abroad. For boys, the availability of sports like football, where heft was at a premium, further promoted attention to abundant eating. For girls, by the later part of the century, widely publicized reports of anorexia nervosa similarly encouraged parents to continue to believe that their main obligation was to encourage eating, not to guide it.

Tolerance of children's eating habits also resulted from the real commitment to providing pleasure. It was so easy to think of food as a legitimate reward for being a child when a parent was too busy to offer more elaborate entertainments or felt guilty about not having enough time to spend. At the least, the weekly shopping cart could be loaded with sugary drinks and fat-coated chips and cookies. Not surprisingly, as pressures to provide pleasure continued to intensify even as adult commitments to work increased in the final decades of the century, the incidence of childhood obesity mounted. It was hard, in the American context, to frame this trend as one of the childhood vulnerabilities that made parents truly anxious. Elemental pleasure was more important.

The most systematic result of the obligation to entertain showed, of course, in the clash with the concerns about the quality of commercial fare for children, for both impulses were very real. Quite clearly, many parents decided that, given the need to offer fun, a substantial dollop of commercialism was preferable to regulation and denial of commercial fare. And this, along with the power of commercial interests in politics, helps explain the substantial failure of one reform effort after another. Worries did not disappear, and many parents did make substantial efforts to square the circle, providing entertainment that was relatively free of commercial taint. But the clash of goals was undeniable, and, on the whole, fun won out.

Most popular child-rearing manuals encouraged an accommodating stance, at least up to a point, without, however, letting parents off the hook. Dorothy Baruch, for example, explicitly took issue with the regulators, noting that radio programs, comics, and movies, though "far from desirable," were not the "cause of the aggression in our youngsters." She did insist that parents must provide "active outlets" to get children's feelings out; this would automatically lessen the "pull of the comics" or the radio shows. But there was no reason to prevent or punish exposure to commercial entertainment, and, by implication, a bit of access would do no particular harm. Children, indeed, needed to develop the skills to handle media signals if they were to become law-abiding members of society. Seipt was even more tolerant. "Of course, too much listening to radio and too much TV could be harmful for children, as anything can be harmful that is indulged in to excess. But mothers and fathers can, and I believe they should, exercise supervision over the programs which their children listen to and see." For there was no real way to prevent exposure, if not in one's own home, then in the homes of friends; guidance, and provision of periodic alternatives, was the key. And there were some very good programs, which had the additional merit of "keeping the attention of the children engaged" while Mother was preparing supper. The implication was, of course, that while a bow to the reality of maternal duties was essential, at other times mothers might be more active. Finally, however, fun was all right:

"You did not bring the radio or television set into your home to be an agency for teaching. You meant it for pleasure for all the family, and that is what it should be." Seipt took a similar stance with comics, urging parents to make sure children did other reading but exercising some tolerance otherwise: "A moderate amount of comic-book reading will not hurt a growing child if you, Mother or Father, will exercise some control over the quality and quantity of this reading."[47]

Most parents clearly agreed with this approach, finding television or other commercial entertainments a vital outlet, for example, when a child was alone or the weather bad. The need to entertain had to override the strictest purism, save in a very few heroic households (of which there were just enough to make more tolerant parents nervous). But there were problems attached: how much was too much, and was the parent exercising enough supervision about program choice? Was there sufficient effort to provide healthier, more educational alternatives?

Some manuals took a stricter approach, thus maintaining the tension that most parents felt at least to some degree. Sidonie Gruenberg, in 1958, offered a long chapter on play for "your active boys and girls." While Gruenberg urges the importance of teaching children how to enjoy themselves, acknowledging that "what we do with our leisure time is what makes life worth living," her whole emphasis is on developing "the active, absorbing interests that can enrich their lives now as well as later." No passive entertainment here, because good leisure was self-improving, active leisure. Television was not in the cards, though it should be preempted rather than banned. In one example, mother faced her six-year-old on a rainy Saturday. Television was an option, but the mother "did not think it good for a child to sit hypnotized before the screen for hours on end." So she suggested making Christmas cards instead and simply turned over the rest of her own day to this activity. "It was [the daughter's] happy introduction to the planning and giving side of Christmas, and it led her to new skills and creative experiences she had never tried before." Gruenberg admits that these activities are not always possible but says there are hobbies, reading, museums—a host of things parents can share to instill their own best leisure interests in their children. The bulk of the chapter focuses on how to provide in organizing skills, the materials needed for constructive play, and hosts of lessons that will give children "fun," which is what they most want, while adding value. Subsections detail how to draw children into art lessons (with the elaborate materials that would support this interest);

music lessons (including how to keep interest lively enough to maintain a practice schedule by keeping "the fun of music alive"—a joint responsibility of teacher and parents); collecting and other hobbies; craft and skill with tools; and sports training and opportunities. The chapter ends with a page and a half on parties, noting that they often turn into disappointments unless parents keep the guest list small and the activities to be provided simple in comparison to the really elaborate injunctions that accompany the lessons and hobbies rubrics. This is entertainment with a purpose, and parental guidance is fundamental to launching and sustaining healthy interests.[48]

Few parents approximated this degree of seriousness, but many approached the model. From the 1920s on, reports of highly programmed children surfaced in the middle class as parents, particularly mothers, shuttled them from school to lesson to lesson in search of genuine but noncommercial leisure. Parallel studies in the 1970s and again the 1990s showed that mothers played a disproportionate role not only in taking care of organized leisure activities (67 percent of soccer parents in the 1990s were mothers) but also in choosing the activities in the first place. Mothers made 60 percent of all selections of recreational services, according to one study, with fathers and children about equal in their minority shareholder roles. While children had slightly greater voice in a final decision—perhaps helping to decide which tennis coach or piano teacher to select—neither they nor their satisfaction counted much concerning the types of lessons to be imposed. Nor did their satisfaction count much in parents' assessment of whether the leisure activities were fruitful, and parents in this context routinely misconstrued children's reactions.

A mixture of activities was common as parents selected certain activities with their own goals in mind but then felt obliged to sponsor more passive entertainment fare as well, to reward and compensate. Small wonder that research on the role of children's or family leisure in parental satisfaction generated complex results. On the one hand, shared leisure could be genuinely pleasurable; it is important, once again, not to overplay the anxiety theme. Many parents delighted in children's fun and relived some of their own childlike joys in the process. Revealingly, however, mothers were unlikely to rate family leisure time as leisure, for their sense of responsibility and sheer busyness overrode the enjoyable elements. Fathers, with a smaller overall role but one in which leisure provided a larger component of the connection with children, reacted more positively: sharing in children's leisure was a definite plus. For mothers, however, the definition of leisure as freedom from normal constraint simply did not apply, for the level of obligation manifestly increased when children were at play.[49]

CONCLUSION

The twin worries about children's leisure—guarding against commercial corruption and ensuring a level of entertainment that would ward off boredom—loomed large in 20th-century parenting. Compromises reduced parents' anxiety, and parents who relaxed on television and snacking avoided some of the day-to-day worries of the active impresario. The redefinition of childhood to include some fun morality could promote fruitful interactions—for example, between fathers and children—and could develop children's leisure capabilities in ways that would enliven adulthood. The change in orientation was significant. It unquestionably promoted new sets of worries and almost unresolvable tensions. But it could be managed.

Still, there were some intriguing twists. Summer was redefined, for many parents, into a time of unusual stress. With children not committed to much work, at least until they could seek employment on their own account, the question of what to do with the kids with their release from school became truly pressing. Entertainment obligations, further fueled by nostalgic imagery of the summer as a special time for children's fun, added to the pressure. The increasingly child-oriented family vacation was one clear response, and it could at best truly generate family bonds and memories, reducing parental guilt in the process. But the amount of vacation time tended to stagnate in the United States, which left the rest of the summer a yawning gap, a prime opportunity for the bored child to vent his discontent. An amazing proliferation of camps filled the breach to some degree. Camps offered parents the satisfaction of providing entertainment without requiring personal involvement, save in paying the often impressive bills, while being assured that their children would have a worthy leisure experience. For camps not only promoted contacts with nature but also built into hectic daily schedules exactly the mix of hobbies, crafts, arts, and sports that the best self-improvement manuals recommended.

Yet even camps rarely filled the entire space, and for the remainder there was little alternative but to relent on more commercial options, sponsoring trips to increasingly tasteless movies or whatever fare could limit the boredom. The new and expanding obligation to entertain exposed parents to the most direct evaluation of their adequacy by children themselves. Combined with other adult commitments, the result could be a barely controlled frenzy.

A symbol of the year 2000 was revealed by the perfecting of mechanical devices to catch drivers who ran red lights. The most frequent violators by far were parents, usually mothers, racing to pick up their children from a game or lesson or speeding to the next delivery. It was hard to keep up, but vital to try.

The commitment to provide quality leisure ratcheted up among the middle class in the 1980s and 1990s with more organized activities, particularly for grade schoolers. Time and money spent on lessons and groups soared, despite—but really because of—the fact that parents were also spending more hours on the job.

Play is an understudied topic, but it is exceedingly complex. In a classic essay, *Homo Ludens*, Johanna Huizinga rails against modern forces that are destroying play as a spontaneously creative, social act, even among children, who have greatest feel for play. Critics of mass culture debate the subject, as well. What should play be? Are we destroying it with passive commercial entertainment on the one hand and restrictive, work-oriented self-improvement on the other?

Often unwittingly, in daily decisions about children's leisure, 20th-century parents have participated in the complexities of the debate. They have not resolved it, any more than they have in their own leisure lives. The voices of children themselves, with their own, though sometimes manipulated, ideas of fun and their laments about boredom, add to the uncertainty. No sudden crisis here, to be sure, but a recurrent sense of doubt and parental self-criticism.

FURTHER READING

Lisa Jacobson, "Revitalizing the American Home: Children's Leisure and the Revaluation of Play, 1920–1940," *Journal of Social History* 30 (1997): 581–97. On consumerism more generally, Peter N. Stearns, *Consumerism in World History: The Global Transformation of Desire* (New York, 2001). Roland Marchand, *Advertising the American Dream: Making Way* for *Modernity* (Berkeley, 1985). There is surprisingly little work on the history of boredom, with the important exception of Patricia Spacks, *Boredom: The Literary History of a State of Mind* (Chicago, 1995), which brilliantly uncovers the initial context for the concept. The discussion offered in this chapter suggests the main lines of a follow-up history on one of the real emotional forces in modern life. See also Richard P. Smith, "Boredom: A Review," *Human Factors* 23 (1981): 329–40; Orrin Klapp, *Overload and Boredom: Essays on the Quality of Life in the Information Society* (Westport, CT, 1986); Franz Hetzel, ed., *Boredom: Root of Discontent and Aggression* (Berkeley, 1975); Haskell Bernstein, "Boredom and the Ready-Made Life," *Social Research* 42 (1975): 512–37.

On commercial recreations and media and their critics: Steven Starker, *Evil Influences: Crusades against the Mass Media* (New Brunswick, NJ, 1989) is a splendid overview. See also Amy Nyberg, *Seal of Approval: The History of the Comic Code* (Jackson, MS, 1998); James Gilbert, *A Cycle of Outrage: America's Reaction to the Juvenile Delinquent in the 1950s* (New York, 1986); E. E. Dennis and Edward Pease, *Children and the Media* (New Brunswick, NJ, 1996); Diane Levin, *Remote Control Childhood* (New York, 1997); George Comstock and Haejung Paik, *Television and the American Child* (San Diego, 1991); Madeline Levine, *Viewing Violence: How Media Violence Affects Your Child's and Adolescent's Development* (New York, 1996); Jens Waltermann and Marcel Machill, eds., *Protecting Our Children on the Internet* (Guetersloh, 2000); Donald Roberts, "Adolescents and the Mass Media," *Teachers College Record* 94 (1993): 629–44; Jeanne Funk, Geysa Flores, Debra Buchman, and Julie Germann, "Rating Electronic Games," *Youth and Society* 30 (1999): 283–312; Robert Liebert, John Neale, and Emily Davidson, *The Early Window: Effects of Television on Children and Youth* (New York, 1973); Rochelle Gurstein, *Repeal of Reticence* (New York, 1996); Marie Winn, *Children without Childhood: Growing Up Too Fast in the World of Sex and Drugs* (Harmondsworth, UK, 1984); Peter Baldwin, "'Nocturnal Habits and Dark Wisdom': The American Response to Children in the Streets at Night," *Journal of Social History* 35 (2002).

On parents and play, Martha Wolfenstein, "The Emergence of Fun Mortality," *Journal of American Sociology* (1951): 15–25; Dennis Howard and Robert Madrigal, "Who Makes the Decision: The Parent or the Child? The Perceived Influence and Parents and Children on the Purchase of Recreation Services," *Journal of Leisure Research* 22 (1990): 244–58; Karla Henderson, "A Feminist Analysis of Selected Professional

Recreation Literature about Girls/Women from 1907–1990," *Journal of Leisure Research* 25 (1993): 165–81; B. C. Green, "Enduring Involvement in Youth Soccer: The Socialization of Parents and Child," *Journal of Leisure Research* 29 (1997): 61–77; Claude Fischer, "Changes in Leisure Activities, 1890–1940," *Journal of Social History* (1994): 453–96.

On children and commercial recreation: David Nasaw, *Coming Out: The Rise and Fall of Public Amusements* (Cambridge, MA, 1993); Cindy Aron, *Working at Play: A History of Vacations in the United States* (New York, 1999); Peter N. Stearns, *Fat History: Bodies and Beauty in the Modern West* (New York, 1997); Lance Van Auken and Robin Van Auken, *Play Ball! The History of Little League Baseball* (State College, PA, 2001).

7

Conclusion

The Impact of Anxiety

THERE HAVE BEEN great joys in 20th-century parenting. No history of new anxieties should becloud this crucial truth. Some of the pleasures attach directly to the distinctive styles developed during the course of the century. The effort to share more in children's leisure can be immensely rewarding, an obvious point confirmed by research on parental satisfaction. While worry can dim a recognition of childish wonder, many parents preserve or even enhance their appreciation of their children's curiosity. The growing commitment to schooling raises concern about children's progress, but it can yield great pride when children achieve. Many men have found the reconnection with children and with child rearing a true blessing that adds considerably to the rewards of life. While fathers vary greatly in their commitment, and while sometimes their involvement may be forced or stressful, their pleasure can be quite real. On another front, while parental concerns about children's health are fierce, and the guilt for major illness tremendous, the normal relief from child mortality is tremendous for contemporary parents compared to parents at any other time in history.

There is great variety in 20th-century parenting, which means that anxieties vary, as well. A father drops a son off for his freshman year at college, tearfully pleading with a university orientation official to take care of his treasure. Another father, same scenario, cheerfully drops his child off and tells the same official, "See you in four years." No history of anxiety should omit this vital divergence in level of parental worry. Parenting styles are not defined by some blanket, uniform anxiety.

Nor, finally, is parental anxiety the greatest problem in the story of 20th-century American childhood. For many groups, structural factors clearly outweigh it; poverty and racial discrimination have had far greater impact in distorting many childhood experiences. The expansion in the number of American children living below the poverty line during the 1980s and early 1990s (up to a full quarter of the total) makes it clear that anxiety about children has not led to consistently solicitous national policies—which means, again, that anxiety itself should not be overrated as a factor in directly shaping childhood experiences.

But the anxiety has been palpable, nevertheless, affecting childhood and, even more, adult experience alike. From Rudolf Dreikurs, in 1958: "the situation is especially difficult when love for one's child is mingled with anxiety. Discouraged individuals are prone to overestimate the frailty of human nature and the hostility of the surrounding world. When they become parents, they are doubly anxious about their offspring. . . . Every moment holds the threat of dangers, and [many parents] are unwilling to face any risks. Parents are attached to their children, and the loss of a child would be a dreadful blow to any one of them. . . . You may live in constant fear of neglecting some important aspect of your duty, and magnify every little fault of your child until it seems a sure sign of his ultimate ruin." But, in typical expert fashion, Dreikurs combines an effort at reassurance with another attack on parental self- confidence: "Excessive concern over the child's welfare is a personality fault." And: "There is no doubt that most parents feel keenly their inadequacy in their relations with their children." Indecision and oscillation between excessive praise for a precious child and anxious criticism of his deficiencies typically reveal their "most striking expression" in widespread parental nervousness. Hence the great need for many parents to seek advice, perhaps themselves to undergo counseling, but hence also some serious doubts that any remedy can really heal the underlying anxiety.[1]

From historians of 20th-century advice literature: Michael Zuckerman, writing about Dr. Spock's success as a popularizer: "in one sense, there is nothing unusual at all in the modern American obsession with child-rearing. Americans have been ill at ease about the younger generation, and preoccupied with it, for centuries. But in another sense there is something odd indeed about this extravagant anxiety. Few parents anywhere have ever put themselves as hugely and hopefully in the hands of child-care counselors as American parents of the aspiring classes have in the twentieth century. And few parents anywhere have ever had so hard a time raising their children." This is a strong claim, but one that is easily supported by evidence from the various categories of parental worry and by the fundamental attachment to the new idea of the child as vulnerable, compounded by belief in the child as precious.[2]

During the 20th century, American parents bought one copy of *Infant Care* and, after the mid–1940s, one copy of Dr. Spock for every first child born. And this is not to mention the vast array of other advice titles, many of them with healthy sales. The advice was needed because parents worried so. But, on the whole, the experts compounded the worry. The behaviorists told parents that children could easily be damaged beyond repair. They disagreed about what the right course of action was, exacerbating parents' anxiety. Even Dr. Spock, who countered the behaviorists with a more positive valuation of children's nature, continued to invoke the specter of "parental ruination" often enough to remind parents to their tremendous responsibility. A single angry or thoughtless word might undermine the child's confidence and set him on a downward spiral "forever." A single incident could be devastating: a 1959 manual, largely written in a permissive tone, told of a child who woke up to a new babysitter, resulting in "serious sleep problems" and nightly hysteria—with the clear implication that conscientious parents should hesitate before leaving the house at all. The need for parents to turn to outside professional assistance was clear even in the most reassuring paragraphs, for the boundary between minor problem and pathology was tenuous indeed. The obligation to let children vent their emotions and to make sure they were positively entertained and motivated, constituted Dr. Spock's contribution to raising the bar of parental performance, even with his apparent permissiveness. The assumption that parents, or at least mothers, would devote massive amounts of time to their children ran through the writings of even the most benign experts.[3]

Rooted in the idea of the vulnerable child, the whole package of parental worries was truly impressive. The child who was easily bored, the child who had problems making friends, the child who seemed burdened by school—any or all could elicit stark appraisals. Everything and anything could be laid at the parents' door. A child who seemed retarded was really the result of "the [inadequate] amount of stimulation he's received from those around him."[4] A given parent might escape one category of worries—I myself, for example, was never concerned that schools would overburden children, tending, academic fashion, to assume that children could and should measure up. But worries about boredom could catch me, along with concerns about my children's chore performance and anxiety about their physical and mental health. Another parent might have a different mix, with more worries about school pressures but a better handle on chores than I ever managed. It was the sheer number of potential anxiety targets that was significant, all duly highlighted by one popular expert or another. Given the range of possible deficiencies, it was hard to feel reassured.

And it was not just the popular manuals and frequent newspaper articles that put the pressure on. Mass American consumerism clearly played on parental guilts, urging this or that acquisition to make children's hard lives easier. By the 1980s, colleges were even organizing sweets-filled care packages that could be purchased for students, a way for parents to provide reassurance but also a reminder that they had plunged their offspring into a world full of troublesome stress.

The new tensions that arose between conflicting parental goals contributed actively to the anxiety quota. Was the chief worry debasing media or providing fun, as far as entertainment was concerned? Too much school pressure or children who might not perform well? Prevention of work burdens that were inappropriate for children or the structuring of suitable chores? The polarities in these key areas reflected the novelty, as well as the complexity, of 20th-century childhood trends. We have seen that subtle compromises emerged in all the areas (e.g., the emphasis on self-esteem as a way to combine schooling and child protection), but they hardly prevented continued worry. Debates about appropriate disciplinary styles added another area of uncertainty.

Furthermore, as we have noted, the children themselves had their role to play, enhanced by parents' beliefs about their own childhood experience. The widespread conviction that many of life's difficulties could be traced back to some parental inadequacy developed particularly widely in the United States—ironically, far more widely than in many societies where life's difficulties, at least in the material and political sense, were much greater. Believing that one's own parents had messed up might inspire parents to make remedial efforts in their own parenting, but almost always at the price of heightened anxiety. And if this was not a sufficient spur, children were quite ready to seize on the dominant culture to point out that they were bored and that parents should do something to entertain, or that school was getting them down unfairly, or that their emotional life was awry.

To be sure, many parents were able to adapt to the pressures, which was why there was real and frequent joy in contemporary parenting. But it was hard entirely to resist the array of reminders in view of the range of potential concerns. The level of worry in the United States ran high, compared to that among the French or Chinese. A society that was using 90 percent of the world's Ritalin supply by the 1990s was clearly obsessed with children's problems in some distinctive ways. The distinction showed in bookstores, as well, with far larger sections in U.S. outlets devoted to parenting manuals and commentary on children's problems. New sources of anxiety, the openness to expert advice, and a culture long a bit edgy where children were concerned added up to an unusual national package.

Moreover, there was no clear relief. In 1952, the pollster Daniel Yankelovich predicted that "various factors seem to be working toward increasing parents' self-confidence." He argued that parents were getting accustomed to contemporary standards, aided by the move away from behaviorism to a more natural, permissive style. Generational disputes would diminish, he predicted; suburban parents, in any event, were finding it easier to talk with each other about how to handle problems. Finally, Yankelovich contended, experts and counselors were more readily available and supportive; their information, "given ahead of time and with professional sanction, should ease parents' anxieties and be helpful generally in broadening the public's conception of the infinite ways in which children can vary and still be healthy in personality." But this forecast, reasonable enough at the time, was simply inaccurate. Parents, if anything, grew more worried, not less, as the 20th century continued.[5]

Anxiety is, of course, a tricky term. The sociologist Alan Hunt has recently reminded us of how loosely social scientists and historians use the notion of anxiety to explain social behaviors, from persecutions for witchcraft to temperance crusades. He urges us to be more precise, and the injunction is a good one. Parental anxieties in the 20th century have been widespread but have remained at fairly low levels in terms of any widespread social expression—not the stuff, for the most part, of witch hunts. We're talking more about a collection of individual anxieties, rather than a social movement. A broader social dimension does crop up, most obviously in recurrent exaggerations of threats to children.

The stubborn belief in the corruptive possibilities of the media or in the existence of new waves of sexual predators, without consistent evidence to support it, is a case in point. And the willingness of most parents to accept exaggeration as fact can lead to genuine hysteria among some.[6]

For the most part, parents' anxieties have flowed from fairly specific situations; they have not depended on wider social currents that demand a symbolic release. For example, there have been real changes in schooling, work habits, and consumerism. Parents may well exaggerate the their influence as far as children are concerned, but they are transferring worries based on a real social phenomenon. It is possible, to be sure, that anxieties about children have sometimes mirrored anxieties about wider social changes. There has been a temptation to transfer to parenting some problems associated with the trends of "modern life," such as worries about Americanization among immigrant parents and concerns about consumerism for almost everyone. Worries about children's emotions have sometimes reflected adult tensions; an example is jealousy projected back onto children at a time when gender contacts and the attendant potential for jealousy were expanding rapidly in adult social life. The causes of anxious parenting, then, are found mainly but not exclusively in the actual settings of contemporary childhood. Correspondingly, the outcomes derive mainly, though not always exclusively, from the experiences of children and parents themselves.

There are, to be sure, some wider ramifications worth considering, particularly in the policy sphere. By the late 20th century, the contrast between parents' continued anxiety about their own children, and to some extent children in general, on the one hand and the clear neglect of children in the policy arena on the other was striking. A nation that consumed volumes of child-rearing advice was oddly immune to concern for the growing levels of poverty or the absence of health facilities that impact many children. A number of factors entered in, including the myopia of the prosperous in dealing with the poverty of the minority, compounded by racial prejudices. The fact that a growing number of adults had passed the stage of active parenting and were more concerned about the impact of taxes on their lives as retirees was another component. The increase in the number of working women reduced women's availability to serve as political activists for children's causes; such activism was a key element in achieving reforms in the 19th and early 20th centuries. But anxiety may have entered in as well, in two senses. In the first place, anxiety about their own children might have reduced adults' political concern for children in general, who could be seen as competitive threats to their own fragile offspring. And, while attachment to their own children persisted, adults often readily dismissed children in general as nuisances or deficient, in either case not warranting government redress.

Certainly the reputations of children in general did not benefit from a century of parental anxiety. Concern about the deterioration of the next generation is not a 20th-century invention; similar expressions were common in the 19th century, as well. And it was still possible, even amid the ongoing anxiety, to revisit statements about the promise of youth and the shining examples of young America—a commencement speech staple, among other things. But there were so many new reasons to worry, some of them quite real, some of them, fed by anxiety clearly exaggerated but nonetheless vivid. It was harder to be optimistic about American children, as a category, in 2001 than it had been in 1900. American adults were quite willing to believe that school performance was deteriorating, though in fact the record was more often mixed to encouraging. They were quite willing to believe that children in general were being corrupted by the media and by consumerism. They worried loudly about character, not only in relation to the corrosive media but also as a result of the unresolved tensions over work performance. Many American adults, at many points in the 20th century, clearly believed that childhood frailty, juxtaposed with the downside of modern life, added up to a new generation less virtuous, and perhaps less talented, than its predecessors. These general attitudes did not necessarily translate into beliefs about one's own children, where the evidence was clearer and where parental affection colored judgment. But even here, these attitudes fed anxiety, for the challenge of keeping one's own offspring safe from the descending spiral experienced by others in their generation was considerable.

Finally, there seemed little doubt that adults' experience of childhood itself worsened over the century. In a 1979 poll, 37 percent of all parents contended that contemporary children were not as happy as children once were, compared to only 16 percent who were prepared to argue that they were happier. And, here, the problems hit home; the respondents were not just talking about children in general. While 74 percent of those polled argued that most American parents were doing a good job, only 63 percent expressed real confidence in their own performance.

Again, there was no massive anxiety here, and certainly no uniformity. But the willingness to express worry about one's own adequacy was surprisingly widespread. Self-evaluations interacted with larger judgments about how children were doing. And, to the extent that there were general problems, American parents resoundingly contended that parents themselves, not broader social forces, were the primary villains. A deepseated American cultural inclination to attribute problems to personal fault, rather than to blame society at large, clearly applied to parenting, reflecting and confirming parents' anxiety. Revealingly, a majority of parents (72 percent) in this same polling group expressed dissatisfaction about the society around them in answering another question about the context for family life but felt that the main obligation to respond rested with parents, not with some larger entity.[7]

CHILDREN OF ANXIETY

What were the results for children of this contemporary parental anxiety? It is important to be cautious here. Parents were far from being the only influences on their children's lives. And, neurotic exceptions aside, their anxiety levels were not usually extreme and were softened by real affection and pleasure.

It is not clear, in fact, that persistent levels of parental anxiety have had a deleterious impact on children in general. Many, of course, would disagree, and the question is huge. Conservatives often argue that parental anxieties, in leading to a new permissiveness, led to a decline in traditional values, which was in turn responsible for the deterioration of the American character. They easily seize on evidence about children's shallow consumerism or on accommodations made to school programs to bolster children's self-esteem as signs of worried permissiveness out of control. Parental guilt, exploited by children, is another obvious political target. In 2001, in Colorado and other states, a movement for "parents' rights" amendments to state constitutions, insisting on their "inalienable" authority over education, values, and discipline, expressed the traditionalists' sense that anxiety had run amuck. But it was not just conservatives who worried about trends. In the late 1970s, the historian Christopher Lasch won attention from President Jimmy Carter with his arguments about the deteriorating American character, rooted among other things in a lack of parental self-confidence and a vulnerability to the confusing blandishments of outside experts. Here, from the liberal side, was another statement that worry was eroding appropriate standards.

Yet, children, in the main, continue to make transitions into reasonably respectable, achieving adulthoods. The work ethic has not collapsed, despite children's successful resistance to chores. School performance has probably improved overall, to judge from steadily rising academic standards—which does not of course mean that it is as good as it should be. Consumerism has gained ground, with children's distaste for boredom translating into parents' propensities to spend in search of distraction. But the results are not necessarily dreadful, and they play a vital role in sustaining a complex economy. Crime and violence have not gained ascendancy; they even retreated, in the 1990s.

The point is twofold. First, judgments about the most important results of anxious parenting, on children and on the adults they become, are tremendously difficult to make and are shaped more by subjective factors than by clear evidence. Second, granting that there is room for dispute, a claim of a definite deterioration in the outcomes of childhood would be hard to sustain. Even children's processes using parents' anxieties as levers in avoiding chores, ducking discipline by claiming that they feel guilt or complaining of boredom, are not necessarily bad. They're distinctive, and they warrant evaluation, but they may give kids some desirable space.

But this does not mean that children have not been affected by the contours of parental anxiety. First, children have been strongly shaped in directions parents helped to sponsor. During the century, they have become steadily more school oriented, however diverse the results. The assumption that high school attendance is normal has become almost universal, and more than half the cohort is committed to college attendance. Second, the assumption that boredom can be used as a measure of life has increased, sometimes in tense juxtaposition with the role of schooling. A 1996 study showed how many children confounded boredom with stress: "The weekend [is worst.] I get bored and if I don't have anything to do and, ah, that can, ah, I can get stressed from that cause I am really bored and I want to do something, go somewhere, and there is really nothing, nothing going on." Male adolescents, particularly, often combined a sense of time stress, when there was schoolwork to do, and boredom, a need to be positively entertained. "Yeh, like if I have nothing to do, like I am sitting at home and there's nothing to do, I phone up one of my friends and we go out and can't find nothing to do we usually just walk around. It gets really boring." Changes of this sort, headed by schooling, are significant. The way parents have decided to measure children has much to do with the new ways children measure themselves and their life. Here, too, childhood in 2000 was much different from that of a century prior.[8]

Parental anxiety has affected children's behavior at various stages of their development. The late grade school years, have become a time of peak child-parent interaction, with some shared chores and much shared leisure, followed by a growing gulf during adolescence. Precisely because of anxious parental hovering, though in combination with the lures of the peer culture and of youth consumerism, children have developed new levels of need to differentiate themselves in ways that can support their independence and identity. It becomes imperative for them to have music and, often, clothing and body styles that separate them from their parents by annoying them. In adolescence, it is additionally essential to create even further space by frequent absence from home—thanks to the ubiquitous car—and by embarrassed withdrawal from most family leisure. Margaret Mead and others have noted how new levels of parental emotional intensity complicate contemporary adolescence; the parental control efforts associated with countering adolescents' perceived vulnerability merely add to this effect.

The chief effect of parental anxiety has been to create a host of new restrictions on children, which replace but in many ways surpass those that used to be imposed by the demands of child labor. It is intriguing, for example, that the 1996 study showed that a large minority of adolescents felt they had no control over their time, even though, from an adult perspective, they seemed to have a great deal of leeway outside school hours. An *Atlantic Monthly* article in 2001 referred to the "Organization Kid" as a contemporary counterpart to the midcentury Organization Man. The author, pointing to the growing proliferation of lessons and other parent-sponsored activities, argued that current constraints on children's time contrast with the freer-wheeling childhood of the 1960s, but in fact the trends toward anxious regulation of childhood began earlier. Indeed, lifestyle rebellions, which formed a major component of the sixties generation, have operated precisely in this context. Efforts to regulate children in the interests of health and safety go back to the earliest decades of the century, and concern about monitoring children's emotional expressions and happiness led to new levels of parental participation and oversight after World War II. It was at this point, also, that interest in socializing children for positions in corporate management and a service economy led to a new premium on developing children's people-pleasing skills, a new component of parental goals. While parents often believed that children were gaining new latitude and crafting new ways to defy them, the basic trends in fact ran the other way, particularly prior to adolescence. Small wonder that, again in 2001, the dean of admissions at Harvard commented on "over-scheduled" college students, who found decisions and spontaneity difficult because of a childhood spent under parental control. His reference, of course, was to unusually high achievers, not to the middle class as a whole, and to the particular activity pattern that had built up in the 1980s and 1990s, when parents in middle-class families increased the time they devoted to children and reduced television watching in favor of sponsored recreations. (It was in 2002 that a New Jersey town promoted a no-activities day to encourage spontaneity by and with children . . . but they had to organize it.) But, some elements of the dean's description rang true for the century more generally, when the combination of schooling and parental commitment to improving leisure took shape. A society that so often worried about undersupervised kids was actually moving toward the opposite extreme.

Again, the result was not necessarily bad, though the Harvard dean argued that overscheduled children needed an unusual period of uncertainty in early adulthood to shake off the constraints and to find themselves. Clearly, however, anxious parenting did have its effects, shaping children's experiences differently from those of children in the past. These experiences differed also from the images parents often maintained of children too free from constraints, too vulnerable to the wider world around them. In fact, anxious parenting, combined with schooling, led to a growing association between childhood and structure.

A final link is more speculative. Anxious parenting also involved an unusual effort to ensure children's happiness—defined, to be sure, in parental terms, at least in part. The goal was admirable, but it also encouraged children to take their own emotional temperature more often than before, possibly to find it wanting. It indirectly induced some children, eager to shake off parental controls but impeded by the fact that their parents' intentions were benign, to pull away through unhappiness. The second half of the 20th century saw a growing incidence of depression among children. Partly this reflected improved diagnosis, partly a psychological vocabulary shared with adults. But some depression may have resulted, however obscurely, from anxious parents' insistence on happiness. The disease was real and agonizing, but its channels may have been partly constructed by the new parental culture. Again, the impacts of parental worries deserve serious attention in descriptions of the complex recent history of American childhood. Anxious parenting generated unusual constraints on children, many of which could be successfully navigated, but also some troubling reactions.

The summary is admittedly complex. Parental anxiety encouraged some desired results—more accommodation to schooling, for example, and better socialization for a life in the corporate world. It also misfired in some cases; unprecedented commitment to children's happiness did not produce clearly happier children, and the anxiety factor helped create the disjuncture. Children were changed by more anxious parenting, but the end results were not necessarily worse, in terms of childhood experience or preparation for adulthood. Granting the delights of more purely editorial commentary—most recently from conservative critics of contemporary character—a neutral statement is most accurate: the balance of plusses and minuses was different from what it had been before, where childhood was concerned, but there remained a balance. It is often difficult to recognize significant change that does not add up to either definite progress or deterioration, but this is the description that best captures the interactions between anxious parents and their children during the 20th century.

PARENTAL RECOIL

The new levels of parental anxiety inevitably affected parents themselves. While the main point of parenting is children, the adult experience deserves assessment, as well, as a significant part of 20th-century life. And here the stark fact is that parental satisfaction declined during much of the 20th century. The change reflected the availability of other life goals that might seem more attractive than parenting. It reflected a larger environment in which control over children, particularly adolescents, seemed more difficult. But, above all, it reflected the burdens of anxiety itself.

Anxious parenthood meant, quite literally, an emotional experience that seriously affected reactions to the role, particularly when reinforced by additional specific responsibilities for entertainment, or compensatory chores, or emotional monitoring. Measurement of satisfaction is difficult, of course, in the blissfully poll-free decades of the early 20th century, but it begins to accumulate for the years since the 1930s.

At the end of the 1930s, for example, a Lewis Terman poll on marriage satisfaction revealed that parents with children and those without were equally happy. This poll was focused not directly on parenting, to be sure, but, rather, on marriage. Still, Terman himself found the parity surprising, and he was right. It seems very probable—though not provable—that a comparable inquiry forty years earlier would have revealed a much higher margin in favor of children, if only because of the prestige attached to motherhood and the paternal satisfactions in being a provider. Parenthood may already have been slipping by the 1930s, even on the verge of the extraordinary baby boom.

From this point on, the trends are definite: every inquiry from 1950 on shows a decided margin in favor of childlessness as the happier state. The 1930s parity, itself probably novel, eroded steadily in favor of childless adulthood. And the gap tended to widen with time. Both individuals and couples without children professed greater satisfaction than parents. Parents themselves were much more sanguine about their role after their children had left home than before. Divorced fathers who had only occasional contact with their children were much more positive about parenting than were fathers in undissolved marriages or mothers of any sort. Whatever way the parenting cake was cut, the satisfaction slice was smaller for the active parent.

Changes particularly affected the middle class. For, on balance, parental satisfaction decreased inversely with social level, despite that fact that strictly material concerns ran the other way. Various studies from the 1920s on show a bifurcation in views among American parents; some took a highly traditionalist view and were bent on exacting religious faith and obedience from children, and whereas others accepted more "modern" approaches and were concerned with developmental issues. The division tracked social class fairly closely, with more affluent and educated parents consistently in the more modern, permissive group. This correlation held in a 1946 study, and again in 1977. But it was the more modern group that was particularly dissatisfied, worried about their children, eager to innovate, but also concerned about defining parental obligations too broadly—a very difficult double bind. This was a group, in sum, working for newer standards for children but unwilling to define parenthood as the whole of life. Two other points are relevant. First, in terms of trend, the percentage favoring the "modern" orientation increased with time, which means, once more, that their dissatisfaction grew, as well. Second, even "modern" parents tended to argue that the "good old days" were better for children and expressed nostalgia for "more traditional standards of family life and responsibility," even as they resolutely moved toward more contemporary concerns. The inconsistency is striking on its face, but not when the level of anxiety associated with contemporary parenting goals is taken into consideration.

The most vivid demonstration of the trend toward a growing unhappiness with the parental role came in two parallel studies, headed by Joseph Veroff, which took Americans' attitudinal temperature in 1957 and again in 1976.

Veroff and his research team found only one category of American parent—divorced fathers—that did not report far more problems and feelings of inadequacy in the 1970s compared to a similar group two decades earlier. Divorced women and married people of both sexes reported a dramatic decrease in overall positive responses. Both negativity and ambivalence had soared. The change was universal, though single mothers reported particular worries about money resources and married men worried about children's lack of obedience. Revealingly, the overall decline in satisfaction was accompanied by an increased emphasis on the interpersonal and emotional aspects of parenting—how one relates to one's children, and how one deals with intensity—rather than on more material criteria. Again, the newer signals about parenting were mixed, with some growing distress.[9]

Evidence of growing parental dissatisfaction during the 20th century, while it precisely maps the effects of anxiety, may need some qualification. Opinion polls are interesting, but they are not everything—and even the polls reveal many parental joys. Further, questions about happiness or satisfaction may be too superficial. Many parents may be less comfortable in their role than their predecessors, or than their childless counterparts, but they may still feel a sense of fulfillment that they would not trade. Robert Bellah, in his study of contemporary character, shows how individual parents can adjust personal goals to gain meaning from parenting. Certainly, Americans—even most highly educated Americans—continue to have children at a rate that surpasses that of many other industrial countries. It is possible, furthermore, that parental rewards increased at the century's end. Certainly, the amount of time spent with children went up, as parents in particular devoted more attention to the area of leisure and recreation. Soccer moms were real people, and, while they certainly exuded anxiety, if only about juggling schedules, they may also have reflected some general renewed satisfaction in parenting. Even earlier, in the 1970s, when gripes were frequent, 90 percent of the parents surveyed said they would decide to have children if they had it to do over again.

Still, the discontent was significant. Even the 90 percent tended to add "but they would wish for more support."[10] This could refer to frustration with the other spouse, or it could represent a vague plea to some other agency. In one respect, certainly, anxious American parents were trapped, compared to parents elsewhere. On the one hand, their redefinitions of parental obligations did leave them feeling overburdened. On the other, their very anxieties made them more reluctant than most Europeans to use facilities like day care centers, since they were more fearful of leaving their precious but vulnerable charges to others. Europeans routinely expressed greater confidence in facilities outside the family and to that extent both reflected and experienced less anxiety than their American counterparts.

Adults in most industrial societies certainly made new choices that pressed on their roles as parents, particularly in the second half of the century. Rising divorce rates inevitably complicated care for children and created new levels of guilt. They may also, in some cases, have reflected the tensions generated by contemporary definitions of child care. Did Americans' divorce rates, the highest in the industrial world, have anything to do with distinctive degrees of parental anxiety? Disputes over children were hardly new, but, with worries rising and marriages more fragile for other reasons, it was tempting to vote with one's feet, as some individual mothers, and, even more, fathers, clearly did. The odd polling results—that divorced parents not primarily responsible for the children felt particularly good about parenting—in this sense did not constitute an anomaly. Decisions by women to work outside the home, another key trend, resulted from many factors, including the extent to which child rearing was no longer a totally fulfilling role for women. Here, too, the change, while rewarding in many ways, added to parental stress. Small wonder that the childless option seemed more straightforward.

It was hard to escape some new vicious circles. Lower birth rates and greater adult life expectancy inevitably repositioned the role of parenthood in life. With new anxieties added in, as in the United States, choices became particularly complex, easily generating additional concerns. It was unfortunate, but true, that during much of the 20th century this still important component of life turned less pleasurable.

LESSONS FROM HISTORY

It would be brash to claim that the history of anxious American parenting suggests a precise list of desirable reforms. Lessons from history are usually complicated, for it is difficult to move from an understanding of past trends and causes to a widely agreed-upon set of measures for the future. Parenting is particularly slippery, because its contours result from so many different, often private, decisions.

It would also be easy to be fatuous. The 20th-century record could easily justify the simple suggestion that parents stop worrying so much—but the same record shows how and why it will be difficult to ease up.

Some fairly clear recommendations do, nevertheless, emerge. The obvious policy issue involves provision of greater support for anxious parents. Employers vary greatly in their tolerance for child-related flexibility demands. Many parents—mothers, for the most part—have already decided against work careers or opt for only part-time jobs because full-time jobs simply do not provide the necessary give. The dearth of publicly sponsored child care facilities is another issue. Expansion in these areas will require significant financial resources. Parents themselves need to decide whether they will actually use some of the opportunities that might be available—whether they can reduce their anxieties sufficiently to place greater trust in others, for example. But knowledge of the levels of anxiety that exist, and the impact they have on the experience of parenting, just might prompt renewed discussion of these issues, not just for the poor but for the middle class, as well.

Parental anxiety in the 20th century has been indissolubly linked to experts, media, and popularizers, who have played, with whatever intentions, on parental guilt. We have not argued, in this book, that experts have created worries from nothing; there was abundant parental clay to work with. But media signals have undoubtedly exacerbated parental concerns and in some cases have shamelessly exploited them.

To deal with this, almost certainly, we need both more parental backbone, to reject unwarranted guilt trips, and more decency on the part of commercial and therapeutic voices. The former is crucial, because the latter may not be forthcoming otherwise. I do not think that outside expertise has undermined parenting, as Christopher Lasch has argued, but I certainly believe it has enhanced parental worrying and reduced their confident pleasure. Claims that kids are measurably deteriorating or that parents are primarily responsible for what does go wrong need far more discounting than we have seen at most points during the past century. A Parents' Response Group might not be a bad idea, not to try to censor criticism but to respond to it with as much objective data—and historical insight—as possible.

It is vital to recognize that contemporary parents have not been intentionally participating in some massive movement toward either neglect or diminished standards. Obviously, patterns of parental contact with children have changed, particularly because of the diminution of family work and the emphasis on schooling. But the range of parental responsibilities for children has actually increased, with the need to attend to emotional development, recreational habits, and more aspects of safety. Of course, there are neglectful adults, and also situations, such as the "latchkey" child of working parents, that deserve evaluation. But efforts to persuade contemporary parents as a whole that they are guilty of some dereliction of duty are inaccurate and should be rejected.

Nor have 20th-century parents abandoned standards. They have changed them; intensified school demands are one obvious example. They have reduced emphasis on passive etiquette and sheer obedience in favor of more subtle forms of emotional socialization and control. They have waffled, collectively, in the face of the difficult pressures posed by commercial entertainment. But they have in many ways increased the demands they place on children, not the reverse. Again, their choices can be contested; there may be components of character that deserve more emphasis (and some, perhaps, that deserve less). Some individual children fail to meet appropriate expectations, and this, too, warrants evaluation. But expert comment, often politicized, that implies some parental collapse is off the mark and should be rejected. It is as important to discuss overregulation as underregulation.

It is important, as well, to get a better fix on how much parents are to blame when things go wrong, in a society that likes to assign blame and prefers individual responsibility wherever possible. It is important, finally, to reduce the exploitation of parental anxiety.

Parents themselves might usefully reevaluate some categories of anxiety in light of the actual trends of the 20th century. There is a range of choice. The competitiveness of some parents concerning their children's scholastic or athletic performance has often been criticized for its impact on children; it should also be evaluated for its reflection of parental tension and for its harmful impact on parents themselves. The college entrance pressures exceed common sense, though the game will be hard to bring under sounder control. College education is important; different colleges do have different strengths and weaknesses. But young people can, and do, thrive at a variety of institutions, and the investment in college rankings not only puts pressure on children but needlessly enhances adult anxiety. The frenzied commitment to keeping children entertained is another category that might be relaxed a bit. Might we also work toward a bit more agreement on what kinds of commercial entertainment really merit parents' anguished concern, and what types are both inevitable and probably fairly harmless? A tough assignment, admittedly, but, with a century of abortive and often excessive campaigns behind us, we might review our reactions. The same holds for the chores category. It's clear that children's chores have diminished faster than expectations about them, and that the work ethic has not as a result been fatally damaged. The next target would be reducing adult frustration, (or bucking contemporary history by getting more help from kids). It's worth some effort to realign our standards with reality.

Three points underlie this invitation to personal and collective rethinking. First, we really do need to consider our commitment to the concept of children's vulnerability. Do we undervalue children's resiliency, their capacity to generate adequate self-esteem? This is a tough area, to be sure, for children *are* vulnerable, and we have made some positive strides—for example, in health and safety—on the basis of this emphasis. The whole imagery has become deeply lodged in our culture, but arguably we overdo. We hem children in with safety restrictions, for example, far more than other countries, without any appreciable result other than worried parents and annoyed kids. We create a number of self-fulfilling prophecies, for example in the self-esteem area, where we undermine self-confidence by fussing about it so much. And we certainly make aspects of the parenting process more anxious-producing in the process. The vulnerability image was invented; it has not been a constant in our history. So, in principle, it can be modified. It deserves some thought, as we ponder the burdens that the image of the fragile child places on parents and on children themselves.

The second point warrants more confident assertion: we definitely need to rethink our nostalgia about children and parents past. We too easily fall into the trap of assuming that things were better back then: parents more loving, children happier, characters firmer. I would hesitate to argue that we have made progress in all these areas, but I see no need to argue for deterioration, either. Yet polls show that parents have been sold the deterioration model, and the result is an uphill battle toward assurance and enjoyment in the parental role. When did young boys stand on opposite sides of construction sites, throwing mudballs occasionally laced with a sharp stones at each other? Not in the regulated 1970s or 1990s but in the presumably more sedate 1940s, when young kids were actually more likely to do moderate violence to each other than is now the case. When did Halloween routinely occasion minor vandalism by middle-class kids? Not in the carefully monitored children's world of the late 20th century. Pranks, in fact, have markedly declined in all sorts of childhood contexts. When did experts blast high school students who could identify only 33 percent of "the simplest and most obvious facts of American history"? Not in the anxiety-laden education reports of the late 1980s or the anxious reconsiderations of the Sputnik era—but in fact in 1917, after a test of 668 Texas high school students revealed that fewer than a third could identify 1776 as the date of the Declaration of Independence.[11]

The point is not that knowledge of history has necessarily improved; it is still a concern, as is children's violence. But we do beat ourselves up unnecessarily when we routinely think that, where children are involved, the past was better and that therefore, as parents, we have some new and awesome responsibility to battle against basic forces of modern life. A study of the series of White House Conferences on Children makes the same point, even for experts: each succeeding conference tended to ignore the difficulties described by its predecessors, claiming that the earlier conferences had "simpler" problems to deal with, when, in fact, there has been no clear pattern of intensification at all. We need a better grasp on the past to temper our anxieties about the present.

When tempted to believe that we have slipped from some higher standards, there are two simple rules first. First, be skeptical. Second, find out what the historical record actually is, as best we know it.

This reevaluation of historical perspective is truly important, whatever one thinks of history as a subject. On many topics, we overdo the optimism about modern advances—but not where children are concerned. Somehow, in thinking about family matters, including parenting, we've fallen into a trap of ignorance and pessimism. We simply don't know what huge problems parents faced in the past, so we see every new concern as an unprecedented challenge. We then compound this reaction with a kneejerk sense that every new twist is a further slide downhill from some golden past. And so we belabor ourselves unnecessarily. The impulse is both inaccurate and unnecessary.

And, finally, as we think about anxieties, let's dare to advance a parental pleasure principle. Parenting does entail responsibility. It is not always fun, and fun is not the best measure of the reasons to be a parent. But, as the polls suggest, it's legitimate to urge that we learn to ease up a bit and enjoy the process more than many American parents now do. It's not wrong to consider support arrangements that would make parenting easier. It's not wrong to think about reducing the list of anxieties. It is legitimate to work on parental enjoyment and to see whether we can't reverse a really troubling 20th-century trend that can't in the long run be good for children and certainly is not good for family life.

The ultimate tool is perspective, and the latitude it provides. American adults in the 20th century—teachers, experts, popularizers, and parents above all—encountered fundamental, intertwined changes in the nature of childhood, and therefore of parenthood. They had to deal with the consequences of lower birth rates. They had to incorporate schooling as the quintessential child role, along with the dramatic decline in children's work. They had to mediate the encounters between commercial media and consumerism on the one hand and childhood on the other. They complicated these tasks with new assumptions about children's frailty, new uncertainties about discipline, and new adult behaviors such as frequent divorce and women's work outside the home. Small wonder that anxiety was one result, though Americans seem to have upped the ante here compared to other societies that experienced the same great transitions. The redefinitions of childhood were sweeping, and they have not been completed. Grasping our recent history is essential if we are to consider parental formulas that might prove more definilive and more comforting than those we have produced to date. The process is not over. Contemporary parenting can become more enjoyable, without hurting the kids or retreating from the gains of the past century. It's a goal worth seeking.

FURTHER READING

Michael Zuckerman, "Dr. Spock: Confidence Man," in Charles E. Rosenberg, ed., *The Family in History* (New York, 1975), pp. 179–207; Joseph Veroff, Elizabeth Douvan, and Richard Kulka, *The Inner American: A Self-Portrait from 1957 to 1976* (New York, 1981); CQ (Congressional Quarterly), *Teens in America* (Washington, DC, 2001); National Education Association, *The Status of the American Family* (Washington, DC, 1979); Daniel Yankelovich, *New Rules: Searching for Self-Fulfillment in a World Turned Upside Down* (New York, 1981); Mary Jo Bane, "Review of Child Care Books," *Harvard Educational Review* 43 (1973): 669–80; Sara McLanahan and Julie Adams, "Parenthood and Psychological Well-Being," *Annual Review of Sociology* 5 (1987): 237–57; Rachelle Beck, "The White House Conferences on Children in Historical Perspective," *Harvard Educational Review* 43 (1973): 653–68; David Brooks, "The Organization Kid," *Atlantic* 287 (2001): 40–55; Peter N. Stearns, *Battleground of Desire: The Struggle for Self-Control in Modern America* (New York, 1999); Alan Hunt, "Anxiety and Social Explanation: Some Anxieties about Anxiety," *Journal of Social History* 32 (1999): 509–28; Robert Bellah and others, *Habits of the Heart* (Berkeley, 1996). On another range of problems associated with social inequality, see James Q. Wilson, *The Marriage Problem: How Our Culture Has Weakened Families* (New York, 2002).

Appendix

*Most Widely Consulted Childrearing Manuals
(from 1927 onward)*

Millie Almy. *Child Development* (New York, 1955).

Rhoda Bacmeister. *Your Child and Other People* (New York, 1950).

Dorothy W. Baruch. *Parents Can Be People: A Primer for and about Parents* (New York, 1944).

———. *New Ways in Discipline* (New York, 1949).

Agnes E. Benedict and Adele Franklin. *Your Best Friends Are Your Children* (New York, 1951).

Bruno Bettelheim. *Love Is Not Enough: The Treatment of Emotionally Disturbed Children* (New York, 1950).

Smiley Blanton and Margaret Gray Blanton. *Child Guidance* (New York, 1927).

Marion Breckenridge and Vincent E. Lee. *Child Development: Physical and Psychologic Growth through the School Years* (Philadelphia, 1943).

Children's Bureau. *Infant Care* (Washington, DC, successive editions).

Rudolf Dreikurs. *Coping with Children's Misbehavior* (New York, 1948, 1958, 1972).

———. *The Challenge of Parenthood* (New York, 1948; rev. ed., 1958).

Rudolf Dreikurs and Loren Grey. *Logical Sequences: A New Approach to Discipline* (New York, 1968).

Rudolf Dreikurs and Vicki Solz. *Children: The Challenge* (New York, 1964).

James Lee Ellenwood. *Questions Parents Ask* (New York, 1955).

Marion L. Faegre and John E. Anderson. *Child Care and Training* (Minneapolis, 1928, 1929, 1930, 1937, 1938).

Thomas Gordon. *P.E.T.: Parents Effectiveness Training: The Tested New Way to Raise Responsible Children* (New York, 1970).

Sidonie Gruenberg. *The Parent's Guide to Everyday Problems of Boys* and Girls (New York, 1958).

Paul A. Hauck. *The Rational Management of Children* (New York, 1967).

Francis Horwick and Reinald Weinerath Jr. *Have Fun with Your Children* (New York, 1954).

James Hynes, Jr. *Understand Your Child* (New York, 1952).

Leo Kanner. *In Defense of Mothers: How to Bring Up Children in Spite of the More Zealous Psychologists* (Chicago, 1941).

John D. Krumboltz and Helen B. Krumboltz. *Changing Children's Behavior* (New York, 1972).

Grace Langdon and Irving W. Stout. *Bringing Up Children* (New York, 1958, 1959, 1960).

David M. Levy. *Maternal Overprotection* (New York, 1943).

Carl Renz and Mildred Renz. *Big Problems on Little Shoulders* (New York, 1934).

Robert Sears, Eleanor Maccoby, and Harry Levin. *Patterns of Child Rearing* (1957).

Irene Seipt. *Your Child's Happiness: A Guide for Parents* (Cleveland, 1995).

Benjamin Spock and Steven Parker. *Baby and Child Care* (1946, 1957,1968, 1976, 1985, 1992, 1998 [7th ed.]).

Frances G. Wickes. *The Inner World of Childhood: A Study in Analytical Psychology* (New York, 1927, 1955, 1966).

Notes

NOTES TO CHAPTER I

1. Theresa Richardson, *Century of the Child* (Albany, NY, 1989); Ellen Key, *The Century of the Child* (New York, 1907); David Macleod, *The Age of the Child: Children in America 1891–1990* (New York, 1998).

2. Richard Sennett, *Families against the City* (Cambridge, MA, 1970); Elaine Tyler May, *Homeward Bound: American Families in the Cold War Era* (New York, 1988).

3. Judith Warner, "Who Knew? The French Got Femininity Right," Washington *Post*, Style section, June 3, 2001.

NOTES TO CHAPTER 2

1. Children's Bureau, *Infant Care* (Washington, 1929), pp. 4–5; D. H. Thom, *Child Management* (Washington, 1925), pp. 12–15.

2. Philip Greven, *The Protestant Temperament* (New York, 1977).

3. American Institute of Child Life, *Problems of Temper* (Philadelphia, 1914), pp. 1–5.

4. Michael Zuckerman, "Dr. Spock: Confidence Man," in Charles Rosenberg, ed., *The Family in History* (New York, 1975), pp. 179–207.

5. T. S. Arthur, *Mother's Rule* (Philadelphia, 1856), p. 288.

6. John B. Watson, *Psychological Care of Infant and Child* (New York, 1928), p. 45; see also Mrs. Theodore Birney, *Childhood* (New York, 1904).

7. Benjamin Spock, *The Common Sense Book of Baby and Child Care* (New York, 1946), pp. 196–97.

8. "What to Do When Your Child Is Afraid," *Parents Magazine* 2 (Mar. 1927), pp. 25–27.

9. Walter Truslow, *Body Poise* (Baltimore, 1943), p. 136; G. E. Thomas, "Postural Defects of the Toddler," *The Practitioner* 173 (1955), pp. 257–66.

10. Dorothy Brock, "Some Practical Ideas about Posture Training,"

American Physical Education Review 29 (1923), pp. 331–35; Ellen Kelly, *Teaching Posture and Body Mechanics* (New York, 1949), p. 17; Zella van Ornum Glimm, "The Way to Good Posture," *Parents Magazine* 6 (Nov. 1931), p. 28.

11. "Another Order of the Bath," New York *Times*, August 17, 1927, p. 23.

12. Vincent Vinikas, "Lustrum of the Cleanliness Institute, 1927–32," *Journal of Social History* 22 (1989), pp. 613–30, citing materials in the Soap and Detergent Archives, New York; W. W. Peter, P. H. Hallock, and Grace Hallock, *Hitchhikers: Patrolling the Traffic from the Mouth and Nose* (New York, 1930), pp. 47–50; Grace Hallock, *A Tale of Soap and Water: The Historical Progress of Cleanliness*, 2nd ed. (New York, 1937).

13. Cited in Thomas Daniel and Frederick Pollins, eds., *Polio* (Rochester, NY, 1997).

14. Peter, Hallock, and Hallock, *Hitchhikers*; see also Ernest R. Groves and Gladys Groves, *Wholesome Childhoods* (Boston, 1931); Norma Cutts and Nicholas Moseley, *Better Home Discipline* (New York, 1952), pp. 64–67.

15. Charles Nam, Isaac Eberstein, and Larry Deeb, "Sudden Infant Death Syndrome as a Socially Determined Cause of Death," *Social Biology* 36 (1989), pp. 1–8; Abraham Bergman, *The "Discovery" of Sudden Infant Death Syndrome: Lessons in the Practice of Political Medicine* (New York, 1986).

16. "Children's Day," *Safety* 9 (Oct.–Nov. 1922), p. 218; "The Nation's Needless Martyrdom," *Literary Digest* 75 (Oct. 28, 1922), p. 29.

17. Vivian Weedon, "Mother Is a Teacher, Too," *Home Safety Review* (Aug.-Sept. 1947), pp. 3, 14–15; Jeanette Townsend, "Parent Wise—Infant Safe," *Home Safety Review* (Dec. 1949–Jan. 1950), p. 296.

18. Ida Tarbell, "Who Is to Blame for Child Killing?" *Collier's* 70 (Oct. 7, 1922), p. 12; *Focus on Children and Youth: A Report of the Council of Parental Organizations on Children and Youth for the 1960 White House Conference on Children and Youth* (n.p., 1960), p. 174.

19. G. Stanley Hall, *Adolescence*, 2 vol. (New York, 1903–4).

20. Christopher Lasch, *The Culture of Narcissism: American Life in an Age of Diminishing Expectations* (New York, 1979).

21. "No Naturally Bad Children," *Literary Digest* 56 (Oct. 31, 1925) p. 21

22. John Watson, *Care of Infant and Child* (New York, 1928), pp. 9–73; Lucy Wood Collier, "The Child, Its Bed and the School," *Sunset Magazine* (July 1923), p. 58.

23. Summarized in Washington *Post*, Style section, August 24, 2001.

NOTES TO CHAPTER 3

1. Constance Foster, "Why Boys and Girls Misbehave," *Parents Magazine* 28 (1953), p. 57.

2. Ruth Benedict, *The Chrysanthemum and the Sword* (Boston, 1946).

3. Dorothy Canfield Fisher and Sidonie Gruenberg, *Our Children* (New York, 1932), pp. 119, 177; Carl Renz and Mildred Renz, *Big Problems on Little Shoulders* (New York, 1934), p. 86.

4. Benjamin Spock, *The Common Sense Book of Baby and Child Care* (New York, 1946), pp. 195–96, 438.

5. Fisher and Gruenberg, *Our Children*, pp. 119, 177.

6. Renz and Renz *Big Problems*, p. 84.

7. Fritz Redt, *When We Deal with Children* (New York, 1966), pp. 136–37.

8. Fisher and Gruenberg, *Our Children*, p. 178; Foster, "Why Boys and Girls Misbehave," p. 37.

9. John B. Watson, *Psychological Care of the Infant and Child* (New York, 1928), p. 111.

10. Watson, *Psychological Care*, p. 136.

11. Julia Grant, "Caught between Common Sense and Science: The Cornell Child Study Club, 1925–1945," *History of Education Quarterly* 34 (1994), pp. 442–47.

12. Rhoda Bacmeister, *Your Child and Other People* (New York, 1950), pp. 53–54.

13. Foster, "Why Boys and Girls Misbehave," p. 84.

14. Sidonie Gruenberg, *The Parent's Guide to Everyday Problems of Boys and Girls* (New York, 1958), p. 231.

15. Robert Sears, Eleanor Maccoby, and Harry Levin, *Patterns of Child Rearing* (New York, 1957), p. 337.

16. Gruenberg, *Parent's Guide*, p. 274.

17. Smiley Blanton and Margaret Blanton, *Child Guidance* (New York, 1927), pp. 185–96.

18. Spock, *Common Sense Book*, p. 195.

19. Rudolf Dreikurs, *The Challenge of Parenthood* (New York, 1958), p. 133.

20. David M. Levy, *Maternal Overprotection* (New York, 1943), pp. 42–43.

21. Grace Langdon and Irving Stout, *Bringing Up Children* (New York, 1959), p. 143.

22. Dreikurs, *Challenge*, p. 86.

NOTES TO CHAPTER 4

1. Sam Wineburg, "Making Historical Sense," in Peter N. Stearns, Peter Seixas, and Sam Wineburg, eds., *Knowing, Teaching, and Learning History* (New York, 2001), p. 306

2. Tait Mackenzie, "The Influence of School Life on Curvature of the

Spine," *American Physical Education Review* 3 (1893), pp. 274–80; Walter Truslow, *Body Poise* (Baltimore, 1943), p. 130.

3. Edward Bok, "A National Crime at the Feet of American Parents," *Ladies' Home Journal* 17 (1900), p. 16.

4. *Annual Report of the Board of Education of Los Angeles 1899–1900* (19800), p. 17, cited in Brian Gill and Steven Schlossman, "'A Sin against Childhood': Progressive Education and the Crusade to Abolish Homework, 1897–1941," *American Journal of Education* 105 (Nov. 1996), pp. 27–66; Edward Bok, "First Step to Change the Public Schools," *Ladies Homes Journal* 30 (Jan. 1913), pp. 3–4.

5. Jay Nash, "What Price Home Study?" *School Parent* 9 (May 1930), pp. 6, 12.

6. Kathleen Hoover-Dempsey, Otto Bassler, and Rebecca Burow, "Parents' Reported Involvement in Students' Homework," *Elementary School Journal* 95 (1995), pp. 436–49; Harris Cooper, J. J. Lindsay, and Barbara Nye, "Homework in the Home," *Contemporary Educational Psychology* 25 (Oct. 2000), pp. 464–87.

7. Sanford Bell, "The Significance of Activity in Child Life," *Independent* 55 (1903), pp. 9, 11; Adeline Dartt, "What Can I Do with Johnny?" *Mental Hygiene* 10 (1926), p. 54.

8. Agnes Benedict and Adele Franklin, *Your Best Friends Are Your Children* (New York, 1951), p. 48.

9. Gertrude Driscool, "What's behind Naughtiness?" *Parents Magazine* 10 (June 1935), p. 26

10. Martin Stewart, "Hyperactive Children," *Scientific American* (April 1970), p. 96; Lucy Kavaler, "If You Have a High- Strung Child," *Parents Magazine* 36 (Mar. 1961), p. 120.

11. Stephanie Garber, M. D. Garber, and Robyn Spizman, "Is Your Child Hyperactive?" *Redbook* (Oct. 1990), p. 32

12. Gregory Cizek, "Pockets of Resistance in the Assessment Revolution," *Educational Measurement: Issues and Practice* (summer 2000), pp. 16–23; Julia Wrigley, "Do Young Children Need Intellectual Stimulation? Experts' Advice to Parents, 1900–1985," *History of Education Quarterly* 29 (1989), pp. 41–75.

13. David Brooks, "The Organization Kid," *Atlantic* 287 (2001), pp. 40–55.

14. Thurston Blodgett, Yale Psycho-Clinic, cited in Ellen Herman, "The Paradoxical Rationalization of Modern Adoption," *Journal of Social History* 36 (2002), p. 115

15. Theresa Richardson, *The Century of the Child: The Mental Hygiene Movement and Social Policy in the United States and Canada* (Albany, NY, 1989); Alexander Siegel and Sheldon White, "The Child Study Movement: Early Growth and Development of the Symbolized Child," *Advances in Child Development and Behavior* 17 (1982), pp. 233–85.

16. Stanley Coopersmith, *The Antecedents of Self-Esteem* (San Francisco, 1967), p. 45.

17. Ibid., p. 68.

18. Sidonie Gruenberg, *The Parent's Guide to Everyday Problems of Boys and Girls* (New York, 1958), p. 192.

19. Jianjun Wang, Betty Greathouse, and V. M. Falcinella, "An Empirical Assessment of Self-Esteem Enhancement in a High School Challenge Service-Learning Program," *Education* 119 (fall 1998), pp. 99–105.

20. Wang, Greathouse, and Falcinella, "Empirical Assessment," pp. 100–2.

21. Wayne Lanning and Peggy Perkins, "Grade Inflation," *Journal of Instructional Psychology* 22 (1990), pp. 163–68.

22. Stephanie McSpirit, Ann Chapman, Paula Kopacz, and Kirk Jones, "Faculty Ironies on Grade Inflation," *Journal of Instructional Psychology* 27 (2001), p. 106.

23. Edward Levine, "Grade Inflation in Higher Education," *Free Inquiry in Creative Sociology* 15 (1987), p. 186; McSpirit, Chapman, Kopacz, and Jones, "Faculty Ironies," pp. 105–107.

NOTES TO CHAPTER 5

1. Angelo Patri, *The Questioning Child and Other Essays* (New York, 1931), p. 112

2. Ellen Key, *The Century of the Child* (New York, 1907).

3. Alexander McKelway, "The Needs of the Cotton Mill Operatives," *National Child Labor Committee Papers* (Washington, DC, 1909), Mar. 29, 1909; for state legislative debates, see Viviana Zelizer, *Pricing the Priceless Child: the changing social value of children* (New York, 1985).

4. Raymond Fuller, *Child Labor and the Constitution* (New York, 1923), pp. 37–41, 46–47.

5. *Steber v. Norris*, 199. Wisc. 366.

6. Letter to the editor, New York *Times*, Aug. 13, 1921.

7. G. W. A. Ireland, "Under the Twentieth Amendment," Columbus (Ohio) *Dispatch*, Jan. 20, 1925. See also *The Manufacturer's Record*, Sept. 11, 1924.

8. Sherwood Anderson, *Dark Laughter* (New York, 1925), p. 25; Woods Hutchinson, "Leisure and Work," *Saturday Evening Post* (1922), p. 46. See Tom Lutz, "'Sweat or Die': The Hedonization of the Work Ethic in the 1920s," *American Literary History* 8 (1996), pp. 260–81.

9. International Circulation Managers *Proceedings* (35th year, 1933), pp. 138–39, and "San Francisco News Circulator Writes on Editing Junior Papers," International Circulation Managers *Bulletin* (Nov. 1933), p. 15. Cited in Todd Postol, "Creating the American Newspaper Boy," *Journal of Social History* 31 (1997), pp. 327–46.

10. David Stern, Sandra Smith and Fred Doolittle, "How Children Used to Work," *Law and Contemporary Problems* 39 (1975), pp. 94–104.

11. Smiley Blanton and Margaret Blanton, *Child Guidance* (New York, 1927), p. 173,; Marion Faegre and John Anderson, *Child Care and Training* (Minneapolis, 1928), p. 284.

12. Blanton and Blanton, *Child Guidance*, pp. 190–92.

13. President's Research Committee on Social Trends, *Recent Social Trends in the United States* (Washington, DC, 1933), vol. 2, pp. 663, 670.

14. Benjamin Spock, *Baby and Child Care* (New York, 1976), pp. 322, 464–66.

15. Benjamin Spock and Steven Parker, *Baby and Child Care* (New York, 1998), pp. 464–66; see also Spock, *Dr. Spock Talks with Mothers* (New York, 1961), pp. 116, 198.

16. David Levy, *Maternal Overprotection* (New York, 1943), p. 72.

17. Sidonie Gruenberg, *The Parent's Guide to Everyday Problems of Boys and Girls* (New York, 1958).

18. Gruenberg, *Parent's Guide*, p. 255.

19. Agnes Benedict and Adele Franklin, *Your Best Friends Are Your Children* (New York, 1951), pp. 60–62.

20. Benedict and Franklin, *Best Friends*, p. 61.

21. Bruno Bettelhim, *Love Is Not Enough: The Treatment of Emotionally Disturbed Children* (New York, 1950), p. 44.

22. Rudolf Dreikurs, *Coping with Children's Misbehavior* (New York, 1972), pp. 30, 80–81.

23. Dorothy Baruch, *New Ways in Discipline* (New York, 1949), pp. 43, 141–42.

24. Dorothy Baruch, *Parents Can Be People: A Primer for and about Parents* (New York, 1944), pp. 192–93.

25. Rudolf Dreikurs, *The Challenge of Parenthood* (New York, 1958), pp. 156–26.

26. Thomas Gordon, *P.E.T.: Parent Effectiveness Training: The Tested New Way to Raise Responsible Children* (New York, 1970), pp. 64–68.

27. John D. Krumboltz and Helen Krumboltz, *Changing Children's Behavior* (New York, 1972), pp. 17, 46, 81, 101, 113, 125, 177.

28. Jane Smiley, "The Case against Chores," *Harper's Magazine* (June 1995), pp. 28–29.

29. Sampson Blair, "Children's Participation in Household Labor," *American Academy of Pediatrics Bulletin* (1991), pp. 241–5.

30. Joann Vanek, "Time Spent in Housework," *Scientific American* 231 (Nov. 1974), pp. 116–20.

31. Robert Lynd and Helen Lynd, *Middletown: A Study in Contemporary American Culture* (New York, 1929), pp. 133–69, 522.

32. D. B. Harris, K. E. Clark, A. M. Rose, and F. Valasek, "The Relationship of Children's Home Duties to an Attitude of Responsibility," *Child Development* 25 (Mar. 1954), pp. 29–33.

33. "Busy Parents Let Kids Off the Hook When Assigning Chores," *Wall Street Journal*, Apr. 17, 1996.

34. See the suggested readings at the end of the chapter for various studies on trends in chores.

35. "Busy Parents," p. 76.

36. S. William Stephens, *Our Children Should Be Working* (New York, 1979).

37. David Elkind, *The Hurried Child* (New York, 1988), pp. 40–41, 150–51.

38. Ellen Greenberger, *When Teenagers Work* (New York, 1979), pp. 202–4.

NOTES FOR CHAPTER 6

1. John Burroughs, "Corrupting the Innocents," *Independent* 61 (December 1906), p. 1106; Angelo Patri, *Child Training* (New York, 1922), pp. 21–22; Patty Smith Hill and Grace Brown, "Avoid the Gifts That Over-Stimulate," *Delineator* 85 (Dec. 1914), pp. 22–32.

2. Ruth Frankel, "Child Leisure—A Modern Problem," *Hygeia* 9 (July 1931), pp. 613–16; Ethel Howes, "Home—A Project," *Child Study* 7 (Dec. 1929), pp. 73–74; Elizabeth Cleveland, "'If Parents Only Knew': The Vital Importance of Play," *Children, the Magazine for Parents* 3 (Mar. 1928), p. 12.

3. Frankel, "Child Leisure," p. 614; Ernest Calkins, "Children as Hobbies," *Parents Magazine* 9 (Dec. 1934), p. 56. See Lisa Jacobson, "Revitalizing the American Home: Children's Leisure and the Revaluation of Play, 1920–1940," *Journal of Social History* 30 (1997), pp. 581–95.

4. Valeria Freysinger, "Leisure with Children and Parental Satisfaction," *Journal of Leisure Research* 26 (1994), pp. 919–26.

5. Anna Richardson, *Standard Etiquette* (New York, 1925), p. 95; Eliza Leslie, *Miss Leslie's Behavior Book* (New York, 1859), pp. 198–99.

6. Emily Post, *Children Are People* (New York, 1940), p. 29; Ralph Bergengren, "To Bore or Not to Bore," *Readers Digest* 1 (1922), p. 51.

7. Frank Richardson, *How to Get Along with Children* (Atlanta, 1954), pp. 128–29.

8. Sarah Canstock, "The Significance of Playthings," *Good Housekeeping* 69 (December 1918), p. 35; see also Beatrix Tudor- Hart, *Toys, Play and Discipline in Childhood* (London, 1955).

9. Cited in Evelyn Geller, *Forbidden Books in American Public Libraries, 1876–1939* (Westport, CT, 1984).

10. F. S. Churchill, "The Effect of Irregular Hours upon the Child's Health," in *The Child in the City; a Series of Papers Presented at the Conferences Held during the Chicago Child Welfare Exhibit* (Chicago, 1912), p. 311.

11. "The Comic Nuisance," *Outlook*, March 6, 1909, pp. 527–29; "Crime against American Children," *Ladies' Home Journal* (Jan. 1909), p. 5; Mary Pedrick,

"The Sunday Comic Supplement," *Good Housekeeping* (May 1910), pp. 625–27. See Steven Starker, *Evil Influences: Crusades against the Mass Media* (New Brunswick, NJ, 1989)

12. Gershom Legman, *Love and Death* (New York, 1963), p. 28; Coulton Waush, *The Comics* (New York, 1947).

13. "The Children's Hour," *The Nation* (Apr. 5, 1933), p. 362; Arthur Mann, "The Children's Hour of Crime," *Scribner's* (May 1933), pp. 313–315; Worthington Gibson, "Radio Horror: For Children Only," *American Mercury* (July 6, 1938), p. 294; Starker, *Evil Influences*, pp. 107–27.

14. "Radio for Children—Parents Listen In," *Child Study* (Mar. 1933), pp. 193–98.

15. Gibson, "Radio Horror," p. 294; "Radio Gore Criticized for Making Children's Hour a Pause That Depresses," *Newsweek*, (Nov. 8, 1937), p. 26.

16. Frederic Howe, "What to Do with the Motion Picture Show: Shall It Be Censored?" *Outlook* (June 20, 1914), pp. 412–16; Fred Eastman, "What Can We Do about the Movies?" *Parents Magazine* (November 1931), pp. 19, 52–54; Starker, *Evil Influences*, pp. 89–105.

17. Jane Addams, *The Spirit of Youth and City Streets* (Chicago, 1909); William McKeever, "A Primary School for Crminals," *Good Housekeeping* (Aug. 1910), p. 181.

18. Herbert Blumer and Philip Hauser, *Movies, Delinquency and Crime* (New York, 1933).

19. Frederic Wertham, *Seduction of the Innocent* (New York, 1954), pp. 118–20.

20. Wertham, *Seduction*; Frederic Wertham, "The Comics . . . Very Funny!" *Saturday Review of Literature* (May 29, 1948), p. 27.

21. Wertham, *Seduction*, pp. 396–97.

22. Frank Riley and James Peterson, "The Social Impact of Television," *Survey* 86 (1950), p. 484; Starker, *Evil Influences*, pp. 125–42; Norman Cousins, "The Time Trap," *Saturday Review of Literature* (Dec. 24, 1949), p. 20; P. Witty and H. Bricker, "Your Child and TV," *Parents Magazine* (December 1952), pp. 36–37, 74–78.

23. Donald Roberts, "Adolescents and the Mass Media: From 'Leave It to Beaver' to 'Beverly Hills 90210," *Teachers College Record* 94 (1993), pp. 629–44.

24. Mediascope, Inc., *National Television Violence Study, 1994–5* (Studio City, CA, 1996).

25. Jeanne Funk, Geysa Flores, Debra Buchman, and Julie Germann, "Rating Electronic Games: Violence Is in the Eye of the Beholder," *Youth and Society* 30 (1999), pp. 283–312.

26. Derbra Buchman and Jeanne Funk, "Video and Computer Games in the '90s," *Children Today* 24 (1998), pp. 12–15.

27. Children's Bureau, *Infant Care* (Washington, DC, 1942), pp. 59–60;

Martha Wolfenstein, "The Emergence of the Fun Morality," *Journal of Social Issues* 7 (1951), pp. 15–25.

28. Children's Bureau, *Infant Care* (Washington, DC, 1945), pp. 52, 95.

29. Smiley Blanton and Margaret Blanton, *Child Guidance* (New York, 1927); Irene Seipt, *Your Child's Happiness: A Guide for Parents* (Cleveland, 1955), pp. 159–60.

30. Frances Horwick and Reinald Weinenrath Jr., *Have Fun with Your Children* (New York, 1954), pp. 34–56.

31. Erna Bunke, "My Hobby Is Hobbies," *Survey* 63 (February, 1930), p. 580; see also Arthur Pack, *The Challenge of Leisure* (Washington, DC, 1934).

32. James Hymes, *Understanding Your Child* (New York, 1952), and particularly Von Haller Gilmer, *How to Help Your Child Develop Successfully* (New York, 1951).

33. Seipt, *Your Child's Happiness*, pp. 161–67.

34. Rudolf Dreikurs and Loren Grey, *Logical Sequences: A New Approach to Discipline* (New York, 1968), pp. 3–4; Seipt, *Your Child's Happiness*.

35. James Gilbert, *A Cycle of Outrage: America's Reaction to the Juvenile Delinquent in the 1950s* (New York, 1986).

36. Blanton and Blanton, *Child Guidance*; Grace Langdon and Irving Stout, *Bringing Up Children* (New York, 1960), ch. 9.

37. Seipt, *Your Child's Happiness*, p. 159.

38. Amy Vanderbilt, *Amy Vanderbilt's Etiquette* (Garden City, NY, 1952), pp. 437–38.

39. Thomas Galloway, *Parenthood and the Character Training of Children* (New York, 1928), pp. 85, 88; Max Seham and Grete Seham, *The Tired Child* (Philadelphia, 1926), pp. 45–46; Hymes, *Understanding*.

40. Benjamin Spock, *The Common Sense Book of Baby and Child Care* (New York, 1946), p. 327; see also Zoe Benjamin, *The Emotional Problems of Childhood* (London, 1948), pp. 152, 154.

41. Sidonie Gruenberg, *The Parent's Guide to Everyday Problems of Boys and Girls* (New York, 1958), p. 136.

42. Spock, *Common Sense*, p. 493.

43. Seham and Seham, *Tired Child*, pp. 45–46.

44. "Hi and Lois," in the Washington *Post*, July 1, 2001.

45. Dennis Orthner and Jay Mancini, "Leisure Impacts on Family Interaction and Cohesion," *Journal of Leisure Research* 22 (1990), pp. 125–37. See also John Watt and Stephen Vodanovich, "Boredom Proneness and Psychosocial Development," *Journal of Psychology* 133 (1999), pp. 303–14.

46. "Call It 'Kid-fluence,'" *U.S. News and World Report* (July 30, 2001), p. 32.

47. Dorothy Baruch, *New Ways in Discipline* (New York, 1949), pp. 199, 202; Seipt, *Your Child's Happiness*; see also Robert Sears, Eleanor Maccoby, and Harry Levin, *Patterns of Child Rearing* (New York, 1957), pp. 290–91.

48. Gruenberg, *Parent's Guide*, p. 136 and ch. 6.

49. Elke Zeijl, Yolanda te Poel, Manuela du Bois-Reymond, Janita Ravesloot, and Jacqueline Meulman, "The Role of Parents and Peers in the Leisure Activities of Young Adolescents," *Journal of Leisure Research* 32 (2000), pp. 281–302; Dennis Howard and Robert Madrigal, "Who Makes the Decision: The Parent or the Child?" *Journal of Leisure Research* 22 (1990), pp. 244–58.

NOTES TO CHAPTER 7

1. Rudolf Dreikurs, *The Challenge of Parenthood* (New York, 1958), pp. 6–7, 13–14.

2. Michael Zuckerman, "Dr. Spock: The Confidence Man," in Charles Rosenberg, ed., *The Family in History* (New York, 1975), p. 179. See also Mary Jo Bane, "A Review of Child Care Books," *Harvard Educational Review* 43 (1973), pp. 669–80.

3. Benjamin Spock, *Baby and Child Care* (New York, 1968); Grace Langdon and Irving Stout, *Bringing Up Children* (New York, 1959), p. 94.

4. George Gardner, *The Emerging Personality* (New York, 1970), p. 75.

5. Daniel Yankelovich, cited in Helen Winter and Ruth Kolinsky eds., *Personality in the Making: The Fact Finding Report of the Mid-Century White House Conference on Children and Youth* (New York, 1952), p. 102.

6. Alan Hunt, "Anxiety and Social Explanation: Some Anxieties about Anxiety," *Journal of Social History* 32 (1999), pp. 509–28.

7. Daniel Yankelovich, *The Status of the American Family* (Washington, DC, 1979); Joseph Veroff and Sheila Feld, *Marriage and Work in America* (New York, 1970); Sara McLanahan and Julia Adams, "Parenthood and Psychological Well-being," *Annual Review of Sociology* (1987), pp. 237–57.

8. Susan Shaw, Linda Caldwell, and Douglas Kleiber, "Boredom, Stress and Social Control in the Daily Activities of Adolescents," *Journal of Leisure Research* 28 (1996), pp. 280–83.

9. McLanahan and Adams, "Parenthood," pp. 237–57.

10. Daniel Yankelovich, *New Rules: Searching for Self- Fulfillment in a World Turned Upside Down* (New York, 1981).

11. Sam Wineburg, "Making Historical Sense," in Peter N. Stearns, Peter Seixas, and Sam Wineburg, eds., *Knowing, Teaching and Learning History* (New York, 2000), p. 306.

Index

About the Author

PETER N. STEARNS is Provost and Professor of History at George Mason University. Editor of the *Journal of Social History*, he has written widely on recent social history, both European and American, and on world history. As a researcher, his primary interest has been in exploring new historical topics and, through this, in showing how trends and analyses of the past can explain current issues.